A Labyrinth Walk of Life

Essays on the Belief in Theofatalism

Chartres Labyrinth

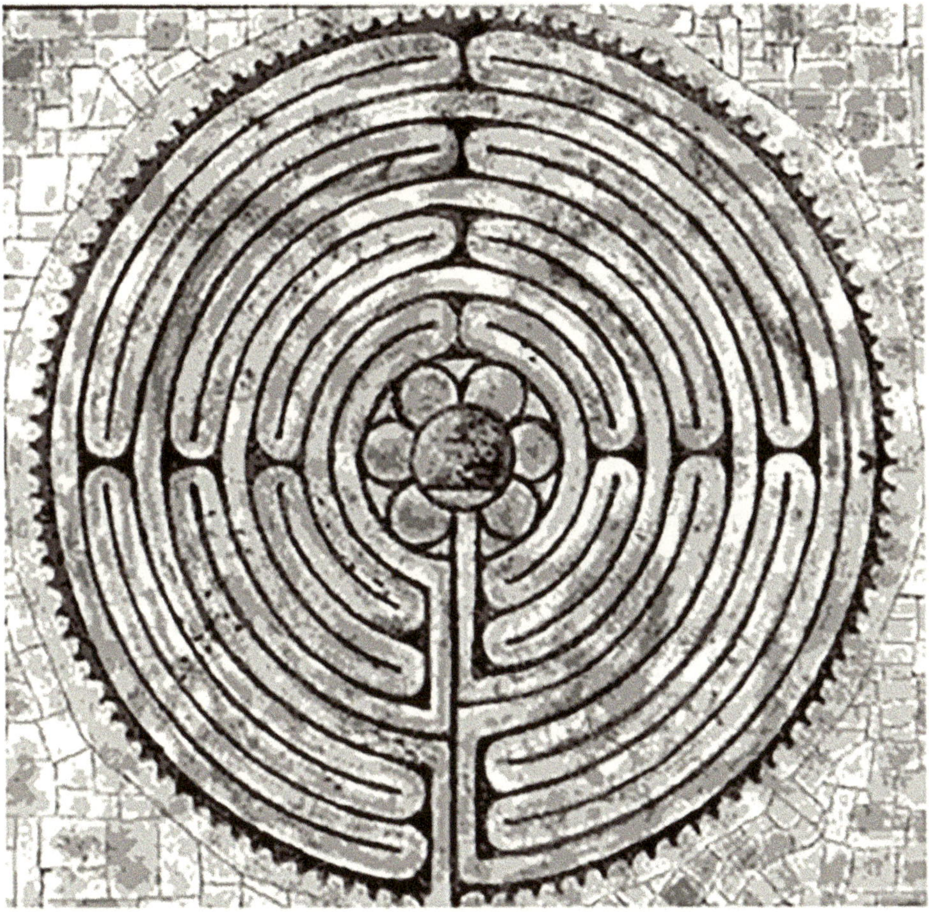

Feel Good Inside No Matter What Happens Outside

LEWIS TAGLIAFERRE

Lewis Tagliaferre

6-05-2019

ISBN 978-1-64140-776-2 (paperback)
ISBN 978-1-64140-777-9 (digital)

Copyright © 2018 by Lewis Tagliaferre

All rights reserved. No part of this publication may be reproduced, distributed, or transmitted in any form or by any means, including photocopying, recording, or other electronic or mechanical methods without the prior written permission of the publisher. For permission requests, solicit the publisher via the address below.

Christian Faith Publishing, Inc.
832 Park Avenue
Meadville, PA 16335
www.christianfaithpublishing.com

The Holy Bible, New International Version®, NIV® Copyright © 1973, 1978, 1984, 2011 by Biblica Inc.™ Used by permission. All rights reserved worldwide.

Printed in the United States of America

Preface

First, I must thank Christian Faith Publishing and the team led by Megan Hancock for the production of this book as it would not exist without their recognition and support. I also thank the many people who provided the information that I was given in the process of learning this belief system. My life was changed in ways I did not anticipate by the previous work of many people long after their lives had passed. Swiss psychiatrist Carl Gustave Jung (1875–1961) said that life is a short pause between two great mysteries, where we came from and where we are going. I have quoted Jung often from various secondary sources because he speaks to me as my personal mentor.

The focus of this personal journal of mine is on applying the ancient symbol of the labyrinth on the cover to the pathway of life each sentient being on earth is given to travel during their lifetime. Its origin is unknown, but this symbol is found in several different forms around the world. The one I used here is obtained from the etching in the floor of the Cathedral of Notre Dame in Chartres, France, constructed around 1200 AD, hence called the Chartres Labyrinth. I discovered this symbol during my search for a belief system I could live with after watching my wife die at her age fifty-two at 7:20 PM on September 3, 1985. The material is challenging to read as it was challenging for me to learn, because it replaces a lot of traditional beliefs that no longer worked. I hope this belief system will be helpful to the readers searching for some inner peace in a world that seems to make no sense. Unless there is some mighty motivation, it is nearly impossible to give up lifelong learning to accept a different concept. But as the late NYC Opera diva Beverly Sills (1929–2007) said, "There are no shortcuts to anything worthwhile."

As I use it here, the pathway of the labyrinth is reversed from the usual entry and exit pattern from the outside in. Instead, we leave the center source at birth and traverse the four segments of the labyrinth outward through life as they are given to each of us: infancy, childhood, youth, and adulthood out into the world—each one building upon the others. Then after midlife, we retrace the pathway in return to the source through integrating stages of maturity, seniority, retirement, and contemplation to approach death, wondering what it is all about. Along the pathway of life, we traverse hills and valleys, fertile fields and desolate deserts, placid streams and raging torrents, storms and serenity, hot and cold, beauty and ugliness, good and evil, grief and happiness, suffering and pleasure. Even though we may be joined by a temporary companion, even a family, everyone must take the walk of life alone for themselves as each pathway is unique. Jung said, "Your pathway is not my pathway. Therefore, I cannot teach you. The pathway is within." The only rules are the following: begin and continue until the final transition emerges while becoming redundant and losing control of your life—or merely giving it up.

Part I is a collection of essays on random topics of contemporary interest that comprise the world as I see it at the time of this writing. You might say they are thoughts I collected along the Labyrinth pathway of my life. Each essay is a theodicy that attempts to reconcile a perfect God with the reality of life on earth. They are not sequential, so you can skip around as you like. Each one leads to the inevitable conclusion of Theofatalism, the belief that God in a different form than the holy books controls everything from atoms to galaxies.

Part II is a discussion of the final stage of life from a Jungian perspective. It discusses personality factors as challenges and resources in aging. At the least, these essays may provide some interesting reading, but hopefully, they may help to stimulate a new belief system that is much needed at this time in human evolution. The topics include matters that many people may prefer to ignore or to avoid. By reading them, your perception of the world will be expanded and enlarged to include reality as it really is, and you may come to feel good inside no matter what happens outside. They may be too academic for some and not enough for others, but I share them in the form that I received them. You may discover that nothing happens outside the will of God, not the god in holy books but the prime mover in the universe: generator, operator, destroyer… GOD. Perhaps this is the "God above gods" proposed by classical theologian Paul Tillich. That would make it a belief system to accommodate all other belief systems.

Jung used the word "god" to refer to the mysterious powers of the universe. "God is the name by which I designate all things which cross my path violently and recklessly, all things which upset my subjective views, plans and intentions, and change the course of my life for better or for worse." This is not a god to be worshipped or loved, but rather one to be feared, or maybe both as one would respond to a father figure who both provides and disciplines (Matthew 6:29–31, Luke 12:4–5). It controls everything from atoms to galaxies, and we all must take what it gives and give what it takes. As it is with individuals, so it is with nations and cultures, which are composed of individuals. If God is in control of everything, agnostics, atheists, and the LGBT community will find themselves in these essays, because God made them too. Everyone is a member of the human community, and no one can resign or be expelled.

You can trace through the labyrinth on this cover with your finger or a pencil or the cursor to begin the experience. As it was used in the Middle Ages, some churches create a labyrinth large enough to walk as a spiritual experience. One such is installed at the

National Cathedral in Washington, DC. For those wishing to know more about the mythical power of labyrinth walking, visit www.labyrinthsociety.org. You can buy one for your own personal use at www.bwatsonstudio.com.

You may wish to introduce *A Labyrinth Walk of Life* to your religious leaders. For further readings in Theofatalism, refer to the following books: *Voices of Sedona, Baby Boomer Lamentations*, and *Theofatalism* by this author as well as the website at www.theofatalism.org and the blog at www.facebook.com/theofatalism.

PART I

Exploring the World

Introduction

The journey through life could be like the orderly walk through the Labyrinth, a mandala or metaphor that symbolizes the walk of life on the book covers by this writer. Unlike the dead ends and random pathway of a maze, the labyrinth has no barriers, and it definitely is not a random walk. The Rev. Lauren Artress (*Walking a Labyrinth*—2011) has said, "Walking the Labyrinth has reemerged today as a metaphor for the spiritual journey and a powerful tool for transformation. This walking meditation is an archetype, a mystical ritual found in many religious traditions. It quiets the mind and opens the soul. Each step unites faith and action as travelers take one step at a time, living each moment in trust and willingness to follow the course set before them."

Those who are able to walk through a symbolic labyrinth often report a spiritual encounter with the divine essence of who they really are. No one can make this discovery for another as it is the ultimate awareness of being one with the universe, insignificant but an indispensable part of the whole—like a drop of water in the ocean. Some of the astronauts who walked on the moon reported such an experience. Unfortunately, modern culture renders most people insensitive to the spiritual or intuitive content of their nature because they are identified with what they do and not who they are. But Jesus declared, "The spirit gives life, the flesh counts for nothing" (John 6:63). This discovery requires that one makes the effort to change the orientation of life from outward to inward—from sensing to intuition, from physical to spiritual. C. G. Jung proclaimed that "those who look outward dream, but those who look inward awake." Most people live on the surface of life and never really probe deeply for the gold nuggets buried in the subconscious mind. Therefore, the essays in this work are intended to focus your attention on a form of subconscious awareness that only a very few may be willing and able to endure—or to contemplate on their labyrinth walk of life.

We may assume many different roles in life, and we present a different persona or identity to the world from time to time as we take the walk of life, wearing a mask as it were a theatrical character. However, all these encounters and persona (false self) are temporary and ultimately leave us with the essential "I AM" that we were at the beginning of life, i.e., the true self. French philosopher Pierre T. de Chardin (1881–1955) said, "We are not humans having a spiritual experience, we are spirits having a human experience." The essence of being a human self accumulates many experiences while walking the labyrinth of life, successes and failures, gains and losses, joy and grief, which make up the experiences of living. As we age, the previous masks must be discarded and assigned to memory to make space for the new ones—until the final one of the old sage. Failing these transitions, the accumulating masks can be overlaid, causing much psychic disorientation. As the late John Lennon learned, life is what happens while we are making other plans. And it all must be necessary or it would be different, minute by minute and breath by breath. As such, there may be no mistakes on the walk of life, merely predestined choices and consequences, all in God's will of course—ergo, Theofatalism.

According to psychiatry professor emeritus Irvin Yalom, this spiritual adventure is so illuminating it is like staring at the sun; it is so dangerous that it can only be absorbed through a dark filter or in very short bursts. So take your time reading the essays that form this inward look at who you really are, insignificant but indispensable to the whole. It may take several readings to fully inform your psyche of this message. Some ideas are presented several times, and that must be necessary or it would be different. Some ideas require repeating. It is like walking the labyrinth, which meanders around and seems to retrace the pathway through the four quadrants. Leon Trotsky (1879–1940) observed, "Life is not an easy matter. You cannot live through it without falling into frustration and cynicism unless you have before you a great idea which raises you above all kinds of perfidy and baseness." Perhaps this is it.

Theofatalism—a contraction of theological fatalism—comes with five principles: (1) everything must be necessary or it would be different, (2) people make unconscious decisions they do not control, (3) the universe is composed of necessary opposites, as in the ancient Chinese symbols of yin and yang, (4) the future is indefinitely uncertain, and (5) GOD—generator, operator, destroyer—is everywhere in everything as immaculate immanence. This is a branch of philosophy that has many proofs, each one quoted throughout these essays. The problem is that very few people can imagine that God causes destruction of his/its own creation, but the evidence is all around if you can see it. C. G. Jung said, "Man's suffering does not derive from his sins but from the maker of his imperfections, the paradoxical God." They also cannot believe that free will is a necessary illusion. We have no free will so we must believe in free will. If you can believe that, this work may be very important to your spiritual growth. With this belief system, you can feel good inside no matter what happens outside—if you work it. All in God's will, of course.

The Newsmakers

Some things in the news can be very troubling… if you get the news. Here are some recent examples:

1) Two college students at Virginia Tech abducted a girl, age thirteen, and killed her for no apparent reason. Another student killed thirty-two people on campus, including professors, without any apparent provocation but his own mental illness. Why would these people ruin their own lives and cause such suffering for so many families unless some force more powerful than they controlled them?
2) A man honored as the best restaurant chef in the world in Switzerland committed suicide at age forty-four from combined grief after both his father and professional mentor died abruptly.
3) Murder-suicides that wipe out entire families are spawned by the poverty and hopelessness in America almost weekly.
4) Rapidly growing diseases of mental illness still suffer from a social stigma and taboo in American culture.
5) Police departments in several cities are under siege for their perceived disregard for the lives of racial minorities.
6) Illegal immigrants are responsible for a rapidly growing number of assaults, murders, and other unpunished felonies, often after being deported and returning several times.

7) The epidemic of drug addictions and illegal human trafficking is being fueled by overuse of legal prescription opioid medicines.
8) The aging of America is stressing the public role of caring for 76 million baby boomers who are not prepared for their retirements.
9) The effectiveness of antibiotic drugs to fight off bacterial infections is rapidly fading as the prehistoric bugs are developing defense mechanisms to assure their survival—caused by the overuse of antibiotics by farmers to increase the production of prey animals for human food.
10) The religion of Islam is being hijacked by ruthless and ungodly zealots who want to dominate the world with sharia as though they are the only true lawgivers, using suicide bombings and beheadings to enforce their beliefs and driving millions of neutral victims from their homes seeking safety as refugees in foreign countries.
11) Countless mentally ill people in the USA are made homeless by the lack of necessary resources to preserve them in adequate housing—except for prisons.

We could add, 12) the insanity that passes for political campaigns to select the next president of the United States. Why would anyone in their right minds want to be president of the United States? There are plenty more events that would shake your confidence in God's benevolence if you only knew what is happening. And we have not even begun to describe the geological disasters like hurricanes, tornadoes, floods, earthquakes, volcanic eruptions, and such plus diseases that plague the world of living creatures, you know, the ones that eat each other for food. For example, a family of ten was wiped out in Arizona when a flash flood swept them all away instantly while celebrating a birthday at a swimming hole after a thunderstorm that occurred eight miles away. This is the world that God has created. "In the beginning, God created the heavens and the earth" (Genesis 1:1).

Most people do not get this kind of news, so they go about their daily lives totally ignorant of the world until something gets their personal attention—which may shock them into reality and stress their coping resources beyond endurance. Anxiety and depression can result after the shock and awe. When the late scientist Albert Einstein (1879–1955) discovered the new laws of physics, he said he felt as though the earth was stripped out from under him and he had no firm place on which to stand. This is the place of anyone who really knows what is happening in the world. Einstein also said we can live as though everything is a miracle or nothing is a miracle, necessary opposites in thought. When you look into a mirror, you may realize that you are a miracle after you contemplate the act of conception and development in the womb that created you and all of your ancestors. The evidence for those who look for it in the workings of your own body points to the conclusion that human beings are no more in control of their own lives than any other species on earth, all of whom are doing both collectively and individually exactly what their creator intends for them to do, moment by moment. American founder Benjamin Franklin (1705–1790) thought the American Revolution was an act of God. He stated, "The longer I live, the more convincing proofs I see of this truth—that God governs in the affairs of men."

The scriptures have much to say about this that you will not ever hear in church because the members might all run for the exits. The Psalm says, "You saw me before I was born and scheduled each day of my life before I began to breathe. Every day was recorded in your book!" (Psalm 139:16). So the scriptural evidence points to the will of God in every aspect of every life of every species on earth—if you can believe it. The key to reading holy scriptures is to ask, what has that got to do with me today? Of course, the necessary opposing humanist force claims that we alone are the determinant of our own futures, and that belief, too, must be necessary or it would be different. "I am the master of my fate, I am the captain of my soul." God never made any one-sided coins. F. Scott Fitzgerald (1896–1940) wrote in *The Crackup* (1936), "A mark of maturity is holding the opposites while functioning normally." Whichever you learn and believe in the time and place where you live must also be the will of some force with power greater than your own mind, whatever is the mind. That force can be called GOD—generator, operator, destroyer—it controls everything from atoms to galaxies, and if you don't get it, you just don't get it. All in God's will of course. Ergo theofatalism.

The Earth from Out There

You may have used the Global Positioning System (GPS) to navigate your way to a destination without realizing how it works. It is a culmination of the most inventive species on earth, *Homo sapiens*. The system was developed by the US Defense Department for military navigation, and it was made available for public use in 2000. The system relies upon twenty-four orbiting satellites positioned about 11,500 miles above the earth, plus a few spares. Each satellite has a life span of about ten years so they must be replaced to keep it working. The amount of information and mathematics compiled into the GPS receivers is far above my pay grade, but suffice to say that it is just one of the many marvels of modern technology. To pinpoint any location on earth, the receiver must use signals transmitted from three or four satellites and make some amazing calculations at the speed of light that could not have been imagined a few decades ago. In just a few years, the GPS navigation system has all but replaced the printed road maps that we used to depend upon for getting from here to there.

If you could look at the earth from out there, as the astronauts in the orbiting space station do, it would seem to be a very placid and apparently peaceful, unoccupied planet. And nothing could be farther from the truth. From the positions of the satellites above the earth, one cannot see any of the life forms or any of the national and political boundaries that separate people into the two hundred or so sovereign nations often at war with each other and within. From out there, one can only see the vast oceans that cover the earth and the variations of green, blue, brown, and white, which designate the continents from the seas. It is all covered with the atmosphere about twenty miles high, a swirling combination of gases that creates the weather and makes life on earth possible. There are unknown numbers of life forms on earth, both on the land and in the oceans from the smallest microscopic cells to the gigantic whales. Some are carnivores and some are herbivores. Consider the miraculous creation of lions, snakes, elephants, sharks, alligators, hummingbirds and butterflies, etc.—only God knows their purposes on earth. The hummingbird is so named because it makes a distinctive sound as its wings beat at fifty times per second, and its heart rate is 1,200 beats per minute but drops to hibernation rates as it sleeps. The European bee-eater is a small bird that captures honeybees in flight and kills them by banging their heads against a rock and then slams the abdomen until the venom is discharged before it is consumed—neat. Did you know there are more than six thousand known species of earthworms?

Plant species also occupy their given places on earth, and some are carnivores too. The pitcher plant oozes a slippery, smelly goo that attracts insects and small mammals that become trapped in the blossom as they are slowly consumed by the plant's digestive juices. Each species preys upon another in a precise dance of survival so that no species becomes dominant in the ecosphere. How they all originated nobody really knows, although science says that it all evolved over some four billion years from one-celled amoebas that emerged from water, if you can imagine that. But what created that original organism? The one thing they all have in common is they must obtain, ingest, and process food to sustain life and pass it on from generation to generation, and then they die. Some living species live only a few weeks and some several years, but in death, they all are equal. For what purpose, nobody knows.

From the most primitive to the most advanced, each individual of all the species seems to be insignificant, and yet indispensable to the whole. Of them all, the species *Homo sapiens* seems to exhibit behaviors that both assure its continuance, but also threaten to cause its extinction. For example, it possesses marvelous abilities to sustain life and to obliterate life simultaneously... both/and. This species exists in a wide variety of forms manifested in various languages, cultures, governance, and society. They are clustered into tribes and nations, some in modern cities and some in primitive villages, each striving more or less for power and control over others, collectively and individually. Whether they accumulate more or less, their individual time on earth is very limited and passes all too quickly. The psalmist pondered this creation and wrote, "What is mankind that you are mindful of them? And yet, you created them just a little lower than the angels" (Psalm 8:4–6).

The Bible says God permitted Satan to demolish the life of Job, a loyal servant, to test his faith. When Job got his desired conversation with God, all he got was a stern lecture on who was the creator and the created. He was so astonished that he uttered, "I am unworthy, how can I reply to you? I put my hand over my mouth. I spoke once, but I have no answer—twice, but I will say no more" (Job 40:4–6). Life on earth is so amazing that some believe it is no accident or random occurrence. It may all be the will of God. Not the manmade god in holy books but the prime mover in the universe...

generator, operator, destroyer… GOD. It controls everything from atoms to galaxies and we all must take what it gives and give what it takes. Ergo Theofatalism.

My Life Story

It is impossible to recount a lifetime of eighty-four years in a short essay, but I must try. I buy high and sell low… that is the story of my life. I was born to immigrant parents at home in Ridgeley, WV, at 4:00 AM during a snowstorm on January 31, 1933, according to my mother. My father had emigrated from Italy with his father at age fourteen on November 30, 1904, to work in WV coal mines, and my mother's family came from Germany. In 1938, my father built a small two-bedroom brick house on twelve acres in an undeveloped location about five miles away, which isolated my mother from her relatives, and she became a depressed recluse, never to leave the house to visit my schools or anything else. Although they were poor and scarcely educated, they seemed to be content with life, even though it was dysfunctional by normal standards. We had a radio and an icebox, and we made our own entertainment on various musical instruments. My mother liked country music, and she bought me a guitar and an instruction book. My father started me on his old cornet, which carried me into the band in high school. My father wrote to me in a letter, "In life, we don't always get what we like so we have to be satisfied with what we get." I was a surrogate husband to my mother as my father worked second shift on the railroad during my teenage years. I did the chores after school while my younger brother got to play. So I never learned how to play. You may have heard about some people whose Midas touch turns everything to gold. Not me. Everything I touch turns to… well, you know. Well, maybe not everything.

A LABYRINTH WALK OF LIFE

My high school love went off and got married while I served four years in the US Air Force (1951–1955) to avoid being drafted and sent to Korea. My mother was devastated and never recovered from my departure until she died of a massive stroke at age sixty-five in December 1960; my father died in October 1972 living in a nursing home, but I never heard him complain. I wanted to be a musician in the air force as I was in high school, but they did not need trumpet players so I volunteered for flight duty on a bomber crew. You may have heard of the B-36, largest bomber ever, but probably not. I did my duty and got regular promotions. I fell totally in love, but the woman I married at age twenty-one on August 14, 1954, forsaking all others, turned out not to like homemaking even though she got a degree in home economics, which was all the rage way back then in the 1950s. She did not really want a full-time career either, you know, one with rising income and a secure retirement. She liked to sew and try different things on a part-time basis as a free spirit. I chose the quick option for a two-year tech education under the GI Bill and that got me a dead-end job, or two or three or four or five. She said what she liked best about me was, "You are very dependable." Meanwhile, we had two kids so I went to college part time for my degree finally at age thirty-five, because I had to earn the living. Between the hours in class and homework and yard work, there was not much time for fun. She made a family life centered around the church where I was a deacon and Sunday school teacher, and we made plans for a cabin in the woods where she liked to camp. But like they say, the plans of mice and men oft go astray.

I did land a good job finally with modest benefits, including a pension, at age thirty-eight, and I was challenged by new managers twenty years younger than me at my age of fifty-four. I *barely* survived the technology revolution. My wife got breast cancer at her age of forty-two, so that messed things up after she had a radical mastectomy. She lived for ten years, and the kids and I did the best we could to act normally with the elephant in the living room. After I watched her die at age fifty-two at 7:20 PM on September 3, 1985, the church members abandoned me because it turned out they were her friends and not mine. I invested my whole being in her—as becoming one—and her loss shattered my life in addition to the kids also. Our house was always full of music, but after her death, it became a cold, dark tomb. Sometimes, life really sucks. When somebody enters your heart, they never leave. I tried, really hard, to replace her about ten times, but none of it ever worked out for long. I hope those temporary partners have some fond memories of me as I do of them. The two kids never married and both struggle in life, totally estranged from each other perhaps to avoid the memories that I wish I could forget. The job included travel to some nice places. One of them was Sedona, AZ, where I began the spiritual journey of this lifetime to survive the grief that threatened my life. The old belief system no longer worked. One personal journal led to another as I compiled several books leading to the awareness of God as generator, operator, destroyer. This is not a god to worship or to love, but one to fear. Jesus declared, "Fear him who after killing the body has the power to throw you into hell" (Luke 12:4–5). "You aren't interested in offerings burned before you on the altar. It is a broken spirit you want, remorse and penitence… a broken and contrite heart O God you will not ignore" (Psalm 51:16–18).

    I made an average living, but never made a lot of money because I could not be ruthless, and my meager investments all fluttered at takeoff and fell back to earth during the Great Recession of 2009. I barely won the race between obsolescence and retirement, health issues included. Regardless what I have done, it does not seem to be good enough to assure my kids a reasonable inheritance. Now at age eighty-four, my peers, relatives, and such are all dead or relocated, and I live alone only with memories and my pet dog, Ellie, who also is nearing the end of her life. Too many funerals. My desire to leave my savings intact to my two children is threatened by immanent medical and custodial care, creating acute anxiety. So I think about preemptive suicide. Like the Buddha said, life is difficult and life is always temporary and changing, and what comes after nobody knows. Poet laureate, Robert Frost (1874–1963) concluded, "It is hard to get into this world and hard to get out, and what lies in between makes no sense." He lost his wife and five of six children by his age of sixty-four and then lived until age eighty-nine to think about it. He wrote, "Lord, please forgive my many little jokes on thee and I will forgive thy great big one on me." So it all must be God's will or it would be different. Ergo Theofatalism.

The Power of Words

Did you ever think about the power of words? Words are thoughts converted into conscious awareness. Could there be any thoughts without words? In every language, words are used to convey thoughts and feelings, ideas, dreams and nightmares, pain and pleasure, joy and suffering. Without words, there would be no connections between individuals. Although they may not follow the common rules of understanding and usage, words between humans and their pets also convey ideas, moods, desires, and wishes. I know when my dog wants to go out or to get fed because she tells me so. Words can make or break people with either encouragement and hope or insults and bullying. What most people want from friends are words of praise, empathy, attention, and approval—PEAA. Deliver the opposites and you could make an enemy. The late poet, Maya Angelou observed that people may forget what you say or do, but they will never forget how you made them feel.

Words in English can be very confusing when they sound alike but have different meanings—bread and bred or past and passed or great and grate, for and four and threw and through or done and dun and sine and sign—for examples. Words must have been one of the very first inventions of human life on earth, and maybe even before. The Bible declares, "In the beginning was the Word, and the Word was with God and the Word was God" (John 1:1). Theologians have been trying to figure out what that means ever since it was written. The very idea of God is beyond human understanding. Some say the Word refers to Jesus of Nazareth and declares him to be God. Whether that is true or not nobody knows. What is known is that the words in the Bible translated into many languages have created and sustained two of the world's primary religions, Judaism and Christianity. Similarly, the words in the Quran created and maintains the other great world religion, that of Islam. People live and die by the words in these great faiths. Some folks go so far as to claim that words make the future happen, so be careful what you speak. They say if you speak or even think doom and gloom words that is what will happen, and if you use words of optimism and accomplishment that also will happen. Thus, you create the future by your words, so they say. You may recall that God scrambled the languages of people at the Tower of Babel, so they would not be able to share knowledge and become like the Gods (Genesis 11:1–9). But they developed interpreters, so that did not work.

Jesus claimed, "My words are spirit and they are life" (John 6:63). But words also describe pain and suffering—even push vulnerable people into suicide. Even kings are not exempt. Shakespeare wrote this instruction in *The Tragedy of Macbeth*, "Give sorrow words, the grief that does not speak knits up the oer-wrought heart and bids it break." Perhaps that was the beginning of the modern form of therapy because sharing your painful thoughts and feelings does appear to be helpful in sustaining human tragedies. Words also can be used by con artists who fleece gullible people out of their money, even when the odds are obviously overwhelming, like they are in the gambling lotteries and fraudulent Ponzi schemes. We often think of words as spoken sounds, but also they can be shared in writing, as with this essay. The world is full of books and blogs now on the Internet. (The Internet was originally developed by the US Government and labs in the UK to allow university research computers to communicate directly and was made available for commercial use by Internet Service Providers in the late 1980s. Virtually all electronic information transfer employed the Internet by 2007. All in God's will of course.)

For those so handicapped, words can be felt as coded blips on a page, waves of the fingers in air, and even taps in the palm of a hand. Words are compiled in writing by the great authors, but the masses in the world have always been led by people of great oratory—consider Adolf Hitler and US presidents for example. Writers may convey theories and information on the Internet, but it appears that only verbal skills can move people to actions, whether in religion, business, politics, or warfare. Someone said great people talk about ideas, average people talk about things, and little people talk about other people. Someone else, maybe Abraham Lincoln, said it is better to remain quiet and be thought a fool than to speak and remove all doubt. You can draw your own conclusions about politicians—which means "many tongues." They can fool some people all the time and all the people some of the time, and that's enough. It appears that political discussion rapidly is becoming a war of tweets on social media, 142 characters at a time.

As society changes, new words are created to accommodate the need to express new thoughts and things. Think of all the new computer jargon, i.e., apps, texting, selfies. New words are being created all the time as knowledge increases. Obviously, words evolve to support changing cultures, and words move some people more than others, as in religions, political campaigns, and revolutions. Ideas contained in words must become contagious, i.e., memes, if they are to be useful. How memes are born and transmitted, nobody knows. The trouble with words is they can only be defined by using other words—app means application, which means a computer program that means… etc. And we all interpret words through a filter of human personality, experience, and culture. Now, one may ask, who creates the power of words and how is it distributed among the masses? How and why this works must be the will of God. Not the manmade god in holy books but the prime mover in the universe… generator, operator, destroyer… GOD. It controls everything from atoms to galaxies and we all must take what it gives and give what it takes… Ergo Theofatalism.

The Greatest Miracle

You may think the greatest miracle was the virgin birth of Jesus and his resurrection. Or maybe the belief in it. Or maybe it is human conception and birth after gestation in the womb. Or maybe it was Moses parting the sea to save the Jews from slavery in Egypt or maybe Noah and his mythical ark. Or maybe it was the prophet Muhammad who founded Islam, or the prophet Joseph Smith Jr. who founded the Church of Jesus Christ of Latter-Day Saints, a.k.a. Mormons. Or maybe the invention of numbers and mathematics… paper, rubber tires, or maybe the atom bomb… or concrete and anesthesia… ballpoint pens, personal computers, Internet and worldwide web, and 3-D printing. All these events are driven by some preceding one or several in a long chain of events from the beginning leading up to here and now—which makes everything inevitable because any different link in the chain would have produced a different result. The Bible says it all began with and by God. "In the beginning God created the heavens and the earth" (Genesis 1:1).

A LABYRINTH WALK OF LIFE

There are many inventions and discoveries that seem to be miracles, but they all originated in the mind of some human being, after God put them there—including this book. Therefore, the greatest miracle in the world may be that of human imagination—because that is where it all begins. Nothing is created that is not first imagined—like the Rubik's cube. (This 3-D puzzle was created by Hungarian architect Emo Rubik in 1974 and has spawned a worldwide cult of solvers and mimics, including computerized robots.) Albert Einstein thought that imagination is more important than knowledge, "The intellect has little to do on the road to discovery. There comes a leap of consciousness, call it intuition or what you will, and the solution comes to you and you don't know how or why. The intuitive mind is a sacred gift and the rational mind is a faithful servant. We have created a society that honors the servant and has forgotten the gift."

C. G. Jung said intuition is perception through the subconscious. He saw a danger to mankind in overconcentration on the technology-based society absent a necessary balance in the arts. Napoleon Bonaparte (1769–1821) concluded, "Imagination rules the world." Nothing can be done until it is first imagined, whether good or bad. Consider the plans by SpaceX Inc. to build a rocket ship that will take passengers on a cruise into space as a commercial business for a mere $250,000 per trip. It would not be possible without the imagination that enabled astronauts to explore the moon in person, which began with the invention of rockets by German engineers to attack London during WWII, which originated in the imagination of Wernher von Braun. It is now possible to experience virtual reality in computer games that literally put the user into a new realm of pseudo space, such as the 3-D games developed by Linden Lab, *Second Life* and *Sansar*.

The future development of artificial intelligence is beyond imagination. Now, some inventors are developing the driverless car and pilotless passenger aircraft as an extension of military drones.

Imagine that. And Jeff Bezos, founder of Amazon.com, is planning for millions of people living and working in space through his company, Blue Origin. Imagine that. On the other hand, consider the imagination of Adolf Hitler and his inspiration for military conquest that propelled Europe into World War II. War is the genesis of many new inventions later adapted for civilian use, including medical treatments, the Internet, and the GPS navigation system. But they are not cheap. The F-22 Raptor fighter plane costs about $340 million each and $42,000 per hour to operate, and its mission is to shoot down other similar planes of enemy nations. The high-tech features of this plane are unimaginable.

For C. G. Jung, imagination was the evidence and manifestation of the intuitive function in personality—possibly even the window into the unconscious and the spiritual realm—which he saw as a necessary balance in human society between sensing and intuition in danger of being lost. He called it the ability to see around corners. All the holy books and all the human inventions are products of imagination, as well as the art, music, poetry, drama, dance, and creativity of mankind. Imagination usually moves in small steps from one discovery to another, but occasionally, it takes a giant leap for mankind—consider the atomic bomb and man walks on the moon. Could there be any better example of one man's imagination than the communications products conceived by the late Steve Jobs (1955–2011), co-founder of Apple Inc. that no one realized they needed until after they bought one? Historically, imagination created the Empire State Building, Hoover Dam, the Golden Gate Bridge, the Eiffel Tower, Facebook, concrete, gunpowder, classical music and novels, crack cocaine and anesthesia, the GPS navigation system, rubber tires, glass and paper and plastic, driverless cars, smartphones, and weapons of war. Imagination took men to the moon, and now it is making plans to take people to Mars… honest. Nothing happens that is not first imagined, and no one can predict all the amazing things to be created in the future. Some people see things are they are and ask why, a few see things as they could be and ask why not. So I ask why not a new belief system to accommodate all other belief systems.

But there is a rub. Human imagination can be used both for creation and destruction as it has no moral compass of itself. Oil can be used to fuel transportation, which pollutes the atmosphere, and to make plastics, which pollutes the earth. Nuclear power can be used to generate electricity or to make atomic bombs. Imagination put men on the moon, but it cannot seem to ensure peace on earth, while the weapons of war become ever more unimaginable. Even sin first must be imagined before it can be done. Did not God create sin so that he could have something to forgive? Jesus challenged those who judged a woman taken in adultery to imagine their own guilt first (John 8:3). He declared there is no difference between the imagination of adultery and the deed (Matthew 5:28). Religious faith rests upon the existence of this human function called imagination or intuition. Faith is more than mere belief because it prompts actions. Jung said, "I don't need to believe in God, I know." Apostle Paul declared, "I know whom I have believed…" (1 Timothy 1:12). The world might be very different if all Christians obeyed the absolute passivism taught by Jesus of Nazareth (Luke 6:1–7) compared with the militant conquests of Prophet Muhammad (peace be upon him) and the believing faith of their followers, all based upon imagination. Russian author Leo Tolstoy described in his book *The Kingdom of God is Within You* (1894) an imagined world based in nonviolent protest taught by Jesus that motivated Martin Luther King Jr., but it has never replaced the violent kind.

Possibly, the worst part of imagination is contemplating your own mortality and the suffering that most likely will precede your death. Many people seem to feel terror at the thought of dying because they cannot imagine what comes after, or they imagine the worst case of eternal suffering in hell, so they don't think about it and go outside to play. Faith in some afterlife after life seems to drive all sorts of imagination about it. With faith, no proof is necessary, and without faith, no proof is sufficient. Personally, I fear terminal suffering that often precedes death connected up to mechanical contraptions in some hospital intensive care unit. The worlds of intuition and knowledge are forever changing, flowing like a river that navigates through white water and over waterfalls on its way to the sea of information, which is never full. Each generation adds its blend to the whole, and each individual is both indispensable and insignificant. This book and the proofs for theofatalism are gifts of my own imagination and intuition, because I certainly cannot account for them otherwise. But imagination and its resulting knowledge comes with a caveat. This is why King Solomon lamented, "I applied myself to the understanding of wisdom, and also of madness and folly, but I learned that this, too, is a chasing after the wind. For with much wisdom comes much sorrow; the more knowledge, the more grief" (Ecclesiastes 1:17–18). All benefits come with burdens. All in God's will of course. Ergo Theofatalism. Imagine that.

The World of Spirit

Who do you think you are… I mean really? That is not just a rhetorical question because whenever you think about it, the answer is not so simple. Of course, you were given a name or you chose one, and when you look into the mirror, some image seems to be there. By the age of two, children realize they are separate from mother and become conscious of "you" and "me," what is called the awareness of self. Actually, throughout life we display many different images or persona for the various transient roles we play in relationships—child, sibling, spouse, parent, worker, soldier, manager, neighbor, etc.

We often refer to ourselves with the preface "I am," and we use the possessive pronoun in describing ourselves as in my body, my hair, my foot, my voice, my brain, my fingernails, and even go so far as to say "my thoughts," "my soul," and "myself." But who is it that owns your brain or your body parts or your soul? And what is the self? Pierre Teilhard de Chardin (1881–1955), the French philosopher and Jesuit priest, wrote, "We are not human beings having a spiritual experience. We are spiritual beings having a human experience." Jesus said, "The spirit gives life, the flesh counts for nothing" (John 6:63). Once you accept the temporary nature of the body, you may become ready to find out who you really are.

This is a very important concept to accept in traveling the spiritual path, which is depicted by the ancient labyrinth used for the symbol of this work, which everyone must walk alone. We begin the walk at birth, exiting from the source out into the world, and then reverse the walk after the meridian is reached to return to the source. Mystics have claimed for centuries that after the body dies, the spirit/soul remains. The laws of physics claim energy can neither be created nor destroyed, so maybe that helps explain the concept of a soul that survives death. How this energy is passed from generation to generation through flesh is a mystery. The fact that some people say that ghosts exist is one of the strongest bits of evidence that the spirit doesn't die, and that "dying" simply refers to spirit leaving the human body to return to the dust from which it is created—but where would they get such an idea from? Unless from the Creator. Clairvoyants seem to have the ability to receive messages from the afterlife, which is very comforting to some of their clients mourning the loss of loved ones. Perhaps they are not lost, but just transformed through some process not yet understood from matter into energy. All in God's will of course.

Under hypnosis, many subjects tell a similar story of events in the spirit world, often recounting multiple lifetimes on earth.

People who report having a near-death experience all report a similar encounter with the spirit world. Jung reported in detail his own such experience during a heart attack in 1944, which included a view of earth from one thousand miles into space, which may have presaged space travel of the 1960s. Is that merely imagination, or what? The Bible seems to use the words *spirit*, *soul*, and *life* as synonyms. Jesus said, "I lay down my life and I can/will take it up again" (Luke 23:46, John 10:17–1). And also, "Do not be afraid of those who kill the body but cannot kill the soul. Rather, be afraid of the One who can destroy both soul and body in hell" (Matthew 10:28). At Calvary he lamented, "My soul is overwhelmed with sorrow to the point of death" (Mark 14:34). In the end on the cross, he declared, "Into your hands I commit/transport my spirit" (Luke 23:46). That undefined something that has the power to possess a spirit/soul/body could be the real you. It is sexless and exists in the same form as angels (Matthew 22:30).

We know from the laws of physics that matter and energy cannot be created but are interchangeable. So the universe could be a closed system as matter is converted from its origins among the periodic table into living flesh on earth with an indwelling energy called life to become a sentient being. Then death becomes a process of reconfiguration from matter to energy while the body sans water reduces to its basic elements, except for its DNA, which seems to survive for centuries. Some claim life is a continuous circular process as in reincarnation while others claim it is a linear process from beginning to ending, because we die only once and after that comes the judgment (Hebrews 9:27). Of course, the atheist and humanist would claim this is all myth, and they and their body are inseparable and ends in oblivion. The key to applying scriptures to modern times is to ask, what has that got to do with me today? Whichever you believe, it must be the will of God—generator, operator, destroyer.

The US government is searching the universe for possible life forms on other planets who may have visited earth in the past. Some researchers now propose the whole thing is some sort of imaginary mirage created by a life force far superior to us. Science may or may not discover other forms of life more or less advanced than us, but here is the thing; the body we possess is a temporary vessel occupied by the real you to carry out your purpose on earth as spirit incarnate, to be discarded when that purpose is finished, no matter what it is. And you don't have to search for your purpose because you cannot avoid it. Thus, I have a body, but I am not my body; I have a brain, but I am not my brain; I have a heart, but I am not my heart; and I have a soul, but I am not my soul. While death may be an ending in one sense, in another it is a completion to be celebrated no matter how it happens, because it is the culmination to the labyrinth walk of life. This is true of all sentient beings, plant and animal alike. Think of that next time you kill a bug or eat a fish or enjoy a steak or pick an apple. So if someone asks who you are, think carefully before you reply. "The spirit gives life; the flesh counts for nothing" (John 6:63). All in God's will of course. Ergo Theofatalism.

The Façade of Civilization

Can the US federal government survive when an armed minority that disagrees with its policies by duly elected officials is willing to disobey that authority, whatever the consequences? America was born in revolution and formed in civil war. From its beginnings with the Declaration of Independence, America has been on shaky ground because the very issues that caused its separation from the crown of England are embedded in its own structure. There might be good reasons why Canada did not join the revolution. The fundamental conflicts between individual freedoms and the governing roles of local, state, and federal governments are constantly being tested. The original US Constitution was scarcely ratified by nine of the thirteen states (nee colonies) provided that it would be amended to describe in a Bill of Rights the obligations and limitations of the governed as well as the governing. Thus, the first ten amendments were compiled and issued to meet that challenge, but not without opposition and confusion before final ratification in 1791. A reading of history discloses that the wrangling and debates that took place within and among the founders produced a document that was compiled from political expediency as much as rational discourse. American politics has been "the art of the possible" from its beginnings. The Civil War and the aborted amendment on prohibition of alcohol shows that it is not a perfect constitution, but one striving for "a more perfect union." If the American republic is so exceptional, many other countries would have adopted this form of government, and none have. Perhaps that is what makes it exceptional.

The fact that many decisions of the US Supreme Court are rendered by a 5–4 vote shows that the US Constitution still is subject to interpretations, which are based in politics. Since the Supreme Court itself is a creation of politics, with judges being nominated by the sitting president, it follows that individuals may passionately disagree with governing policies. Thus, the seeds for dissent are there and the second amendment assures that armed rebellion is within the realm of possibility as individual possession of firearms is protected. Never mind that the original intent of the second amendment was to assure "a well-regulated militia," as that presumption was long ago diminished if not totally ignored. Indeed, what seems to be lacking is the organized militia called for in the second amendment and its regulated hierarchy of controls and discipline, which could be the dominant weakness of the representative republic, not a democracy, in which we live. Without such military organization and leadership, the evolution of armed mobs can be anathema to this form of government and the "more perfect union" that it promised.

When you combine the freedom of speech of the first amendment with the right to own and bear arms in the second with the present and growing social trends of flash mobs and street gangs, things could get extremely ugly in America. The façade of civilization is very thin. However, Apostle Paul admonished the Christians in Rome as follows: "Let everyone be subject to the governing authorities, for there is no authority except that which God has established. The authorities that exist have been established by God. Consequently, whoever rebels against the authority is rebelling against what God has instituted, and those who do so will bring judgment on themselves" (Romans 13:1–7). However, neither he nor Jesus could prevent the Jews from rejecting him as Messiah and revolting against Rome. After the final battles of 135 AD, they were vanquished and banned from Jerusalem, fulfilling their destiny. The silence of Christian church leaders is deafening as mob violence and decreased reverence for authority grows in America. What the future holds nobody knows, but it must all be God's will or it would be different. Not the manmade god in holy books but the prime mover in the universe: generator, operator, destroyer… GOD. Ergo Theofatalism.

The Imperfect Union

For the greatest country on earth, the United States of America surely has a lot of problems. It was born in revolution, stressed by civil war, and repeatedly challenged by depression and racial discontent. The capitalist economic system that it flaunts is by no means perfect as people strive in some areas and stagnate in others. By government definition, about 47 million people in this nation of around 315 million live in poverty, and up to 90 million able-bodied adults left the workforce involuntarily after the Great Recession of 2009. Many of them are poorly educated and living in isolated clusters of inner cities, so they make bad decisions and propagate another generation of poor people, and the cycle repeats and expands with each passing generation. Some politicians claim that government handouts that protect the poor from homeless starvation only reinforces such behavior, as when single women get increased benefits for making more children in single-parent families. In some inner cities, fully 70 percent of children are born to black single mothers. These kids learn to survive sans normal social families and disdain traditional success as being like white people, something not valued in their culture, except for the few exceptions who do act like white people. In the world of mammals, single mothers usually raise their offspring alone, so perhaps humans really are not much different.

In every race, the first half to finish always is followed by the second half, and somebody always comes in last. Every bell curve has a bottom half. The late comedian, George Carlin (1937–2008) observed the average American is pretty dumb, and half of the rest are even dumber. Such is the law of statistics. The mid-range of every group contains about 68 percent of the population spread about the middle, which is about $32,000 of annual personal income in America, plus or minus 34 percent. Many of them must spend half or more just on housing alone. Incomes of the middle class have not risen much with the peak being just before the banking collapse of 2009. The bottom half of all workers earns on average $16 thousand per year, which is unchanged since the 1980s. Meantime, the top 1 percent (bankers, lawyers, hedge fund managers, company owners, entertainers, professional athletes, etc.) have seen their incomes triple in thirty years to a minimum of $425,000 by age forty. The top 1 percent gets richer and more powerful, while the bottom half gets poorer, considering inflation. Since the Roosevelt administration created the Social Security (SS) retirement safety net of 1936, the number of people working to support those receiving benefits has declined from about sixteen to about only three. Soon, it will be only two unless some very painful changes are made, which will be necessary.

The SS administration reports making payments to about 48 million retirees and 11 million disabled people funded by about 166 million workers in 2014. In surplus years, money is "borrowed" from the SS trust fund of US treasury bonds to pay general expenses without raising taxes. The total US government accumulated debt is now over 19 trillion dollars with annual interest payments of $600 billion, about 30 percent of the mandatory budget. Politicians and economists say this trend is unsustainable and will not bode well for the future of America. This knowledge of national affairs is enough to worry anyone if you think about it. However, Jesus admonished his disciples not to worry about tomorrow as each day will have its own troubles. "Can any one of you by worrying add a single hour to your life? And why do you worry about clothes? See how the flowers of the field grow. If that is how God clothes the grass of the field, will he not much more clothe you—you of little faith? So do not worry or say, 'What shall we eat?' or 'What shall we drink?' or 'What shall we wear?' For the pagans run after all these things, and your heavenly Father knows that you need them. But, seek first his kingdom and his righteousness, and all these things will be given to you as well. Therefore, do not worry about tomorrow. Each day has enough trouble of its own" (Matthew 6:27–34). Consider that all living things have a natural life cycle, including you. It must be the will of God because it makes no sense otherwise, considering all the poor and homeless wretches in America. Ergo Theofatalism.

Who Do You Trust?

Trusting in God even when all else fails seems to be the bottom line in most forms of religion. They often fail to deliver on promises of health, wealth, and happiness so what is left when you are down and out basically is faith in unproven beliefs which counter normal reasoning. With faith, no proof is necessary, and without faith, no proof is sufficient. You may recall the story of Job in the Old Testament, how all his cattle, servants, and children were destroyed by Satan with permission of God to test his loyalty. Even his health was taken as his body was infested with painful boils. His wife challenged him to curse God and die, but his response was, "Even though he slays me I will trust/hope in him" (Job 13:15). He figured if he could only converse with God to prove his loyalty, all his troubles would end. But when he finally got the interview with God, all he got was a stern lecture on who really controls everything, namely the Creator God. Some scholars think his reinstated family and wealth was added at the end later to make it all come out okay. Each generation seems to produce another cohort of preachers who convince gullible followers that inner peace and prosperity are just around the corner if you believe and contribute more to their personal wealth, and there seems to be no shortage of hopeful disciples. Jesus said there would be false teachers and false prophets who would deceive even the very elect. So beware who you are led to follow. (Matthew 24:24).

There is something about human nature that clings to hope beyond all reason, even when facts indicate the opposite. If they do not put faith in God and celebrity prosperity preachers, people are likely to invest in professional gurus including financial advisors, teachers and professors, medical doctors, and lawyers to help fulfill their hopes and dreams. They want some assurance that the "do this—get that" formula will work in their lives like a mathematical equation, $x = (f)y$. But the Psalms invoke the will of God from birth to death in every detail of human life, "You saw me before I was born and scheduled each day of my life before I began to breathe. Every day was recorded in your book!" (Psalm 139:16). So the scriptural evidence points to the will of God in every aspect of every life on earth during your walk through the labyrinth you are given. Friedrich Nietzsche (1844–1900) concluded, "Hope is the worst of all evils for it prolongs the torments of man." Of course, the necessary opposing humanist force claims that we alone are the determinant of our own futures because people are co-creators with God. The necessary opposite to God's will was penned by William Ernest Henley (1849–1903) in his poem "Invictus," "I am the master of my fate, I am the captain of my soul." The fact is the future is indefinitely uncertain, including what comes after death, and that awareness causes existential anxiety, called angst, if you think about it. Stanford professor emeritus, Irvin Yalom said that facing this reality is like staring at the sun, which drives the mental neurons of the brain into saturation and thus makes people turn away in terror. So they just go outside and play to avoid thinking about it—until they can no longer avoid the anxiety of uncertainty. All in God's will of course. Ergo Theofatalism.

The Servant Has Become the Master

Something is happening that bodes ill for modern society and increasing business for psychotherapists. I refer to the ubiquitous (look it up) and addictive use of modern Internet communications and smartphones, a computer in your hand, which many people cannot seem to live without. It all began with English mathematician George Boole (1816–1864), who developed binary algebra, and American engineer Claude Shannon (1916–2001), father of the digital information age, who developed the ways to make it useful. That was followed by the personal computer, the Internet, and the worldwide web. Liberating personal computers and phones from wires and cables now make it possible for total submersion in a world of virtual relationships in your hand and pseudo knowledge and fake news in an avalanche of information overload 24-7. Information is not a substitute for knowledge and wisdom. This trend seems to be hell-bent on consuming the lives of habitual users who are every bit as addicted to so-called social media as any dope fiend or alcoholic or smoker ever was enslaved by drugs. We can thank the late Steve Jobs (1955–2011) co-founder of Apple Inc. who reportedly quipped, "How will they know they want it, unless we give it to them?" You see them all over as people seem to be glued to the small screen walking their dogs and feeding their kids while eating their meals at McDonald's or grocery shopping and working out at gyms (also in the bathroom and bedroom) like they are afraid of missing something crucial to life without checking it every few minutes. Some kids are becoming so addicted to the small screen they are unable to give up the attachment even during mealtimes. The situation is so bad that the American Society of Pediatrics issued guidelines for parents to restrict use of smartphones by children under age five. Psychologist Jean Twenge reported that kids over age thirteen with smart phones are showing retarded overall social development by three years and greater risk of depression and suicide. A doctor in Colorado has initiated a referendum that would prohibit retailers from selling smartphones to kids below age thirteen. For God's sake, people, get off the damn cellphone and talk to your kids.

The use of emails and text messages is rapidly replacing traditional social interactions. It is like God made thumbs so people could text. Indeed, here is the danger—when people are dependent upon the virtual contact with their wireless devices and texting messages, what will happen to real life relationships and actual dialogue between human beings instead of texting on Twitter with smartphones? Even President Trump is using daily tweets to spread his propaganda, and it is working. His signature campaign pledge was returning exported jobs to America, but no one questions when his daughter is going to bring home the $100 million annually that she exports to other countries for their cheaper labor to make her Trump brand of women's products sold online. Many states have stopped teaching cursive writing, as in personal letters, because people now are using their thumbs for texting—and sexting. Attempts to head off auto accidents by outlawing driving while texting is falling on deaf—or connected—ears. New autos are including online screens that can only distract drivers even more. The new Forty-Niners football stadium is equipped with a Wi-Fi router for each one hundred seats, so the fans can watch the game and stay in touch while submerged in the crowd. Programmable robots have taken over much of manufacturing processes, and now the trend includes machine to machine communications as well. The driverless car seems to be the next major development in artificial intelligence, and airlines are talking about pilotless airplanes. Customer services are now being conducted by automated voice robots, and it is almost impossible to talk to a real human about customer relations. Will human relations soon become obsolete and immaterial in the future? As one who has bridged the transition in one lifetime from cursive writing and three-cent stamps, vacuum tubes, and crank auto windows in cars without air-conditioning to the modern world of instant thumb-texting, I think change is not always for the better. How and why it happens must be the will of God, or it would be different.

The problem is that people may not realize what has been lost until future generations look back in history and wonder where it all went wrong. The servant has now become the master. This trend toward virtual relationships could be fueling the fact that half of American adults live single and half of all children are being raised by single parents. Iceland has all but abandoned conventional families. Soon there will be no more role models for traditional families except what children get on their smartphones, and what comes after that nobody knows. Among the burdens of virtual relationships are stolen identities and hacking into private communications and business and government accounts. Most people use the online banking system without a clue as to how it really works. The rapid trend toward electronic transfers of money makes it much easier for the financial system to be corrupted. Paying your bills online is like sending a stamped check in the mail without the envelope, like an old-fashioned postcard. Money itself is becoming little more than numbers on a computer screen, as we are becoming the cashless society. The new elite class are those nerds who know how to write the millions of lines of codes that make the otherwise dead hardware come to life. The Windows 10 operating system contains more than eight hundred thousand files and six million lines of code. Computer coding is the highest demand job worldwide.

The Internet is a totally unregulated and lawless international network spawning an emerging world war in cyberspace in which the best hackers are likely to win, and average users can easily be scammed. At this time, there are billions of devices connected on the Internet, and most of them are not effectively protected. Any communication over the Internet is open to hackers, including your cellphone. If your online bank accounts have not been hacked yet, they probably will be. And you will not know it happens until after the damage is done. In the worst case, your identity may be stolen and someone may sink you into the worst money pit of your life by taking out loans in your name. Even government networks are not absolutely safe, because perfect Internet security is not possible. Hackers are even able to influence American elections. They can be located anywhere in the world, and they are more effective than any defense systems, which always are playing catch up to their inventiveness. This means the average cellphone user will need to learn and to keep up with all the personal security options. We are in a cyber-war, and we are losing. Russian leader Vladimir Putin has bragged that he could destroy America in thirty minutes with a neutron bomb that would destroy all the personal and business computers in an instant. Actually, he would only need to hack the national electric grid to create social and economic chaos instantly. The burdens of online communications rapidly are outpacing the benefits.

The Bible predicted that human commerce would be reduced to mere numbers in the end times, and it may be close to reality because you cannot live without a personal credit card, or two or three, and each account requires its own ID and account number (Revelation 13:17). Some ideas, called memes, seem to be contagious and take on a life of their own so more than two billion people on earth now are part of the online world. But most of the human beings on earth do not yet depend on electronic social media for their incomes and commerce, so it remains to be seen how this trend to virtual relationships will spread into undeveloped countries. Voice and icon communications likely will serve illiterate people. The attempt by Facebook founder Mark Zuckerberg to place a satellite in orbit that would bring Wi-Fi to Africa was lost in *its* fatal launch. While wireless electronic media certainly has advantages of convenience and speed, the disadvantages of its addictive attachment and instantaneous damage could be overlooked until the event horizon is passed and society is sucked into a black hole from which there is no exit. Indeed, the servant has become the master. All in God's will of course—generator, operator, destroyer—as there can be no other. Ergo Theofatalism.

A Response to Suffering

Of all the perplexing questions mankind is capable of raising, none is more troublesome than why do so many good people suffer and so many bad people prosper. Anger and fear, rage and terror or depression are common responses to such injustice. Suffering seems to be a necessary part of life for everyone sooner or later. But what if suffering is part of the natural plan of God? Some who suffered greatly have testified to feeling the presence of God, which helped them survive the worst and even found inner peace during their deepest trials. Others are broken beyond repair by life and, like Humpty Dumpty, cannot be put back together again. The son of God lamented on the cross, "My God, why have you forsaken me?" (Matthew 27:46, Mark 15:34). So when you ask where is God when we suffer, consider where He was when his only son died on the cross. We like to thank God for the good things of life, but few would even dream of making him/it the source of all that happens. That God—generator, operator, destroyer—is the source of all bad things is plainly stated in scripture (Isaiah 45:7) but many theologians lay the blame for suffering on all humans who are born sinners deserving only of eternal punishment in Hell (Ecclesiastes 7:20, Matthew 10:28, Luke 12:4–5, Romans 3:23, 1 John 1:8, Romans 3:10–18).

Christian writers who deal with this issue reference scriptures that command us to love God and to keep his commandments no matter what happens. The standard theodicy—argument for God in the midst of suffering—is since God is only good and loving we are not to question why good people suffer, but we can feel confident with Job that "though he slays me I will still trust in Him" (1 John 4:8, Job 13:15). They claim that "all things work together for good for those who love God and are called according to his purpose" (Romans 8:28). Notice this is not an unconditional promise, so what if you are not called for his purpose? The idea that mankind's willful original sin by the first man Adam caused it all just does not make sense, because that would mean mankind is more powerful than God, the one who created it all—including sin and belief in human free will.

A LABYRINTH WALK OF LIFE

In response to suffering, Apostle Paul instructed insipient Christians being martyred by Rome to "give thanks in all things for this is the will of God for you" (1 Thessalonians 5:18). If anything should be different, it would be. The Bible says it was God's will for the Jews to reject Jesus as Messiah and were destroyed by Rome because their eyes and ears were closed so they would not repent and be saved, and that was their destiny (Isaiah 6:9–10, Matthew 10:13–15, Mark 4:10–12, 1 Peter 2:8) The greatest gift was the life and sacrifice of Jesus who some claim was God himself come to suffer and erase the sins of mankind—which he created in his own image and likeness (Genesis 1:26; John 1:1, 3:16; Romans 10:9). Jesus declared, "Greater love has no one than this; that a man lay down his life for his friends/disciples" (John 15:13). Those who accept him as Lord and savior are promised bliss in eternal life with him (John 3:16, Romans 10:9). But he said that only those whom God selects/calls/enables will make that decision (John 6:44, 65). Jesus said a man was born blind just so his power of miraculous healing could be demonstrated, and neither he nor his parents had sinned (John 9:1–3). Jesus also said, "Blessed are those who mourn for they shall be comforted" (Matthew 5:4). In the life to come, if any, justice will be done, and it will all come out all right in heaven (Romans 8:32). "For these momentary, light afflictions are producing for us an eternal weight of glory far beyond all comparison and comprehension" (2 Corinthians 4:17). Suffering must be necessary because if everyone enjoyed heaven on earth there would be nothing to hope for in the afterlife, if there is one. "For our light affliction, which is but for a moment, is working for us a far more exceeding and eternal weight of glory, while we do not look at the things which are seen, but at the things which are not seen. For the things which are seen are temporary, but the things which are not seen are eternal" (2 Corinthians 4:17–18).

In Hinduism and belief of reincarnation, present suffering is the just reward for behavior in previous lives and preparation for future lives. In Buddhism, suffering is depicted as the lot of human beings simply as the way things are. They say suffering is caused by discontent, so to remove suffering, just be content with what is no matter how painful and deplorable. Homeless refugees in ravaged countries and disabled veterans from the wars around the world may have difficulty accepting their suffering is the will of God, and justifiably so. The modern dialectical behavior therapy invokes mindfulness from Buddhism to help suffering people navigate their troubled lives—observe and accept all things as temporary without judging, because you cannot defeat God. You have to accept misery to get out of hell on earth. Buddhist nun Pema Chodra wrote in *When Things Fall Apart* (2011) the goal of Buddhism is to allow ourselves to experience fully whatever we encounter in life, to face what is repulsive, to help those who cannot be helped, and to go to scary and dark places for that is the way of personal growth. It is the goal of accepting the extremes or opposites as merely the way that life is—it is what it is because God makes it that way. "The Lord makes poor and makes rich; He brings some low and lifts some up" (1 Samuel 2:6–7). "When a disaster comes to a city, has not the Lord caused it?" (Amos 3:6). "Though you build your nest as high as the eagle's, from there I will bring you down, declares the Lord" (Jeremiah 49:16, Obadiah 1:4).

St. Paul said he had found the secret to feeling content regardless what his circumstances were (Philippians 4:11–12). All burdens come with benefits, so if you are suffering consider that each day is one day less to go. Life is too short to let circumstances determine your joy. You can feel good inside no matter what happens outside. Jesus said, "The spirit gives life, the flesh counts for nothing" (John 6:63). Whether you experience fear and anger or comfort and contentment in life, it all must be God's will, or it would be different. Not the manmade god in holy books, but the prime mover in the universe… generator, operator, destroyer… GOD. Ergo Theofatalism. Can you believe that?

Four Challenges in Aging

Aging happens, death is inevitable, and nobody knows what comes after, which naturally gives people anxiety if they think about it. We all must meet this challenge but very few are prepared for it, and perhaps that is humanly impossible. Professor emeritus Irvin Yalom said facing death is like staring at the sun. But eventually, it cannot be avoided as death intrudes in all families. There are about 2.6 million funerals annually in America, 7,123 per day and 296 per hour, but you would not know it unless your family is one of the statistics. However, we are programmed to live and not to die. The late founder of Apple Inc., Steve Jobs, observed that even those who think they are going to heaven don't want to die to get there. And moviemaker, Woody Allen said, "I don't want to live forever in my work, I want to live forever in my apartment. I don't mind the idea of dying, I just don't want to be there when it happens." Although it is the inevitable end to life, preparation for aging and death still is a taboo in many western cultures so it has not been integrated into normal living. Anthropologist Margaret Mead said we celebrate at weddings, we rejoice at births, but when someone dies, we pretend nothing happened. In some cultures, aging and dying is a family affair integrated into daily family activities. The Bible says the allotted life span of mankind is three score and ten years (Psalm 90:3) but half of the people in America die by age eighty and most of the rest by age ninety, and the final years may not be very pleasant. If dying is a natural part of life, why do we fear it and fight it so much? Perhaps the shock cannot be totally avoided, but maybe it is time to seek a better way.

Each of us is given a labyrinth to walk through life, so let us count the ways of walking through it at the end. There are possibly four—as with four seasons, four points on the compass, four gospels, etc. For this purpose, they are discussed as the physical/sensing, spiritual/intuition, intellectual/thinking, and emotional/feeling aspects of personality. People approach aging with the same resources they used throughout their lives, so these four resources are arranged in a top to bottom ranking of ability and preference by each individual. Your own preference may be different from the order presented here. This discussion follows the personality model called the Myers-Briggs Type Indicator (MBTI(c) CPP, Inc.). Google MBTI for the details. This essay is longer than others, so take your time.

First and most observable are the *physical changes* that are visible and measurable with the senses. They include the obvious changes and slowing down that even exercise and diet cannot deter forever. The hidden challenges may be invisible, but that only makes them more traumatic when they cause physical symptoms to appear. The main problem with dying is something has to kill you. The body becomes more prone to invaders that before were easily repulsed. There are more than six thousand ways to die in America. The most likely are heart disease, cancer, stroke, and diabetes. This aging process seems to be regulated by the length of something called telomeres appended to the chromosomes we are born with. As cells die and are replicated, the telomeres dry up, which controls our individual longevity and senility. What regulates telomeres, nobody knows. Although the advice from experts is to keep on keeping on in the "use it or lose it" mode, the aging transitions may be invisible within cells, but that only makes them more traumatic when they cause physical symptoms eventually to appear. As F. Scott Fitzgerald described in *The Crack Up (1936)*, "There is a sort of blow that comes from within—that you don't feel until it's too late to do anything about it, until you realize with finality that in some regard you will never be as good again." You can accept it or fight it, but you cannot change it. However, some doctors seem to think that aging is a curable illness to be defeated at all costs. When they cure all the diseases, then what will people die from? Actually, people have options for care and treatment of terminal illness but very few are prepared for such decisions without careful preplanning and emotionally charged family discussions, which seldom occur until the final crisis. The body is a temporary vessel to be discarded at the right time. Jesus said, "The spirit gives life, the flesh counts for nothing" (John 6:63).

The *second* challenge in aging comes from the *intuition or human imagination*, which drives all creativity. It can see around corners, and it can anticipate the future. Albert Einstein thought that imagination was more important than knowledge because "The intellect has little to do on the road to discovery. There comes a leap of consciousness, call it intuition or what you will, and the solution comes to you and you don't know how or why." Napoleon Bonaparte (1769–1821) concluded, "Imagination rules the world." It was a delight when the future held promise and accomplishment, but a future leading only to suffering, humiliation, and oblivion eventually may erode the mind and produce anxiety and depression accompanied with anger. Those with a spiritual belief in some blissful life after life may find comfort in their imagined spiritual transition. Religion has its place, but sometimes it is more depressing than comforting. But F. Scott Fitzgerald wrote in *The Crack Up (1936)*, "In the real dark night of the soul it is always three o'clock in the morning." The late pathologist and preemptive suicide advocate, Dr. Jack Kevorkian (1928–2011) resolved his own demise by concluding, "After all, how painful can oblivion be?" And psychiatrist Dr. Victor Frankl (1905–1997) who survived the Nazi concentration camps, said if you have a "why" to live you can tolerate almost any "how." This idea, of course, failed millions of souls who were lost against their own will during WWII. Willis Carrier, inventor of air-conditioning, said, "The secret to happiness is imagining the worst that can happen and planning to accept it." Some people may find comfort in their faith as did Job, "Though he slays I will still trust in him" (Job 13:15). Apostle Paul accommodated his own aging thus: "We glory in our sufferings, because we know that suffering produces perseverance; perseverance, character; and character, hope… Though outwardly we are wasting away, yet inwardly we are being renewed day by day. For our light and momentary troubles are achieving for us an eternal glory that far outweighs them all" (Romans 5:3–4, 2 Corinthians 4:16). If you believe that, say amen.

The *third* challenge in aging is *intellectual or cognitive.* Learning new stuff becomes more difficult and tedious and less rewarding—keeping up with all the new technology becomes less and less exciting. Memories of the past, both the pleasure and the pain, intrude upon your thoughts. Once done, nothing in the past can be redone differently. Dreams can invade your restless sleeping cycles, leaving you more tired when you awake and troubled by their mysteries. Thoughts of pending disability and worries about the impending future can invade normal life so that activities once pleasurable lose their zest. In the worst cases, one forgets who they are as the mind retreats into a dark cave where no one else is allowed entry—but other terminal diseases are just as frightening and gruesome when you think about them. Normal mental resilience that met and resolved problems of living in the past now can induce irritability, anger, and depression as the options become less and less desirable. The Roman first century stoic Epictetus taught that events do not disturb men's minds, "but their thinking does." C. G. Jung observed, "I have seen many people who suffered from all sorts of ailments of the body simply on account of wrong convictions." Changing thinking to accommodate aging reality is the goal of cognitive behavior therapy (CBT) and Rational Emotive Behavior Therapy (REBT), which has had mixed success in helping people to accept the unacceptable by resisting raw emotions with logical reasoning. Apostle Paul gave this advice, "Whatever is true, whatever is right, whatever is pure, whatever is lovely, whatever is admirable, if anything is excellent or praiseworthy, think about such things, and the peace of God will be with you" (Philippians 4:7–9). Some people may remain mentally alert and rational while enjoying life until the end and others may not, making demands upon family or caregivers for the personal care they need when the mind (whatever that is) no longer remains in control.

Fourth, the feelings and emotions that were the source of many pleasures and excitement that make life worth living become dull and retreat into a shrunken atrophy. Enjoyment of entertainment and pleasures of the past are replaced with recurring fears and panic attacks as the realization emerges that each day is one day less to live, and what comes after nobody knows. Social support fades away as lovers, friends, and relatives succumb to the grim reaper, one after the other, leaving no doubt about your own impending demise. Giving them up and letting go of your own body may be the last great adventure. Shakespeare advised Macbeth to "give sorrow words because the grief that does not speak knits up the oe'rwrought heart and bids it break." It may be necessary to process the emotional changes with aid of a counselor if relatives and trusted friends are unable or unwilling to help hold these strong feelings and life changes, which they see coming in their own futures.

The range of responses to these challenges in aging is quite broad, from gracious radical acceptance and even possibly welcome as the completion of a live well lived and the escape from suffering, to a cynical and begrudging resistance with the worries of each day piled one upon another, if one feels alone and inadequate to the challenges without social support. The airbrushed models on the AARP magazine covers eventually will all become the true image of aging—like the portrait of Dorian Gray. The late author and atheist Christopher Hitchens said the hardest part about dying was realizing the party is going on without you. Some people may leave something for history, but most people scarcely leave any ripples in the waters of life. The longer you live, the faster time seems to pass; as the years pile up, each one becomes a shorter interval of your life. Medical resources slowly are acknowledging the special needs of aging as the 76 million baby boomers—born from 1945 to 1965—enter retirement poorly equipped to navigate these troubling waters.

This journey into the unknown could be like walking the Chartres Labyrinth, which symbolizes life on the cover page of the books in this series. We leave the source at birth and traverse the four segments of the labyrinth through life as they are given to each of us, then we retrace the pathway in return to the source beginning at midlife to approach death. Everyone must take the walk alone for themselves. The only rules are begin and continue, putting one foot in front of the other, until the final transition emerges while becoming redundant and losing control of your life. Jesus told his disciple, "When you were young you dressed yourself and went wherever you pleased, but when you are old someone else will dress you and take you where you do not want to go" (John 21:18). So to paraphrase the nihilism of the great king Solomon, enjoy life while it lasts and let it go when it ends, because it is all meaningless in the end. If you can. All in God's will of course. Ergo Theofatalism. More about this in part 2.

The Mysterious Human Brain

The humans on earth are diverse physically and multicultural in language and customs, which leads to continual chaotic wars and struggles for survival and control—not much different than other creatures on earth. In some human cultures, continuous change is worshipped and in others the historical traditions are maintained from generation to generation. Stability and change seem to be necessary opposites. Capitalism is based on continually converting luxuries into necessities, but there are primitive human cultures that have scarcely changed in a thousand years. One aspect of humanity that intrigues me is the unconscious human doings that drive much of their behaviors. Most people are so busy human doing they have no time for human being. Unless they have a preference for intuition, people are unlikely to have much sensitivity of their spiritual life. Many are so busy doing stuff most people never stop long enough to look inward to explore the psychic landscape of ideas instead of things. It is like they are having a party on a houseboat floating down a river heading for a waterfall. C. G. Jung observed that "those who look outward dream, and those who look inward awake." He also said that "inside all chaos, there is a secret order." Searching for this order in human society when it seems to be unreasonable is the goal of contemplative therapy. (*Practitioners of contemplative psychotherapy become experts at recognizing sanity within even the most confused and distorted states of mind and are trained to nurture this sanity in themselves and in their clients.*) One might conclude that chaos is more common than order after observing all the suffering and insanity in the world. Perhaps this is comforting if your life is in chronic chaos… or not.

The necessary opposites of inner and outer intrigue me precisely because, like Jung, my personality is attracted and is fueled by the inner workings of the human brain, what may be termed unconscious mind or introverted intuition. Most of the time people run about in their conscious minds, never realizing it is only the top of the iceberg in human beings. The brain seems to be the only organ that can analyze itself. The others just do what they are programmed to do. The brain of science genius, Albert Einstein, was removed and dissected in attempts to determine what made him different from ordinary people, but the investigators could not tell any difference.

Apparently, the biophysical material does not define the person. But what does?

Brain research has split into three disciplines of psychology, psychiatry, and neurology and neither respects the work of the others—which leaves traditional therapy to licensed clinical social workers. Exploring the human brain with fMRI scans is like mapping the moon through a telescope. It seems to have a mind of its own and apparently can even repair itself after damage in some circumstances. We don't really know how it works, but we can tell when the brain malfunctions because of the behavior that ensues, which may violate cultural norms and threaten personal safety. The diagnostic manual for psychiatry, DSM-V, describes more than three hundred different forms of mental disorders, one of which is termed a spiritual crisis—a confrontation with God. There are so many options that practically everyone could be diagnosed with one or another of them. They still come with stigma and taboos in modern society. Drug treatments prescribed by psychiatrists for mental disorders are poorly understood and applied mostly on a trial and error basis, often with serious side effects because each person has a unique and unpredictable metabolism. It can take months and longer to find the most effective medicine.

Magicians demonstrate that the human brain can be fooled very easily because you really cannot believe your own eyes. Advertisers and merchandisers have learned how to manipulate buyers to make their desired purchases. Print NEW on a product container and people will rush to buy it, or raise the price 50 percent and then advertise it at 25 percent off and buyers will think they are saving money. Researchers found the left and right hemispheres of the brain sometimes have difficulty accommodating different inputs, as with words and pictures. The corpus collosum, which connects the two sides, seems to be more active in women than in men. Movie directors know the background music can help set the mood for what you are watching. Military trainers have learned how to obtain conformity among the recruits who come from diverse backgrounds by controlling behavior, which changes brain activity, changing civilians into soldiers, airmen, sailors, and marines. But when veterans return they often have difficulty readjusting to civilian life. Voters are known to select politicians based on their assumed competence and truthfulness, which is perceived merely by looking at their faces 70 percent of the time—hence the power of television in political campaigns. Job interviewers know that first impressions count, but applicants now need to apply online. So they must carefully include the key words needed to stimulate interest in their resumes.

One confusing human aspect is that of memory, which seems to be a manifestation of *Homo sapiens* not well understood at all. Learning must rely upon memory, and we know that it can malfunction when overlaid with time, but how memory works and where it resides in the brain is a mystery. They say it is normal to begin losing memory capacity after age thirty because the storage capacity gets overloaded and must drop out some information to make space for the new. But with age, some people experience a memory decline more serious. The patient with Alzheimer's disease may recall specific events of youth while not recognizing current family members. How memory, time, and consciousness are related is one of the mysterious unknowns in neurology. It appears that objects, colors, words, sounds, etc., are stored in different parts of the brain and some form of executive function recombines them for recall. Thus, memory is not so much recalling the past as it is reconstructing it. This is what happens in dreams when the brain seems to be processing events like assembling a jigsaw puzzle. Possibly the most amazing example of memory is the way a concert pianist can play classical music from memory without the printed score, or the way stage actors can recite the script for a complex play. But one of the most unreliable uses of memory is the eyewitness testimony used in courts at law.

Experiments show that several people viewing the same scene can see much different things.

Possibly the most mysterious function of the human brain is its ability to imagine what does not yet exist—whether good or bad. Like the people who keep buying lottery tickets with astronomical odds of winning or the inventors who create new products most people never dream of. Napoleon said that imagination rules the world, and Einstein said imagination is more important than knowledge. Research and magic tricks indicate the human brain has a mind of its own when deciphering truth from deception—which often is beyond conscious control. You cannot possibly know and use all the neurons of the brain consciously, so much of human behavior is driven subconsciously, like an iceberg. The top must go where the bottom takes it. The documentary series by National Geographic called *Brain Games* illustrates many actions of the brain that are independent of conscious awareness. Consequently, conscious control of the human brain may be an illusion.

We may not know consciously what we know until we need to know it. But we don't know what we cannot know, like the future. And some things worth knowing are beyond words to describe, as in the energy of life and love—or the nature of God. So many people on planet earth individually and collectively stumble and lurch from crisis to crisis, never really rising much above their lowest common denominator, wealth and fame of the few notwithstanding. In addition, knowledge is expanding faster than possible for everyone to accommodate, and some are more gifted than others with God's favor. "The Lord kills and makes alive; The Lord makes poor and makes rich; He brings some low and lifts some up" (1 Samuel 2:6–7). So we all must carry on from the position in life that we occupy since "we" (whatever that is) do not control our own lives. We all must walk the labyrinth of life each one is given, which includes those in palaces as well as prisons and hospitals and the homeless huddled in the streets and refugee camps. All in God's will of course… generator, operator, destroyer… GOD. American founder Benjamin Franklin (1706–1790) concluded, "The longer I live the more convincing proofs I see of this truth: that God governs in the affairs of men." It controls everything from atoms to galaxies and we all must take what it gives and give what it takes… ergo Theofatalism.

Destiny Calls

This thing called destiny is quite interesting. C. G. Jung wrote, "Nature is awful, and I often ask myself, should one not interfere? But one cannot really, it is impossible, because fate must be fulfilled." How else can anyone explain the skyrocketing career of movie actress Jennifer Lawrence, who never studied acting but knew as a child that she would be famous when thousands of well-trained wannabes mope around Hollywood without ever being discovered. Or the stellar music career of Loretta Lynn, the coal miner's daughter. Or the boxing career of the late Muhammad Ali, a.k.a. Cassius Clay. Or the supermodeling success of Cindy Crawford, worth $100 million though she only attended college for one quarter. Or the unexplainable popularity of Joel Osteen, a motivational speaker disguised as a Christian minister. Or the business careers of Bill Gates, Steve Jobs, Mark Zuckerberg, and Warren Buffet. How about the election of billionaire Donald J. Trump for president, who won the election with dubious tactics and lost the popular vote? Many voters probably forgot that prior to his switch to Republicans, he had supported many Democrats, including John Kerry for president and Nancy Pelosi for Congress. In fact, he changed political parties five times since the 1980s, registered as an independent in 2011, and returned to Republicans in 2012. At least he is being consistent in his inconsistency. His greatest asset as a candidate was saying what he thinks, and his greatest liability as president is saying what he thinks. If it were not for Twitter, perhaps the outcome would be different.

On the other side are the lives ruined through no fault of their own and those criminals who seem to be personified evil. Thomas Paine (1736–1809) was admired by the rebels, including George Washington, as a primary voice for support of the American Revolution with publication of his essay titled "Common Sense" in 1776. But he was reviled and abandoned by his political allies after he wrote *The Age of Reason* (1794) in which he proclaimed suffrage for all, abolishment of slavery, and the rationale for Deism above Christianity. He had stopped preaching and gone to meddling. Adolf Hitler survived combat in WWI and expulsion from architectural school to gain control of Germany in 1933, and more than 55 million people suffered the consequences in WWII. You may remember how President John F. Kennedy was assassinated in 1963, but you may not know that he was saved from drowning during WWII when his PT-109 boat was destroyed by a Japanese cruiser. Presently, millions of civilians have been displaced in Iraq, Syria, and Afghanistan through civil wars conducted as proxies among the nations that support opposing sides. How could such things happen outside the will of God? We do not judge the lion as being evil when it consumes a prey animal for food, or condemn a python for squeezing its prey to death, or condemn God for the sins of its own creation or natural disasters, so why condemn human criminals for being what God created? People do not seem to merit either praise nor blame. Natural disasters are called acts of God, but people are assumed to have free will and to control their own behavior. Not. It is unreasonable to overgeneralize about it, but some clues can be found in religions.

To begin, the Quran, the holy book of Islam, says this about that. "No calamity comes, no affliction occurs, except by the decision and preordainment of Allah" (S:64.11). The Bible claims we all are on a pathway that was conceived before we were born, and the

Jews were destined to reject Jesus in fulfillment of Old Testament prophesy because "this is what they were destined for" (1 Peter 2:7–8, Isaiah 8:14). "God gave them a spirit of stupor, eyes that could not see and ears that could not hear, to this very day" (Romans 11:8, Isaiah 29:10). To make that come true, Jesus taught his disciples in secret parables so the Jews would not understand, repent and be redeemed (Matthew 13:9–14, Mark 4:10–12, Luke 8:9–10). Moreover, "A person's steps are directed by the Lord. How then can anyone understand their own way?" (Proverbs 20:24). Perhaps that pathway was laid out for you as in a labyrinth walk before the world began, "You saw me before I was born and scheduled each day of my life before I began to breathe. Every day was recorded in your book!" (Psalm 139:16). It seems that each of us must fulfill the destiny we are given as there can be no other. You don't have to search for your purpose in life, because you cannot avoid it. This book would not be possible without paper, which would not be possible without trees, which would not be possible without the earth, which would not be possible without the sun, which would not be possible without the universe, which would not be possible without the beginning, and in the beginning, God created the heavens and the earth (Genesis 1:1). You would not be possible without your parents, who would not be possible without their parents, etc., etc., etc. Get it?

There is more. King Saul and his son Jonathan both had to die in battle so that David could become king of Israel and the ancestor of Jesus the Messiah. Moreover, the tens of thousands of soldiers killed by David in his many battles were destined to be his victims (1 Samuel 18:7). Although human free will is inferred by scripture in John 3:16, Jesus declared that no one can come unto him unless the Father enables/calls them (John 6:44, 65). He also said there would be false teachers, false prophets, and false teachings to confuse even the elect—plus, there would always be poor people and wars (Matthew 24:23–25, 2 Peter 2:1–22). Apostle Paul instructed the Christians in Rome to obey the authorities and pay their taxes because that is the will of God (Romans 13:1–7). And he claimed that God is the potter and we are the clay, some to be made for royal use and some for common use (Jeremiah 18:2–6, Romans 9:12). He admonished Christians to "be thankful in all things, for this is the will of God for you" (1 Thessalonians 5:18). That is pretty difficult to accept if life has destined you for criminality, poverty, disability, pain, and suffering. But Paul said he had learned to be content no matter what his situation was in this life, whether sick or well, hungry or fed, in comfort or distress, free or imprisoned (Philippians 4:11–12). That sounds like Buddhism, which claims that acceptance of reality is the cure for suffering—including the reality of who we really are as individuals and as a species. Modern resilience psychology would invoke learning positive thinking to help overcome the automatic negative reaction to adverse events in life. St. Paul said while he was wasting away outwardly, internally he was being renewed day by day (2 Corinthians 4:16–18).

This is also the conclusion of first century stoic philosopher Epictetus who said, "The Stoic sage will never find life intolerable and will complain of no one, neither God or human. The sage lays down the burdens of resentments, regrets, slights, injuries, grudges, and disappointments as they are much too cumbersome for a person of wisdom and contentment. A wise man never fears to die because he is always ready to go. The sage must travel light. Events do not disturb men's minds but their thinking does." Henry Ford (1863–1947) concluded, "Whether you think you can or you think you cannot, you are probably right." But Apostle James proclaimed, "Go to now, you that say, today or tomorrow we will go into such a city, and continue there a year, and buy and sell, and make money: Whereas you know not what shall be on the morrow. For what is your life? It is even a vapor, which appears for a little time, and then vanishes away. Therefore, you ought to say, if the Lord wills, we shall live and do this or that" (James 4:13–15). If Jesus, the only Son of God, could not escape his destiny on the cross, what possible power do we have to escape ours? "Thy will be done" (Matthew 26:42, Luke 22:42, John 6:38).

Pastor Joel Osteen tells of his nephew who overcame teenage depression and went on to become a lawyer. But the son of Rev. Dr. Rick Warren in CA succumbed to depression and committed suicide, as did the celebrated actor Robin Williams and the famous author Ernest Hemingway among thirty thousand or more who take that exit annually, including twenty-two soldiers who commit suicide each day. God gives some people more burdens than they can carry. Everyone seems to occupy their designated place on the bell curve of life like pieces of a jigsaw puzzle, whether they reside in mansions or prisons or mental hospitals, much like walking the labyrinth of life each of us is given. After he lost everything including his health, Job declared, "Naked I came from my mother's womb, and naked I will depart. The LORD gave and the LORD has taken away; may the name of the LORD be praised" (Job 1:21).

Everyone is better off than some others and worse off than some others. So it seems that we all must be where we are or we would be someplace else, always walking the labyrinth of life we have been given, each one to his own destiny. Here is the thing; no one can live the destiny of another, not even our children, because nothing happens outside the will of God, the prime force in the universe. Ergo Theofatalism.

More about the Human Brain

The human body is a miracle of creation that contains several systems all apparently controlled by the brain—and we cannot consciously control any of it. The organs and various systems all seem to know how to perform their functions sans any conscious intervention for their control. The fact that many organs can be transplanted from one body to another several hours after death is declared shows some form of intelligence and communication exists between systems in the body not yet explained by medical science. Biology research indicates that cell death takes time and genetic DNA remains functional for very long times—centuries. The biggest mystery is how the brain seems to be the master controller, but maybe not. The human brain is the most complex organism known, and we take it all for granted so long as it works okay, but only recently have psychology, neurology, and psychiatry been applied to understanding the brain, mind, body complex better. We can put astronauts on the moon, and we can explore the stars and galaxies, and we can transplant organs and even hands and human faces, but we know very little about the brain and its operations. When it malfunctions, the resulting behaviors are so scary and bizarre there is still a gigantic wall of stigma surrounding mental illness. The line between sane and insane is very gray. Since they now can observe the living brain's internal actions from outside with fMRI scans, patterns of normal and abnormal functions are becoming more understood, and even becoming controllable by neurologists and psychiatrists. But treatment for mental disorders still is in very primitive states, and psychiatrists have little treatments to offer except toxic unpredictable drugs and electric shock therapy.

One of the most mysterious aspects of the brain is called sleep. It is a naturally recurring state of mind characterized by cyclical altered consciousness, relatively inhibited sensory activity, inhibition of nearly all voluntary muscles, and reduced interactions with surroundings. It is distinguished from wakefulness by a decreased ability to react to stimuli, but is more easily reversed than the state of hibernation or of being comatose. During sleep, most systems in an animal are in an anabolic state, rebuilding the immune, nervous, skeletal, and muscular systems. You might think the purpose and process of sleeping would be well known by now, but it is not. One of the ways of calming the mind (whatever that is) and experiencing serenity and self-insight is called meditation, or mindfulness, i.e., focusing attention here and now. Mindfulness is a keystone practice in dialectical behavior therapy. This is an ancient practice of brain relaxation having roots in China, Tibet, and India within the traditions of Hinduism and Buddhism, which migrated to the west during the last century. Basically, it calms troubled thinking by concentrating on sensory experience in extensive detail here and now without judging of any kind, sans the past and the future.

Sometimes the brain goes awry with behavioral symptoms of mental illness, which appear to be inherited to some extent. Mental illness still is a taboo that comes with stigma in western society because of its bizarre behaviors. Some of the most compulsive creativity occurs during the manic phase of manic-depression, a.k.a. bipolar disorder. While chemical medications are used in the biological treatment of mental illness, they come with lots of trial and error in practice, serious side effects, and many unknowns about how they work or don't work since everyone has a unique metabolism. The treatment of mental illness in America took a giant leap backward with closing of the mental hospitals in the 1960s, which needed to be modernized but not abandoned. While concern for patient rights and humane treatment was well meant by the US Supreme Court, which concluded they voided the civil rights of the mentally ill, the outcome has made jails and prisons the virtual psychiatric wards in America for many suffering people. Unless you work in the field you probably would be blindsided if a brain disorder—one of several hundred—affected a member of your family. If it has, you know what that means. The hidden numbers are staggering if known because most of the sufferers still are not properly diagnosed or treated. Suicides and lives lost to mental illness are very common, but still are considered taboo even among close relatives. Perhaps they fear it may be contagious—and so it might. We live in the dark ages in brain science regarding mental health.

On the other hand, science is learning to use brain functions to control prosthetic limbs and even to control some car operations by tapping the brain waves and converting them to useful signals. The LGBT community has come out of the closet and achieved neutrality and even social acceptance in America, and now it is time for mental illness to be recognized so effective diagnosis can stimulate more effective treatment and social acceptance for people with sick human brains. The National Alliance for Mental Illness is the primary resource for this effort (www.nami.org). Now is the time. All in God's will of course. Ergo Theofatalism.

Wars and Rumors of Wars

The conflict between Israel and the Palestinians seems to be a continual thorn in the side of both opponents and supporters of the proposed two-state solution. Ever since the incipient United Nations reconstituted Israel at the insistence of President Harry Truman in 1948, the conflict over disputed territory has caused strife and untold suffering for both sides among their relatively small populations of maybe eight million Jews and two million Palestinians. One can find rationale for both sides in the conflict, but the fact is that leaders of Israel still believe they have a divine right to their holy land granted to Moses by God in the Old Testament and Palestinians claim they were there first, which is true because history affirms the existence of Canaanites as early as 2,000 BCE. God caused the problem by granting the bastard son, Ishmael, of Abraham equal and opposite nationalism and then ordering Moses to invade and occupy the land which was home to some six to ten different tribes (Genesis 15:18–20, Exodus 3:7–8). He ordered the killing of all the men, women, and children of each conquered city, and the looting of all personal property (Deuteronomy 3:3–7). However, scholars now believe the assimilation by Israelites of the tribes in the area was very gradual over several hundred years and not by isolated warfare. The present existence of Palestinians is an inconvenient barrier to full occupation by Israel that must be eliminated or at least totally assimilated, never mind any rights to sovereignty the international community may convey to them. Prime Minister "Netty" and his crowd are slowly but surely expanding by building settlements in the disputed territories and using the USA to finance their invasion while they have no intention of ever actually implementing a two-state solution—UN resolutions notwithstanding.

On the other side, the Holy Quran contains many verses that can be interpreted to command Muslims to fight the infidels and People of the Book until all declare Allah is God and Muhammad is his messenger. The Holy Quran proclaims: [4.74] "Therefore let those fight in the way of Allah, who sell this world's life for the hereafter; and whoever fights in the way of Allah, then be he slain or be he victorious, We shall grant him a mighty reward." Israel is surrounded by about 500 million Muslims who all would like to see it disappear. But there are many rich, powerful Jews in America who help to assure that politicians look out for Israel. And so there will be continued resistance from Palestinians and overreactions by the Jews, while the best that can be hoped for is containment of hostility within the holy land in hopes that it will not spread throughout the Middle East. Since God caused it only God can fix it, which would require a complete change of hearts and minds, which does not seem to be on the horizon yet. Jesus said there would always be wars and preparations for wars until the end (Matthew 24:6). Not until his gospel is preached to all nations will it end (Matthew 24:14). Perhaps wars are the ways that God prunes his creation, just as Jesus said he does (John 15:1–2). That, also, is the only logical explanation for all the suffering in the world by innocents. And so it must all be God's will or it would be different... not the manmade god in holy books but the prime mover in the universe... generator, operator, destroyer... GOD. It does whatever it wants with everything from atoms to galaxies and we all must take what it gives and give what it takes. Nothing happens outside the will of God, believe it or not. Ergo Theofatalism.

Daring to Live

In western cultures, we are taught a formula for life that I call the "do this—get that" philosophy. Whether driving to work or taking rides on roller coasters, we are led to believe we control our own lives. It might be derived from our faith in science to cure all ills and discover the universal laws of physics that enabled mankind to walk on the moon and to live in the orbiting space station—or just plain faith in human free will. Science has enabled us to enjoy miracles of discovery including concrete, electricity, computers, smartphones, steel, rubber, plastics, gunpowder, anesthesia, and many other marvelous inventions. But when it comes to human relations, this philosophy ensures false security as it does not always work out as a reliable predictor of results derived from efforts. Control of anything in life, including your life, is an illusion. Possibly the worst case is putting all your faith in "the Lord" only to find that you are seemingly abandoned at the time of your greatest need, as Jesus felt hanging on that cross, "My God, why have you forsaken me?" (Matthew 27:46, Mark 15:34).

The problem is that "do this—get that" does not always work out as planned, x does not always equal (f)y in life. For example, you may choose which stocks to invest in your retirement account but you cannot control how they will perform in the future—and you do not create the stocks or control the stock market. In fact, since 2002 the number of companies with public stock has declined from 5,600 to 3,700, which means more concentration of wealth and fewer options for investments by average people. One private company example is Koch Industries, valued at $92 billion, which is wholly owned by the two Koch brothers. The only thing certain about the stock market is its history, and your choice to buy must be predetermined or it would be different. Actually, about 90 percent of the stock shares are owned by the top 10 percent income segment, so average people are not involved. You can go to college and then be unable to find a job in your chosen field while you ponder how to pay off the student loans. You can take the medicine as prescribed but you cannot control what your body does with it. You can choose your food but you do not control your metabolism. In fact, you cannot create the food you eat either. You may hope to die peacefully at home, but 70 percent of patients die in hospital, often alone and connected up to life extension systems that only prolong suffering.

Often plans do not work out, people disappoint us, we experience pain when we anticipated pleasure, and endings always follow beginnings. You can own a computer or cell phone (which depends on the materials and technology that went into them) but you cannot control the Internet or protect your accounts from hackers. Good things happen to bad people, and bad things happen to good people. Life is just unfair. It requires us to make choices with consequences containing both benefits and burdens under indefinite uncertainty about the outcomes. Some people may need to fail repeatedly to learn this lesson. After Thomas Edison failed a thousand times to invent the lightbulb, he declared, "I have not failed a thousand times, now I know a thousand things that won't work." The instruction to his disciples by Jesus in Luke 6:38 to give unconditionally, and it would be returned to them with good measure packed down and running over is just not true in general. So if you believe that, it must be God's will.

We are taught to take control to make wrong things right, and we have the power to get whatever we want if we just believe we can. Jesus told his disciples with faith like a mustard seed they could cast mountains into the sea (Matthew 17:20). That has yet to be validated. The late Steve Jobs created Apple Inc. and got filthy rich but lived only to the age of fifty-seven, while his cofounder Steve Wozniak left early and took his millions with him, but Roger Wayne, their original partner, sold out his interest early for a mere $800. Trappist monk Thomas Merton (*a.k.a. Fr. M. Louis*) (1915–1968) explained human careers in *No Man Is An Island* (1955), "Some people find in the end that they have made many wrong guesses and that their paradoxical vocation is to go through life guessing wrong. It takes them a long time to find out that they are happier that way." My father wrote, "In life we cannot get everything we like, so we have to be satisfied with what we get, but I think I did the best I could under the circumstances." Here is the thing; we actually do not have any control over anything from atoms to galaxies, including the actions of the brain and body we occupy. You (who or whatever a "you" are) do not control the organs in your body, or even your brain, much less those of any others in your social and family circle.

Experiments by Benjamin Lebet showed the brain initiated hand movement subconsciously about half a second before the subject consciously decided to do so, thus showing that free will is an illusion. In baseball, the batter must begin his swing before he knows what the ball will do, and a football passer must throw into an empty place on the field before the receiver actually gets there. Parents probably can relate if they have children who became pseudo-independent prematurely after puberty, before they actually can take care of themselves. We may raise children to become independent and then feel unhappy when we succeed. Nowadays, many families become dispersed for careers and wind up being separated by great distances, in outlook in addition to miles. It is amazing how children who grow up in the same family can turn out so differently. All in God's will of course.

Every event has a cause and all causes have causes—going all the way back to the original cause in the big bang that created the universe, which makes all present events inevitable. Free will is a necessary illusion to maintain law and order in society, but an illusion nevertheless in spite of those who would argue otherwise. All the choices we make are driven from subconscious processes that we do not control consciously, while assuming the benefits will exceed the burdens. Throughout life, we compile a subconscious library of assumptions, perceptions, and conclusions about the world beginning from childhood experience—called schema—that colors and filters the way we respond to ongoing events throughout adulthood. Perception creates reality. Obviously, children from deprived and abusive or abandoned environments are likely to view the world differently from those raised in affluent neighborhoods. Thus, we are the product of the subconscious perception of the way the world works, through no control of our own. And like an iceberg, the top must go where the bottom takes it which, of course, shatters the belief in conscious control and demolishes the theories of criminality and law enforcement from free will. Of course, there are exceptions, and they must be God's will or it would be different. Occasionally, somebody rises from the ghetto and becomes rich and famous.

Most people never consider the influence of their upbringing, but Socrates said, "The unexamined life is not worth living." Now, schema therapy, developed by Dr. Jeffry Young, seeks to uncover childhood sources of eighteen psychological dysfunctions, reduce their control and develop healthy adult behaviors by limited reparenting—but few people ever get such treatment so most drift through life like the iceberg, never really learning healthy adult behavior. This maladaptive outlook can be seen in numerous personality disorders, criminality, and even wars. The healthy adult forgives the past, no longer sees themselves as a victim but as a survivor, and expresses emotions in ways that cause no harm. Since no one has a perfect childhood, even rich kids, to be somewhat dysfunctional is to be human. You may imagine the dysfunctional society that a population of schema driven people would produce. Just look around. So do not expect human society to change any time soon, unless God wills of course. If you are not depressed and anxious you don't know what is happening, and maybe that is a good thing because what you don't know cannot hurt you. Denial of reality seems to be an effective defense mechanism to help people function in situations beyond their control. But some of us cannot unknow what we are given to know, even if we wish we could. "With much wisdom comes much sorrow, the more knowledge the more grief" (Ecclesiastes 1:17–18).

Science has discovered that observing a phenomenon in physics actually changes it, so there is no security anywhere in nature. Israel prime minister, the late Golda Meir (1898–1978) said that life is like taking an airplane trip, "Once they close the door there is nothing you can do about it." Celebrated humanist Helen Keller (1880–1968) although deaf and blind, wrote in *The Open Door* (1957), "Security is mostly a superstition. It does not exist in nature, nor do the children of men as a whole experience it. Avoidance of danger is no safer in the long run than outright exposure. Life is either a daring adventure, or nothing." Thus, Rome had its gladiators and we have roller coasters, scuba diving, skydiving, NASCAR races, and combative sports in addition to the stock market and the numbers lottery—plus wars of course. The newest challenge sport is called "BattleBots," electro-mechanical two-hundred-pound robot gladiators in mortal conflict for vicarious thrills of their bloodthirsty fans. Trying to avoid uncertainty may be the cause of much mental distress, the antidote being radical acceptance of indefinite uncertainty. But acceptance creates apathy, and discontent must exist to drive progress, i.e., dialectical opposites.

Whether you are content or discontent must be God's will for you, or it would be different. The Bible says, "But who are you, a human being, to talk back to God? Shall what is formed say to the one who formed it, 'Why did you make me like this?' Does not the potter have the right to make out of the same lump of clay some pottery for special purposes and some for common use?" (Jeremiah 18:2–6, Romans 9:16–21). "A person's steps are directed by the Lord. How then can anyone understand their own way?" (Proverbs 20:24). Perhaps that pathway was laid out for you as in a labyrinth before the world began, each to his own. Psychiatrist Carl G. Jung said, "Your pathway is not my pathway. There, I cannot teach you. The pathway is within us." So it all must be God's will or it would be different, down to the last detail minute by minute. Not the manmade god in holy books but the prime mover in the universe… generator, operator, destroyer… GOD, everywhere in everything from atoms to galaxies as immaculate immanence—ergo Theofatalism. Now, go outside and play.

Work like a Slave

You may have noticed that the American dream in which each generation enjoyed a better standard of living has been in stall mode for the past generation. Many pundits have offered causes and solutions, but the trend goes on. Here is my take on it.

The history of labor in America has never been smooth. Workers merely were factors of production during the industrial revolution that was driven by a few oligarchs who monopolized oil, steel, railroads, autos, coal, banking, and the investor class. Their unbridled greed led to the stock market crash of 1929 and subsequent anti-trust and labor laws to create more competition and a healthier economy. It took a world war to create demand for workers that finally broke the Great Depression. When it was over, the generation that won WWII created a bubble that was fueled by pent-up demand, formation of new families, and government support of veterans with education and mortgage benefits. Thanks mostly to organized labor, workers saw increasing incomes and better working conditions and enjoyed the good life. Consequently, the "baby boomer" generation that they created from 1945 to 1965 were spoiled with houses, cars, and credit cards. They never learned the lessons of their grandparents not to take the good times for granted. However, employers used drastic measures to increase profits that included automated manufacturing and outsourcing jobs to countries with lower labor costs and accepting more immigrants for lower-paying jobs. This trend stimulated global transportation, communications, and banking, which increased demand for skilled-knowledge workers and left some heavily industrialized areas of America in shambles.

The federal government responded again with guaranteed student loans that expanded demand for higher education, increasing the cost for said education for jobs that did not exist, creating a new generation of "millennials" now ages eighteen to thirty-five saddled with debts they cannot escape and insufficient wages to repay them and maintain the standard of living of their parents. Long-term job security and secure pensions were replaced with individual saving plans that shifted responsibility to workers who are not able or willing to save the substantial funds needed for retirement. Something had to give, so once again the government stepped in with deficit spending to stimulate economic demand artificially by borrowing money from the international investor class, which overstimulated the stock market. Another bubble was created resulting in the Great Recession of 2009 followed by tepid growth and slackened demand for workers. Meantime, organized labor unions have been demeaned and represent a smaller group of workers in education, government, construction, and manufacturing, leaving the rest to fend for themselves.

Workers today need to realize that career planning and job security is up to them. No one is going to do it for them. Not government, not employers, and not educators. In fact, some educators have become diploma-mill predators, selling debt-financed courses with no guarantee of employment. Students take the courses they like and end up working for whomever will give them a job at whatever income the labor market will bear. They must compete in the "employment at will" market with literally no job security whatever. They may need to relocate to distant places away from families to obtain jobs not existing in their hometowns—and do it repeatedly. Some people are more mobile than others for various reasons, financial and cultural. The highest-paying jobs in professions and technical skills are reserved for the few with special aptitudes and connections not possible for average high school graduates. The growing gap between haves and have-nots probably is contributing to the growing malaise and depression, which fuels drug addictions for self-medication.

The US fought the Civil War to replace slavery with a free market for the working class. Employers are free to hire and fire at will, and they demand loyalty, obedience, and productivity from their workers in return for competitive wages and safe working conditions—but not security. Freedom and liberty do not come with security. The US Department of Labor was established in 1913 to "foster, promote and develop the welfare of working people, to improve their working conditions, and to enhance their opportunities for profitable employment." You can judge its success in achieving its mission for yourself. Apostle Paul had this to say about the employer-employee relationship: "Slaves, obey your earthly masters in everything; and do it, not only when their eye is on you and to curry their favor, but with sincerity of heart and reverence for the Lord. Whatever you do, work at it with all your heart, as working for the Lord, not for human masters. Masters, provide your slaves with what is right and fair, because you know that you also have a Master in heaven" (Colossians 3:23, 4:1). So what has changed, really? All in God's will of course. Ergo Theofatalism.

A Theory of Mind

We use the word "mind" often without thinking much about it. Maybe we should. Great thinkers and scientists have been trying to figure it out for centuries without much success. Even the basic issue, whether mind is some electro-chemical process in the neurons of the brain or some nonmaterial aspect of sentient beings is yet to be settled. Contributions to the theory of mind made by Sigmund Freud (1856–1939) and Carl G. Jung (1875–1961) may be worth some discussion. Freud proposed the mind in three parts: id, superego, and ego. The id is a hedonistic power that says "just do it" without much assessment of the possible consequences. It can lead people into some serious trouble unless it is bridled. The superego says "just say no" and keeps people from venturing into the unknown or exploring the limits of human accomplishments. The ego provides the much-needed balance between the id and superego if it is properly developed and applied to decision making. Sometimes it is appropriate to just say no, and sometimes just do it, but we need the ego to choose. The challenge and goal of psychotherapy by Freud is to bring these three elements of mind up from the unconscious and by making them conscious to enable people to control their behavior, choosing the best option among several alternatives—what Jung called individuation as the main task in the second half of life. It is nothing less than a merger of the physical with the spiritual, the reconciliation of ego-self with the divine.

Although Jung accepted the theory of Freud, he added the idea from his empirical observations of patients that mind exists on three levels: the conscious mind, the subconscious mind, and the unconscious mind. The conscious mind is the repository containing awareness of awareness, which enables people to use its ability to perceive inputs through the five senses plus intuition, then to make judgments using thinking and feeling for the best possible decisions. The subconscious mind lies below the surface and contains individual lifelong collections of memories, learning, values, and orientation, which may not be needed all the time but which can be called into consciousness when useful. The subconscious also contains the details needed to perform many actions that otherwise would be an overload of memory—like riding a bicycle or brushing your teeth or hitting a golf ball or playing the piano or typing on the keyboard of a laptop. The intrusion of subconscious contents into consciousness can occur both voluntarily and involuntarily. The unconscious level of mind contains all the material that is inherited through genetics, which lays the basis for defining what it means to be human—as opposed to being, say, a chimpanzee. Jung said the unconscious contents were expressed in what he called "archetypes," which seem to be present in all human cultures, i.e., the instincts and symbols that are common to all humans throughout the world. In his view, mental distress is the result of conflicts between these three levels of mind, which can be treated by getting them all working together for the common good of individuals and humanity in general. Jung called this process "individuation" and proposed it as the main task during the second half of life. Since it is painful to do, he called it the "divine suffering."

In addition to these theories, the human body seems to have a mind of its own. Organs go about their work daily without any apparent conscious connections with the brain—as they do in all mammals. The lungs process air to extract the needed oxygen and transfer it to the blood, the heart pumps blood around in the veins and arteries, the stomach plays its necessary role in digestion of food, and the kidneys and liver plus the others all go about their functions seemingly automatically—until they malfunction. In the extreme cases, some organs can be transplanted from one body into another and continue functioning. All this activity creates the mind-body problem. How do the organs in the human body know what they are supposed to do and what makes them do it—or what makes them stop? And what role does sleep play in the functions of the brain and mind? If, as some researchers claim, sleep is necessary to calm the mind and reenergize it, where does that energy come from? It is like a battery that recharges itself—or maybe not. Perhaps it is recharged from a cosmic source not yet detectable.

Perhaps the power of the mind is shown by the placebo effect in which a sugar pill can evoke healing results same as the tested medicine in double-blind studies. In the New Age movement, they teach the outer conditions of life reflect the inner beliefs of each person. Think rich and you will be rich, think poor and you will be poor, think healthy and you will be healthy, think sick and you will be sick, think you are a champion golfer and you are. Jesus told his disciples, "Truly I tell you, if you have faith and do not doubt, not only can you do what was done to the fig tree, but also you can say to this mountain, 'Go, throw yourself into the sea,' and it will be done. If you believe, you will receive whatever you ask for in prayer" (Matthew 21:21–23). But of course, the "do this—get that" formula does not always work out as planned in real life. Good things happen to bad people and bad things happen to good people, leaving many people totally confused about the god they were taught was all perfect love. The first-century stoic Epictetus taught that events do not disturb men's minds, but their thinking does. Stoics taught that the path to happiness for humans is found by accepting that which we have been given in life, by not allowing ourselves to be controlled by our desire for pleasure or our fear of pain, by using our minds to understand the world around us and to do our part in nature's plan. Changing thinking to accommodate aging reality is the goal of cognitive behavior therapy, but who or what changes thinking is unknown and maybe unknowable.

Who is the owner/controller of "my body," "my mind," and "my soul," or "my thoughts?" Rene Descartes (1596–1650) declared, "I think therefore I am." The ancient instruction to "know thyself" actually has no meaning. When we say, "I said to myself," who is speaking? Neither psychiatry or neurology or theology has found the answer yet. The psychology of self tries to explain, but it falls short and seems like a dog chasing its own tail. Perhaps the best we can say is "I am, here and now." Repeating that phrase as a mantra can help to induce inner peace no matter what happens outside. Try it: I AM, here and now, I AM, here and now… and repeat. This meditation will help let go of the past and worries about the future while being in the present. To quiet the mind, it is necessary to practice some such meditation for thirty minutes every day, and if you are busy, then it takes an hour. Mind, brain, and consciousness still are unexplained by science, although they are a primary focus of research. The human brain has been evolving for millions of years and yet we know very little about it. There appears to be some command and control function that can change mood by thinking differently. "What is true, what is noble, what is right, what is pure, what is lovely, what is admirable, if anything is excellent or praiseworthy, think about such things" (Philippians 4:8).

This discussion leads to the observation that people all do what they do and think what they think without much conscious control, maybe none. What is below the level of conscious awareness is more powerful than what is apparent and, like an iceberg, the top must go where the bottom takes it. Moreover, everyone seems to be on a pathway that is unique to each one. Jung said, "Your pathway is not my pathway. Therefore, I cannot teach you. The pathway is within." And the Bible says, "A person's steps are directed by the Lord. How then can anyone understand their own way?" (Proverbs 20:24). Perhaps that pathway was laid out for you as in a labyrinth before the world began. All in God's will of course. Not the manmade god in holy books, but the prime mover in the universe as generator, operator, destroyer—GOD. Ergo Theofatalism.

Living the Questions

The Bible presents many challenging questions. It was written across many centuries by many different authors, copied by others and translated by even more, and if you give them all equal authority you get into trouble. For example, Apostle Paul wrote decades before the gospels and said in Romans 10:9, "If you declare that Jesus is Lord and believe in your heart that God raised him from the dead you will be saved." However, later Jesus reportedly said, "No one can enter the Kingdom of God unless they are baptized of water and the spirit" (John 3:5). Several scriptures claim the Kingdom can be seen and entered. But Jesus also claimed the Kingdom was neither here nor there but is within you (Luke 17:21, KJV). John 3:16 seems to imply that people have free will to accept Jesus as Lord, but John 6:65 quotes Jesus saying no one comes to him unless they are called by God. Luke 2:14 says "Glory to God in the highest, and peace on earth to people who enjoy his favor or people of good will!" Compare the following: "Do not think that I came to bring peace on earth. I did not come to bring peace but a sword!" (Matthew 10:34). There is no way to explain the contradiction between John 3:16 and John 6:44, 65. Look it up. One implies you have free will to select Jesus as Lord, and the other one says you don't. There are many such conflicts in the Bible, so which/what/who are you gonna believe?

A LABYRINTH WALK OF LIFE

This confusion has caused the churches of Christianity to split into many different denominations, each with their own interpretations and proof texting of scriptures, often leading to wars and religious atrocities. This practice is called by some "cafeteria Christianity" as in choosing elements from a food buffet, picking what is on your diet and leaving the rest. However, Paul declared that God is not the author of confusion but of peace among all the churches (1 Corinthians 14:33). So it follows that if the Bible contains confusion, as it does, then it must not be authored by God, either directly or indirectly. But Paul also claimed that all scripture is given by divine inspiration of God and "is profitable for doctrine, for reproof, for correction, for instruction in righteousness" (2 Timothy 3:16). At that time, all they had was the Old Testament, and most people were illiterate, so they learned only what they were taught. Be warned because Jesus said there would be false teachers and false teachings to deceive the very elect, and St. Peter also warned that they say whatever is needed to get your money (Matthew 24:23–25, 2 Peter 2:1–22).

So beware of any teaching that conflicts with the voice of Jesus in the several gospels because they and they only contain what the writers thought were his actual words, if you can believe that. But they are inconsistent and leave a lot of questions with no answers. The main question is what to take literally in twentieth-century English and what is symbolic based on the context of its time. I wrote this above, but I am repeating it here because I need to read it again. John 3:16 says, in third person, God sent his son into the world so that whoever believes in him would be saved and enjoy everlasting life… but John 6:44, 65 quotes Jesus in first person saying that only those who are called/enabled by the Father will make that decision. At one point, Jesus told his disciples they could have anything they asked for in prayer if they only believed, but at another, he said that they could not add one day to their lives or one cubit to their stature by thinking about it. Jesus said, "If you do not hate mother and father and brothers and sisters and even your own self you cannot be my disciple" (Luke 14:26). But the writer of 1 John said, "For whoever does not love their brother and sister, whom they have seen, cannot love God, whom they have not seen. And he has given us this command: Anyone who loves God must also love their brother and sister" (1 John 4:20–21). There is no possible reconciliation of such contradictions. In addition to the *Bible*, there are the *Quran, Book of Mormon, A Course in Miracles,* and other sacred scriptures that many people grant the authority of God. How these books obtain such adoration and so many loyal believers is a fundamental question in human psychology of religion.

So what are you gonna believe? Probably whatever you were taught by family and religious leaders where you happened to live who selected the scriptures they wanted you to get and omitted the others. But why so much diversity among the religions of the world? Why do they exist at all? And how come some people reject all of them as merely myths and fables? The only logical conclusion a thinking person may draw is that God must want it that way or it would be different. Not the manmade God of the Bible or any other holy books but the prime mover in the universe. Generator, operator, destroyer—GOD. It controls everything from atoms to galaxies and we all must take what it gives and give what it takes… ergo Theofatalism.

Flash Mobs in Voting Booths

Our freedoms could be killing us. Think about it. Freedom of speech, freedom of religion, freedom to congregate, freedom to own guns… they are two-edged swords. All benefits come with burdens, as God never made any one-sided coins. So long as these freedoms are exercised to preserve and protect the US Constitution they are beneficial. But they can be used to subvert and destroy the society that embraced them. For example, the freedom to own guns in the Second Amendment is preceded by the clause to establish a "well-regulated militia" in each state, which is conveniently ignored by gun advocates and the US Supreme Court decision (5–4) in *District of Columbia vs. Heller* (2008). The late comedian Will Rogers (1879–1935) observed that "whenever Congress makes a law it is a joke and whenever it makes a joke it is a law." Moreover, Americans are free to be stupid and crazy… and they can vote and make babies. Even the highly learned among us can be duped. Jesus said there would be false teachers and false prophets to deceive even the very elect (Mathew 24:23–25). When paranoid nationalism absorbs personal ambitions, the whole society becomes subject to infiltration of ideas that become contagious quickly and bode ill for the future.

Perhaps we need to take a lesson from the history of the Third Reich in Germany under Adolf Hitler, because those who ignore history are doomed to repeat it. Germans fell for the bombastic rhetoric of Hitler promising to make Germany great again. That sounds too much like President Trump. Abraham Lincoln espoused a government of, by, and for the people, but he feared its takeover by corporations who put profits above people. Now, the business of America is business, just as he feared, with no financial limit on the freedom of corporations to influence elections, thanks to the Supreme Court decision (5–4) in *Citizens United vs. Federal Election Commission* (2010). If you want to understand American politics, just follow the money. The founders created a republic with the electoral college system to elect the president because they did not trust the illiterate commoners to make the right decisions. The late comedian George Carlin (1937–2008) observed that "the average American is pretty dumb and half of the rest are even dumber." It seems that many dull voters have been mesmerized by the campaign rhetoric of President

Donald J. Trump. Benjamin Franklin thought it was an act of God. He wrote in his autobiography, "The longer I live, the more convincing proofs I see of this truth—that God governs in the affairs of men." And that must include what occurs in voting booths during elections.

Voters in my state have elected eight Republicans from rural districts and three Democrats from urban districts to the House, two Democrats to the Senate, and Democrats as governor, lieutenant governor, and attorney-general. Four states with Republican governors voted for Clinton in the 2016 presidential election, and the governor of WV, who was elected as a Democrat, switched to Republican. Our government is divided because the voters are divided. Jesus said, "Every kingdom divided against itself will be ruined, and every city or household divided against itself will not stand" (Matthew 12:25). Those who criticize the government should remember who elected them, and usually it is not a majority of registered voters because many of them do not bother to vote. So government of, by, and for the people must be limited to those who actually vote.

America is composed of countless minority groups, each claiming their freedoms guarantee them a voice in the governing process. Indeed, the US Constitution stipulates congressional representation on the number of inhabitants, and not citizens—counting slaves as three-fifths persons (article 1, section 2). Each House member presently represents about 720,000 residents, up from 30,000 stipulated in the Constitution. Peaceful assembly to petition the government is guaranteed, but now we face entrenched groups on the extreme right and left who seem poised for a fight. With the aid of a smartphone, groups can be convened almost immediately as flash mobs illustrate. The potential for harm is at least equal to the potential for good in social media. Such is the nature of necessary and dialectical opposites. Apostle Paul declared that all government is established by God, so the obligation of citizens is to obey that which God has ordained, pay your taxes and hope for the best (Romans 13:1–7). So as you ponder who to vote for, keep in mind that nobody can predict what the future may bring, let alone control it. Only God can do that, generator, operator, destroyer… GOD, the prime force in the universe. If you don't get it, you don't get it. All in God's will of course. Ergo Theofatalism.

Indefinite Uncertainty

God has a lot of explaining to do. The world is full of suffering people who often go unnoticed unless they are part of your own family. Possibly the worst examples are those poor wretches who seem to have done nothing to merit their pitiful existence—the refugees fleeing civil wars and the innocent victims of geological tragedies and medical epidemics. Many millions of Americans are either unemployed or underemployed for no fault of their own. The more you try to find a reason for it, the more your mind becomes befuddled with all the possibilities for causes of human suffering because each cause has its previous cause back to the first cause, so all events seem to be inevitable. You could begin with wondering why people, plus all the other many life forms on earth, exist in the first place. Science is pretty good with questions about how things work, but it fails to address why things are as they are… from atoms to galaxies. That is the domain of religion and philosophy, which are based more on perceptions and interpretations and intuition than they are on logical reason. Thrown into the mix of opinions are attempts to accommodate some kind of loving God as the ultimate and omnipotent cause of all things, which leads into a circular dialogue about human free will or some actual predestined cause of suffering. One explanation lays the responsibility onto God. After all, God created man in his own "image and likeness to rule over the rest of creation" (Genesis 1:26).

The Bible is not much use here because it contains so many contradictions it is totally impotent to solve the problem of suffering. One example is the Christian myth promoted by Apostle Paul that all suffering and death is traceable to the original sin of the first man, such that all are born sinful and deserving of suffering for eternity unless they accept Jesus Christ as their savior (Romans 5:12, 10:9). Try to imagine what the world would be like if there were no death—standing room only. Then he contradicted himself by saying sin committed before the law was given to Moses will not be held against anyone (Romans 5:8). Where there is no law there cannot be any sin. But Jesus disclaimed the notion of willful belief described in John 3:16 by declaring that only those called by God would accept him, and the Kingdom of God would be populated by such as little children, so they must not be born sinners for that to work (John 6:65, Matthew 19:14, Mark 10;14, Luke 18:16). He also declared a man born blind was made so to display the power of God to heal him and neither he nor his parents sinned (John 9:3). But not all of the sick were healed by their faith in him, and not all those who suffer presently are relieved either. Moreover, Cain, the first murderer—of his brother Abel in a fit of jealousy because God preferred his sacrifice of a blood offering—was not punished but was protected by God and made the father of many cities (Genesis 4:15–17). There is no explanation given for the mother of cities.

Death is the great equalizer among all human beings, whether rich or poor, and their sinful nature must be the will of God, or it would be different. Rather than explaining it, Jesus instructed his disciples to comfort and aid the suffering souls because that is also doing it unto him (Matthew 25:34–40). When he was asked in an interview if he believed in God, C. G. Jung replied, "I do not have to believe, I know." In a letter later, he made it clear that he would have given a different response if he had been asked whether he agreed with anyone's particular image of God. Because of the mysterious and incomprehensible nature of God, no image of God will ever be adequate. Jung therefore asserted the inadequacy of all images of God, including his own. He was suggesting we recognize that any and all images of God are always different from the actual nature of God—if any. Once we realize this fact, then, in Jung's view, we have taken a small, practical, but significant step forward in our spiritual development.

The Bible does not provide much hope for those who are suffering, except maybe for some form of afterlife for those who are chosen. Jesus told his disciples, "You did not choose me, I chose you" (John 15:16). Flowing throughout the New Testament is the Kingdom of God, which is mentioned seventy-four times. The Kingdom of Heaven is like unto it, presented thirty-four times, thirty-one of them in the Gospel of Matthew. They seem to be presented as one and the same thing. The Kingdom of God/Heaven is described in ten parables by Jesus, all in the Gospel of Matthew, as something "like" a situation in the common life of the times, with two repeated in Mark and one in Luke. The various different descriptions are very confusing. The Kingdom variously is described by Jesus as here and now, in the future, something that can be seen, inherited, and entered, and something that is inside you, in the midst of his followers, as well as not of this world. Scholars have attempted unsuccessfully to reconcile the various translations and interpretations and to extrapolate the meanings at the time of Jesus into applications for modern times, merely adding more confusion. What it all means is indefinitely uncertain.

The great agnostic, Thomas G. Ingersoll (1833–1899) reasoned, "Is there a God? I do not know. Is man immortal? I do not know. One thing I do know, and that is, that neither hope, nor fear, belief, nor denial, can change the fact. It is as it is, and it will be as it must be." A clergyman once said to an atheist, "If you are correct I have lost nothing, but if I am correct you may have lost everything." So we must live with indefinite uncertainty about why there is so much suffering among mankind. Perhaps one day, the answer will be given and we may or may not like the explanation. All in God's will of course. Ergo Theofatalism.

Something to Worry About

Here is something you might want to worry about. Bacteria are thought to be some of the oldest life forms on earth, maybe even the oldest from which all other species of life have evolved in more than four billion years—and nobody knows just how many there are. What is known is scary. Bacteria are all over the place, including the water and soil and air making up the earth, so your body probably is covered with them. They reproduce so rapidly by dividing cells that a colony can double its population every thirty minutes. Although bacteria are necessary microbes in your gut for digesting food, when they invade the body, they can cause serious life-threatening infections including *E. coli* and gangrene that are getting harder to cure with antibiotic drugs. More and more people are dying of bacterial infections contracted in hospitals that go unreported and untracked by the Center for Disease Control because it would panic the public. Here is why. Bacteria are able to recognize the attack and to set up defense mechanisms called biofilms that defend against the antibiotics, which become less effective the more often they are used. The problem is exacerbated by farmers who have been feeding antibiotics to pigs and cattle to improve their yields, thus helping to create resistant strains of bacteria that now are reaching epidemic levels. The big pharma companies are dropping research on antibiotics because they do not see much future profit in a drug that loses its effectiveness the more it is used. The White House took notice and has requested increased budgets for researching the problem and creating new antibiotics since the profit-driven pharmacy industry has all but stopped such research.

The latest threat was discovery in China of a mutant gene in bacteria that defeats even the last chance antibiotic drug and is sure to migrate worldwide. It has already been detected in North America. In short, antibiotics have seen better days and the anticipated deaths from bacterial infections will likely increase very rapidly unless new drugs are developed very soon. So wash your hands and shower more often and avoid the use of medical tools in hospitals where many of the infections occur. If you do get infected, expect some serious trial-and-error treatments, including possible amputations, against the drug-resistant bacteria. And we may also add the raging epidemics caused by the unrestrained virus invasions that occur from time to time. The latest of these is called the Zika virus—transmitted by mosquitos—which causes cranial disabilities among the innocent infants by infected mothers. But that is another story. Now what was that about humans being the top of the food pyramid? Mmmm? Humans are not at all immune from the many dangers lurking in nature. The immune system has evolved to counter all sorts of mortal invaders, and sometimes it wins and other times it loses. Bottom line is that with aging, the body loses its ability to fight off invaders and eventually the outcome is foretold. All in God's will of course. But you don't have to worry because Jesus declared, "The spirit gives life, the flesh counts for nothing" (John 6:63). Ergo Theofatalism.

The Jesus Cult

The rich folks in all the Christian churches may be in for a jolting surprise. Jesus did not call his disciples to join him in health, wealth, and happiness. Instead, he called them to leave trades and families to follow him loyally and faithfully into suffering and yeah, even death. Sort of like a Jesus cult. In fact, the first Christians in Jerusalem lived in a commune, sharing their resources equally. One couple who withheld some of their wealth were struck dead for their deceit (Acts 2:44–47, 5:1–10). That apparently was a big deal because Jesus declared, "Do not store up for yourselves treasures on earth, where moths and vermin destroy, and where thieves break in and steal. Store up for yourselves treasures in heaven, where moths and vermin do not destroy, and where thieves do not break in and steal. For where your treasure is, there your heart will be also" (Matthew 6:19–21). And "If you love me, keep my commandments" (John 14:15). Read Luke 6 to learn what he taught. Here is one sample: "You have heard that it was said, 'Love your neighbor and hate your enemy.' But I tell you, love your enemies and pray for those who persecute you, that you may be children of your Father in heaven" (Matthew 5:43–44). This instruction seems to oppose human nature, which also was created by God.

There are many teachings of Jesus in the gospels that would drive people out of church if they were taught in Sunday school and preached from the pulpits. The truth is that church leaders cherry pick and proof text what they want people to get to preserve their careers and treasuries. If they preached the full gospel of Jesus, the churches might be empty. Thus, all Christians are hypocrites, more or less.

Moreover, none of his disciples were volunteers—they were all chosen for their roles as martyrs. Need some proof? "No one comes to me unless the Father calls/enables/selects them" (John 6:44, 65). "You did not choose me, I chose you" (John 15:16). "This is the man (Saul of Tarsus) I have chosen to carry my name to the Gentiles, and I will show him how much he must suffer for my name" (Acts 9:15–16). Even Jesus was not a volunteer savior as he prayed in the

Garden for the cup of suffering to be removed. "Father, take this cup from me. Yet not what I will, but what you will" (Mark 14:36). Being his disciples came with a devastating cost. "If you do not hate mother and father and brothers and sisters and even your own self you cannot be my disciple" (Luke 14:26). "Sell all you have and give the proceeds to the poor and come follow me" (Matthew 19:23–25). "It is easier for a camel to go through the eye of a needle than for a rich man to enter the kingdom of heaven" (Matthew 19:24). "Blessed are the poor, the meek, the suffering, and the outcasts for they shall see God" (Matthew 5:3–5). "Whoever does not bear his cross and come after me cannot be my disciple… whoever that does not forsake all that he has cannot be my disciple" (Luke 14:27–33). "There is no greater love has no one than this; that a man lay down/gives up his life for his friends" (John 15:13). His teachings were granted only to those destined to receive them and were denied to those who were not called to repentance and divine selection (Matthew 13:11, Mark 4:12, John 6:44, 65). Of the Jews, the Bible says, "God gave them a spirit of stupor, eyes that could not see and ears that could not hear to this very day" (Romans 1:7–9). Those Jews who rejected him as their savior were destined for their demise (1 Peter 2:7–8).

You won't get this message in churches because that could scare all the wealthy members and hypocrites into stampedes for the exits. Instead, what you get are the opposing messages from prosperity preachers that God is love and wants everyone to be healthy, wealthy, and happy. Moreover, everyone is a sinner who must recognize Jesus Christ as Lord and believe that God raised him from death, or be consigned to hell for eternity (Romans 10:9). "Fear him who after killing the body has power to cast you into hell" (Luke 12:4–5). Oh, and don't forget to join the church of your choice and pay the tithe. By the way, the tithe is derived from tribute paid to King Melchizedek by Abraham from the spoils of war (Genesis 14:18, Hebrews 7:1–2). Jesus prophesied there would be false prophets and false teachings to deceive even the elect (Matthew 24:23–25). And it all must be God's will or it would be different. "All scripture is God-breathed and is useful for teaching, rebuking, correcting and training in righteousness" (2 Timothy 3:16). Ergo Theofatalism. So what does that have to with you today? Maybe nothing and maybe everything.

Friend or Foe

The role of Judas Iscariot as the betrayer of Jesus is commonly known among Christians. He is the disciple who accepted thirty pieces of silver from the temple priests as payment for identifying the Messiah in the early morning ambush by Jewish leaders who wanted him dead. He is presented as the personification of evil and the incarnation of Satan himself come to betray the sacred son of God (Matthew 26:14–16, Luke 22:3–6). It was a dirty job, but somebody had to do it. The Bible says that after the crucifixion of Jesus, Judas was so remorseful that he flung the money back into the temple and committed suicide; one account says he jumped off a cliff (Acts1:18–19) and the other says he hanged himself (Matthew 27:5). Either way, Judas is cast as the worst of the worst in setting Jesus up to be crucified. He deserves neither pity nor forgiveness. But wait a minute, because there is more to the story.

The role of Judas is recognized by scholars as prophesized in the Old Testament, so his action was not an act of betrayal so much as an act of God. It was prophesized, so it had to happen (Zachariah 11:12–13). Jesus himself realized and accepted the necessary role of Judas in the drama that unfolded during the last supper, as he announced that one of the selected ones would betray him and suffer greatly for it. Jesus even encouraged Judas to get on with it to fulfill the prophecy, which he must have known was a necessary prelude to his undeserved inquisition and crucifixion. "What you are about to do, do quickly" (John 13:27). Working backward, one may reason that the resurrection was the necessary climax of his mission and the beginning of the rest of the story. The resurrection must be preceded by the crucifixion, which must be preceded by the inquisition, which must be preceded by the unlawful arrest, which must be preceded by the betrayal. And Judas was the one chosen for this role in the drama. One may also conclude that all the other characters in the final act of the play were portraying their designated and necessary roles in the drama that unfolded. The Jewish temple leaders, the high priest, King Herod, Pontius Pilate, the Roman soldiers, the women disciples; they all played their roles flawlessly. And so did Judas Iscariot. (You can read the story of Judas with some variations in the gospels of Matthew chapters 26–27 and Mark chapter 14 and Luke chapter 26, and John chapter 13–14 and Acts 1:18–19.)

So where are we going with this? If you take the scriptures literally, poor Judas seems to have been given a raw deal. He was cast into a destiny not of his own making, and he suffered terribly for being in the wrong place at the wrong time. If you take the story symbolically, perhaps it says more about God than about Judas. As Shakespeare said, the whole world is a stage and all the men and women merely are actors. And the playwright, the producer, and the director are God. It is a scary/dreadful thing to know your life is in the hands of the living God—who rules with Christ in one hand and Satan in the other (Hebrews 10:31). Saint/Mother Teresa said, "God does whatever he wants with whomever he wants, and we all must take what he gives and give what he takes… with a smile." She suffered greatly for ten years before she died and lamented to Jesus, "If you treat others like you treat me, it is no wonder you have so few friends. My soul is no longer one with you." The late Helen Schucman, scribe of *A Course in Miracles* (1975) wrote, "Disobeying the will of God is meaningful only to the insane. In truth, it is impossible." Which leads us back to the labyrinth walk of life where there are no mistakes, only predetermined choices and consequences. Of course, this could be a false conclusion based upon faulty logic, and Judas might have rejected the money so we would be talking about a different story. But he didn't, and nobody can go back in time to do anything over differently. So if there are some skeletons in your closet that make you feel remorseful about the past, you might consider that it all must be the will of God, or it would be different. Not the manmade god in holy books, but the prime mover in the universe—generator, operator, destroyer… GOD. Ergo Theofatalism.

Freedom versus Security

America is facing a serious demographic challenge to the economy, which is being ignored like the elephant in the living room. The 76 million aging baby boom generation—those born in 1945–1965—changed America with credit cards, ATM machines, and home mortgages refinanced as cash cows. They cared little for their own future security and lived for the here and now, which is here and now. As they enter retirement years, they are beginning to realize they saved too little to live comfortably without massive government aid. Many people seem to avoid thinking about their old age until their fifties. By then, it is too late to save enough for a secure retirement, and so they become dependent upon Social Security. The combined unfunded liability of Social Security and state pensions is estimated by Motley Fool to exceed $20 trillion. One survey by the Motley Fool concluded that 56 percent of the elders more than age fifty have less than $50,000 saved for retirement and a third of them have practically no savings at all. As the employer-provided defined pensions that funded the old age of their parents were replaced by personal responsibility for their aging transitions with 401(k) plans and IRAs, their tomorrow now has become their today, and it is no bed of roses.

Combined with the global outsourcing and impact of automation in manufacturing well-paying jobs have declined, and the aging baby boomers now pose a shock to the economy. Their needs for housing, medical care, and efforts to maintain their lifestyles have been passed on to their children and grandchildren, and the transition is not going smoothly. Moreover, they passed their spendthrift tradition on to the next Generation X, and so their children are not saving sufficiently for their own old age either. How can they, when the cost of living the way they enjoy takes all of their incomes and more, thanks to those ubiquitous credit cards and greedy banks. Poverty is an expanding epidemic in America, the land of the free and the home of the brave.

Experts predict that automation and artificial intelligence will create 15 million new jobs during the next decade but eliminate 25 million—mostly those paying below $30 per hour. Part of the solution was government guaranteed student loans for education for jobs that do not exist. This is nothing less than public subsidizing of higher education, elevating the cost very rapidly and artificially increasing demand. Higher education without commensurate jobs merely creates a lot of disappointed people. The total student debt now exceeds $1.2 trillion and rising, and they cannot escape by declaring bankruptcy. That now bodes ill for another generation of Americans who cannot save for retirement and pay off their debts as well. It also will impact the economy because that is money they cannot spend on personal purchases. About half of recent college graduates live at home with their aging parents, and half of all adults remain single. In addition, the southern border with Mexico was intentionally opened up to expand the economy, encouraging mass immigrations of poorly educated and socially dependent residents who promptly produced a new generation of needy citizens. So we have the worst of all worlds, one with an increasing aging population unprepared for retirement and lower expectations for the younger generation who cannot afford to pay taxes for their own entitlements.

Psychologist Eric Fromm (1900–1980) wrote in *Escape from Freedom* (1941), "If the economic, social and political conditions do not offer a basis for the realization of individuality, while at the same time people have lost those ties which gave them security, this lag makes freedom an unbearable burden. It then becomes identical with doubt, with a kind of life which lacks meaning and direction. Powerful tendencies arise to escape from this kind of freedom into submission or some kind of relationship to man and the world which promises relief from uncertainty, even if it deprives the individual of his freedom." You can have either freedom or security, but not both. The more of one, the less of the other.

Scottish professor and nobleman Alexander Tytler (1747–1813) reportedly predicted in the eighteenth century that all democracies must be temporary because democratic forms of government have a natural evolution from initial virtue toward eventual corruption and decline. "The majority always votes for the candidates who promise the most benefits from the public treasury, with the result that every democracy will finally collapse due to loose fiscal policy, which is always followed by a dictatorship… nations always progress through the following sequence: From bondage to spiritual faith; from spiritual faith to great courage; from courage to liberty; from liberty to abundance; from abundance to selfishness; from selfishness to complacency; from complacency to apathy; from apathy to dependence; from dependence back into bondage." C. G. Jung wrote of the current situation thus: "The infantile dream-state of the mass man is so unrealistic that he never thinks to ask who is paying for this paradise. The balancing of accounts is left to a higher political or social authority, which welcomes the task, for its power is thereby increased; and the more power it has, the weaker and more helpless the individual becomes." President Lincoln wrote his biggest fear was that corporations would gain control of government, and the republic would be lost. Considering the Supreme Court decision in *Citizens United vs. Federal Election Commission* (2010), which removed the cap on political donations by corporations, we seem to be well on the way. Although the US national debt is climbing beyond $20 trillion, the US economy now depends on annual deficits that are necessary to stimulate its flagging growth rate. When you add the debts of states and local jurisdictions, it all adds up to some real money. The United States is the most ethnically and culturally diverse nation in history, and it is an experiment still in process. The US Congress is divided because the people are divided. And we may have reached the point where both political parties must make promises they cannot keep to get elected.

In 2016, discontented American voters elected Donald J. Trump as president, a billionaire with no training or experience for the job, who promised to solve all the problems with the power of a dictator the way he ran his international business empire—hiring and firing people at will. How his administration will work out is still to be determined. Remember this; the first rule in politics is to get elected, and the second rule is to get reelected. His election reminds of the power granted to Adolf Hitler who also campaigned on the goal of making Germany great again. Every society has its dark side—what C. G. Jung called the shadow—lurking in its collective unconscious waiting to cause trouble, hence there are economic depressions, revolutions, and wars. Apostle Paul declared that all governments are instituted by God and should be obeyed (Romans 13:1–7). So it must all be God's will or it would be different. "When a disaster comes to a city, has not the Lord caused it?" (Amos 3:6). "Though you build your nest as high as the eagle's, from there I will bring you down, declares the Lord" (Jeremiah 49:16, Obadiah 1:4). Such was the rise and fall of his religious empire created by the *late* Rev. Robert Schuller in the Crystal Cathedral that he built in Orange, CA, only to see it fall into bankruptcy before he died, leaving about $50 million in unpaid bills. As with people and churches, so with nations. If you are not anxious and depressed you just don't know what is happening. The only antidote may be the serenity prayer offered by the Rev. Reinhold Niebuhr (1892–1971) here paraphrased: "Lord, please grant me serenity and inner peace, grace to accept what I cannot change, the courage and ability to change what I should, and the wisdom to know the difference." All in God's will of course. Ergo Theofatalism.

Balancing Reason with Emotions

Things in life do not always work out as planned. We usually take for granted the decisions we make throughout life, as though we actually have control of them. Some work out well and some don't. People select the options that promise the benefits will exceed the burdens within their personal values. When it comes to making decisions, big or small, both reason and feelings must be engaged in making wise judgments. For some people (mostly men, but not all) thoughts based on logical reasoning are more preferred, and for others (mostly women, but not all) feelings based upon emotions rule the decision process. For you reasoning types, emotions are called love, sadness, shame, guilt, fear, anger, happiness, jealousy, anxiety, envy, anger, depression, and such. Emotions must be necessary elements of human nature or they would not exist. But they can upset your comfortable life and render impotent your logical reasoning, so the challenge is using their benefits and minimizing their burdens. For you feeling types, reason comes in two forms of logic, deductive and inductive. Look it up. A few people who are conflicted enough may seek professional help in sorting out their decisions if their suffering exceeds their threshold of pain.

A LABYRINTH WALK OF LIFE

Modern therapy is based on some very old ideas cast into a new binding. Human nature really has not changed much in two thousand years, and some ancient ideas still are very practical today in seeing our individual lives in the perspective of time and space. The Buddha remarked, "Life is a creation of the mind." Some might say that God is a creation of human minds. First-century stoic philosopher Epictetus (who was a man) taught you can be happy inside no matter what happens outside because, "Events do not disturb men's minds, but their thinking does… No man is happy (or sad) who does not think himself so." C. G. Jung observed, "I have seen many people who suffered from all sorts of ailments of the body simply on account of wrong convictions." Psychologist Albert Ellis observed, "Humans create fairly sophisticated languages which not only enable them to think about their feeling, their actions, and the results they get from doing and not doing certain things, but they also are able to think about their thinking and even think about thinking about their thinking. Because of their ability to think about their thinking, they can very easily disturb themselves about their disturbances and can also disturb themselves about their ineffective attempts to overcome their emotional disturbances."

Consider this Stoic wisdom from Roman Emperor Marcus Aurelius: "Why do you hunger for length of days? The point of life is to follow reason and the divine spirit and to accept whatever nature sends you. To live in this way is not to fear death, but to hold it in contempt. Death is only a thing of terror for those unable to live in the present. For all things fade away, become the stuff of legend, and are soon buried in oblivion. Mind you, this is true not only for those who blazed once like bright stars in the firmament, but for the rest. As soon as a few clods of earth cover their corpses, they are out of sight, out of mind. In the end, what would you gain from everlasting remembrance? Absolutely nothing. Do not then consider life a thing of any value. For look at the immensity of time behind thee, and to the time which is before thee, another boundless space. In this infinity then what is the difference between him who lives seven days and him who lives seven decades? So what is left worth living for? This alone: justice in thought, goodness in action, speech that cannot deceive, and a disposition glad of whatever comes, welcoming it as necessary, as familiar, as flowing from the same source and fountain as yourself. You have power over your mind, not outside events. The happiness of your life depends only on the quality of your thoughts. Pass on your way, then, with a smiling face, under the smile of him who bids you go."

Usually, this process of decision making using feelings and reasoning goes on in the subconscious mind without conscious awareness. Options are chosen for the assumption that benefits will exceed burdens, except when they don't. The opposite function of what you most prefer—what Jung called the shadow—will predictably be troublesome, whether thinking or feeling, when it is called into use under extreme stress if this process is not understood and made conscious. Thus, feelings can be trouble for reasoning types and reasoning will upset the feeling types under conditions of stress and crisis. Confusion, divorces, criminality, revolutions, and even wars can be the results. The bottom line is people make the choice among options unconsciously that seems to provide more benefits than burdens, using both reason and emotions. Once you become aware of this process at work in your personal makeup, the commander in chief residing in the frontal lobe of human brains can be invoked to overrule the primitive process and yank it into effective use—what is called wise mind—providing a balance in use of reason and emotions. That process can evolve slowly through life experience or other forms of self-education, through dialectical behavior therapy, or sometimes quickly with an imminent crisis that drives them into counseling seeking the key to controlling the uncontrollable. Some people prefer feelings and some prefer reasoning, and both have their place. Here is the thing: The key to happiness is letting go of the uncontrollable, which is just about everything, and assuming you did the best you could under the circumstances. As with an iceberg, the tip of consciousness must go where the base of unconscious takes it.

If you understand yourself and others in these terms you (whoever "you" are) may be able to change the brain you were given to perform differently and enjoy a happier perception of life, no matter what is the reality of it. Or maybe not. It is all God's will of course, as there can be no other. Ergo Theofatalism.

This Thing Called Love

C. G. Jung said, "The love problem is part of mankind's heavy toll of suffering, and nobody should be ashamed of having to pay his tribute." Poet Alfred Lord Tennyson wrote, "Tis better to have loved and lost than never to have loved at all." Some may disagree. All beginnings come with endings, some sooner than later. That seems to be a necessary law of opposites in life. Even if you are prepared for it, the sting of grief following a major loss can be catastrophic. We grieve in proportion to the value of the loss, the peak of stress being death of a spouse followed by divorce. Some losses are imposed and some are willful, but they all have in common the need to process what is called the grief of loss. Grief is assumed to be a natural response to loss and follows a constructive process in the normal course of bereavement, even though its impact can seem like the disruption of life as we knew it. We grieve in proportion to how much we have loved. There are five tasks to be worked through: (1) acknowledging the loss occurred, (2) allowing the feelings of loss and remorse to flow until they dissipate, (3) detaching from the investment we had in attachment to the object of loss, (4) finding ways to substitute for what was provided in our lives by the loss, and finally (5) reconstructing a new life based upon a different concept of what is normal. The antidote to loss seems to be loving again as it was expressed by Roman Emperor Aurelius in the second century: "Accept the things to which fate binds you, and love the people with whom fate brings you together, and do so with all your heart." Easy to say but can be extremely difficult and painful to accomplish, often taking years of life to process.

The most complicated and difficult part of the transition from beginning to ending is finding a new meaning to make life worthwhile when it seems to be worthless and without hope after loss of a loved one or treasured object or lifestyle. The resulting post trauma shock can disable the brain and cause lasting impairment if not properly treated. Unfortunately, such suffering of loss seems to be the genesis of compassion for others in pain. If we had no grief perhaps there would be no empathy for others in distress. The genesis for charity may be in loss. "Now there remain faith, hope and love/charity. But the greatest of these is love/charity" (1 Corinthians 1:13, KJV). "Love" is translated "charity" in the King James Version—which differentiates it from *cathexis*, the human animal instinct for reproduction. Of that procedure, Lord Chesterfield opined, "The position is unseemly, the pleasure is momentary, and the consequences are abominable." Sexual cathexis is likened to an addiction because it elicits similar changes in the brain, disabling reason and replacing it with feelings invested in a person. Erotic novelist Anais Nin observed that the nature of women is to want to be filled and the nature of men is to want to be emptied, both rewarded with the ultimate pleasure. Interesting how that works to assure procreation of the human species.

"Love is different. Love is patient, love is kind. It does not envy, it does not boast, it is not proud. It does not dishonor others, it is not self-seeking, it is not easily angered, it keeps no record of wrongs. Love does not delight in evil but rejoices with the truth. It always protects, always trusts, always hopes, always perseveres. Love never fails" (1 Corinthians 13:4–8). Cathexis is all about conditional getting while love is all about unconditional giving. When two people share love, each one helps to fill the needs of the other, and so they "become one."

Psychiatrist Victor Frankl, who survived but lost his family in Nazi concentration camps, wrote in his logo therapy that man can live with practically any "how" if he has a necessary and sufficient "why" of life. A wise sage said to be happy, people need someone to love, something to do that they love, and something to hope for in love. The normal human process of grief and anxiety requires living somehow even when you don't want to or don't know why. The existential question of where is God when we suffer loss of a love conjures up the image of Jesus dying on the cross lamenting, "My God, why have you forsaken me." Painful feelings of loss are an inevitable part of love. You can't have one without the other. The only choice is between the pain of love and the pain of loneliness. To be human is to suffer. That, of course, requires radical acceptance of reality—right down to your soul—because if someone enters your heart, they never really leave. Like Humpty Dumpty who fell off the wall, some things that are broken cannot be fixed, only endured. That is why there are wheelchairs, cemeteries, and junk yards. It may be difficult and even impossible to accept the pain when you are suffering the brokenhearted loss of a love, but this too will pass. Apostle Paul instructed to "give thanks in all things, for this is the will of God for you" (1 Thessalonians 5:18). Not the god of religions, but the prime mover in the universe; generator, operator, destroyer… GOD. Once more—Theofatalism.

Holding the Opposites

Here is something to think about. God created all life on earth, and life on earth includes suffering and death, predators and prey, so therefore God created suffering and death, predators and prey (Genesis 1:1). In fact, you can believe that nothing happens outside the will of God, including atheism. Not the manmade god in any holy books but the prime mover in the universe... generator, operator, destroyer... GOD. It does whatever it wants with everything from atoms to galaxies... ergo, Theofatalism. Can you believe that?

Or perhaps you choose to believe all life on planet earth is a random process with no purpose, or at least none that we can know for sure—what is called nihilism. Such would be the opposite of belief in Theofatalism, which claims there is no need to search for your purpose in life because you cannot avoid it. And God never made any one-sided coins. St. Clement of Rome said God rules with two hands, Christ in one and Satan in the other. As such, everyone is doing the will of God, as there can be no other. So when bad things happen, God still is the cause. Saints and criminals are part of the world that God has made. But hey, the five principles of Theofatalism include the principle of necessary opposites as in the laws of physics and dialectical therapy. For every action, there is an equal and opposite action, and for every thought, there is an equal and opposite thought. Joy and pleasure are necessary opposites to have pain and suffering. Sour is necessary to discern sweet, hot to discern cold, etc. It seems necessary to feel grief to feel compassion. Each day of your life is one more and one less. One may speak of a unity in opposites because they complement each other. Get it? So the mark of maturity is holding opposites and functioning normally. Whether you do or you don't, it all must be God's will or it would be different. Think about it.

A LABYRINTH WALK OF LIFE

Black Holes and Other Cosmic Mysteries

Some things are beyond knowing. Take the origin of the universe for one. Science says that looking backward in time concludes with an event that made all the elements at one instant more than 13 billion years ago to appear with a force from nothing that still is driving the stellar objects away from each other at increasing speeds creating an ever-expanding universe driven by some as yet unknown energy, and where it all goes nobody knows. But where did the material elements originally come from? The answer often given is nothing. It all came from nothing… or maybe it came from energy which can neither be created nor destroyed, whatever that is. Moreover, the earth and all of its inhabitants are made of the same universal elements as all the other stellar objects. But there is a difference on earth. It is composed of both animate and inanimate matter. Something called life is added to sentient beings on earth that makes them emerge from the elements, interact for a time, and then return to the elements when life is ended. Individuals of each species appear to be indispensable but also insignificant. Or are they each insignificant but indispensable. Is life on earth unique or is it present throughout the universe—maybe other universes? But what is life? It appears to be undefinable. Scripture says that spirit gives life, the flesh counts for nothing (John 6:63). But what is spirit? Humans have attempted to explain the unknowables with words that can only be explained by mathematics. Equations defining ideas. What is thinking and what are thoughts? Where do thoughts come from? How is mind different from brain and who or what is it that owns them—as in "my brain" or "my body"? Think about it long enough, and you will go mad.

There seems to be both matter composed of elements and nonmatter composed of thoughts. Science now says the universe possibly contains more than twenty times the known elements in some undetectable form called dark matter fueled by dark energy.

So perhaps there are two universes, the material and immaterial… or maybe even an infinite number of universes, with many dimensions beyond human understanding. Some cosmology predicts that the infinite gravity of a black hole existing at the center of all galaxies where nothing escapes, not even light, could be the tunnel into other universes. As such, maybe our universe is the offspring of some parent universe that was spawned through its black hole. Another theory in quantum mechanics predicts that matter and anti-matter must co-exist—and if it were to combine, the results would be total annihilation of everything, i.e., zero or nothing. The mysteries go on and on. It is all completely unknowable. But mankind must continue searching anyway. King Solomon thought about such things and concluded, "With much wisdom comes much sorrow, the more knowledge the more grief" (Ecclesiastes 1:17–18). So be careful what you ask for. You can ponder this or just go outside and play. All in God's will of course. Ergo, Theofatalism.

No Pain, No Gain

History is worth knowing to help keep things in perspective, else we are bound to repeat it. The United States of America was settled by invaders from Europe, principally England, France, and Spain as well as others after the explorations of Christopher Columbus and Amerigo Vespucci in the early sixteenth century. The invaders systematically displaced the natives living here for thousands of years and installed replicas of their culture from back home. During the late eighteenth century there began a massive wave of immigrants including the Dutch, the Irish, Germans, Italians, Swedes, and people from many other countries, including involuntary slaves imported from Africa unwillingly. They brought not only their cultures and diseases but their religions also, which saw the many protestant denominations as well as the Roman Catholic Church implanted throughout the states. The original colonies rebelled against the English crown in 1776 and set up a republic form of government as recited in the Pledge of Alllegiance—not a democracy—with semi-independent states. During the nineteenth century, the invading settlers from throughout Europe argued for "manifest destiny" to justify forcing the native tribes into concentrated reservations, which nearly exterminated them. The new invaders spread across the plains and mountains to the west coast like a wave of rampaging locusts, buying up the central plains from France and driving the Spanish south below the Rio Grande River and totally out of Florida.

Then came immigrants to the west coast from Asia, the Chinese, Japanese, and others who also brought their cultures and religions. The country was ravaged by Civil War in 1861–1865 to abolish slavery and unify the nation to meet periodic international challenges to its continued existence during its birthing process, which still is ongoing in the ultimate social experiment. After President Abraham Lincoln, the country split into two political parties that have remained adversaries ever since. Millions of lives were lost and millions more were maimed for life in its incessant wars. How it ever managed to survive and grow to the premier world power composed of the most diverse ethnic society on earth must be the will of God or it would be different. A few oligarchs rose to rebuild the nation in a new form with steel, railroads, coal, electricity, banking, oil, and automobiles all on the backs of intimidated and abused immigrant workers (Morgan, Mellon, Carnegie, Rockefeller, Vanderbilt, Edison, Ford, et al.). A new wave of Hispanic immigrants entered illegally across the southern border, which really is no border at all. The US Constitution gives them all freedom to practice their religions, including Islam, from coast to coast.

Now, there seems to be a rediscovery of Buddhism—more a psychology than a religion—sweeping from the west coast to the east coast of America, possibly through such mediums as the popular Dialectical Behavior Therapy (DBT) and its relation to the reality of suffering among the masses. (DBT attempts to improve lives by teaching skills in mindfulness, distress tolerance, interpersonal relations, and emotion regulation.) Founded in India during the fifth century BC, Buddhism says that suffering comes from being discontent with what is. Since it was founded among peasants with little hope of better living, it follows that to remove suffering one must be content and nonjudgmental with what is, no matter how painful. Its theme is radical acceptance of reality—even when reality is unacceptable. Apostle Paul may have been influenced by Buddhism because he said that he had learned to be content in all circumstance, sick or well, hungry or full (Philippians 4:11–12). English philosopher and the most prolific liberal of his age, John Stuart Mill (1806–1873) stated, "I have learned to seek happiness by limiting my desires rather than attempting to satisfy them." Also, he concluded the accumulation of capital is dependent on excess income (profit) and the desire to defer future spending to present saving. The thing is that national growth and personal development must be stimulated by discontent because contentment breeds stagnation. Someone said the Stone Age did not end for lack of stones. Perpetual and sustained discontent is what has driven changes in America, and without change there is no growth.

American capitalism is driven by converting luxuries into necessities—as with the progression of wireless cell phones to replace landlines and electric windows and GPS receivers in cars, which replaced horse carts, to be augmented next with self-driving automatic navigation. In contrast to Buddhism, this reasoning means that we must accommodate perpetual suffering of discontent to grow. If you are not hurting, you are not growing. No pain, no gain. If anxiety is the normal reaction to indefinite uncertainty, it must be rampant in American culture where freedom to succeed or fail is the mantra of ultra conservatives, never mind the cause and effect relationships at work in each life. Stability and change are incompatible opposites because you cannot have both at the same time in the same place. Just ask all the native Americans living in those squalid reservations—except the ones thriving on gambling casinos. All in God's will of course. If God wanted history and change to be different, it would be. Not the manmade god of holy books but the prime mover in the universe... generator, operator, destroyer... GOD. It does whatever it wants with everything from atoms to galaxies. Hence, Theofatalism.

Staring at the Sun

The main problem with dying is that something must kill you, and there are thousands of ways for that to happen. The young may die and the old must die—that is just the way it is. It never is easy so people try to avoid it by not talking about it in many families until the final crisis. Professor emeritus Irvin Yalom said confronting death is like staring at the sun, and it is dangerous to your mental health to face it prematurely. You can ignore it but you cannot change it. Death can be slow and traumatic or quick and traumatic. There are no general principles about coping during terminal illness because each situation and personality involved are different. The earth is a very dangerous place to live, and eventually we all succumb to it. In addition to accidents, wars, diseases, murders, and natural disasters there are untold numbers of infectious microbes who live by human deaths. The earth is populated by more bacterial carnivores than medicine can fight off. They are very smart too. Since antibiotics have been developed to kill them off they have developed the uncanny ability to recognize a threat and to create a defense mechanism for self-protection. Some of them respond soon as they detect they are being attacked. Space does not permit listing all the many and diverse mortal enemies of humans, but if you think we are the top of the food pyramid, think again. Unless you work in medicine you probably are not aware of the many threats to human lives unless something happens in your family to get your attention.

When we realize that mortal threats are all around, the resulting stress, anxiety, and depression may be disabling unless you have a belief system that accommodates this reality of life on planet earth. Accepting this reality is a challenge too much for some to bear—so they just avoid it and go outside to play or take a preemptive exit. Practically everything people do, be it work or recreation, is a subconscious attempt to deny and avoid thoughts of their personal mortality. Most families postpone any kind of preparations until death of a member is imminent, and then it is too late for rational planning. Even the choice for palliative care and hospice service are left until the last weeks or days in many cases. Only some of the wealthy and a minority of the rest make out wills and trusts before the need is acute. It is never too late to make plans and the earlier the better, but death still is shocking to everyone involved. Among the carnivorous animals it is kill or be killed and with all the continuous battle to live, humans are not much different from the various mammals among us. But Jesus said, "The spirit gives life, the flesh counts for nothing" (John 6:63). So perhaps there is some purpose to it all, if we could figure out what that is. Up until now it has been a mystery. A mystery that leads to existential anxiety, called angst, if you stop to think about it. All in God's will of course… not the manmade god in holy books but the prime mover in the universe… generator, operator, destroyer… GOD. It does whatever it wants with everything from atoms to galaxies… and people must take what it gives and give what it takes… Ergo Theofatalism.

Fear and Trembling

What is life, and when does it begin and when does it end? These questions have occupied thinkers for centuries and still there are no generally accepted answers or medical standards for defining death. Some may say that life begins at conception, but the egg and sperm are both alive before they unite, are they not. Each conception was begotten by a previous conception. Thus, the origin of life can be traced back to its first cause, whatever that is. And some may say life ends with a silent brain and dormant heart with no blood pressure. But organs can be transplanted several hours after that so at some level life is not limited to brain waves and heartbeats, while dying is more likely a process than an event. Plants are alive but they have neither brains nor hearts. When we harvest a vegetable or pluck a fruit are we not killing a life that God created just as much as slaughtering an animal for food? By the way, the Bible says that God provided tree fruit for human food in the Garden of Eden; there is no mention of eating animals (Genesis 2:16, 3:2). Did you ever wonder how all that water gets into a watermelon? Every individual among all the living species seems to be both necessary and insignificant, and neither science, religion, nor philosophy can seem to reconcile the opposites of birth and death. And what about some life after life? We don't even know if there is one.

    Each organ and system in a living body possesses the knowledge and motivation to conduct their unique roles in life, and we do not consciously control any of it. How the organs in living bodies know to do what they are designed for in the body are unknown mysteries. A few people hope to survive being frozen for several/many years and then defrosted and brought back to life. Jesus said, "The spirit gives life, the flesh counts for nothing" (John 6:63). Whatever we call life is, there still is a lot to be discovered about it. The same goes for God. Maybe life is God in us as immaculate immanence. St. Paul concluded, "Therefore, my dear friends… continue to work out your salvation with fear and trembling, for it is God who works in you to will and to act in order to fulfill His good purpose" (Philippians 11:12–13). If the Bible is the inspired Word of God, you better believe it. Ergo Theofatalism.

The Will of God

People cannot choose where they are born and how they will die, except for suicides, but most people are led to believe they have free will to choose how they will live. When you really look into it there is scant evidence to support that idea and much evidence to suggest that belief in human free will is the greatest hoax in the universe. We have no free will so we must believe in free will. That is the only way to explain life on earth no matter what is the results. Each individual among all the many forms of life on earth seems to be necessary and indispensable, but also insignificant. What if there is some prime force in the universe that controls everything from atoms to galaxies—including belief in free will? Mmmm? Then you may ask what does that power gain by perpetuating the illusion of free will among humans? And the answer is, of course, none of your business because that is God's business. The evidence is plentiful. The Reformation founder, John Calvin (1509–1564), concluded, "By his power, God cherishes and guards the World which he made and by his Providence rules its individual parts. Humans are unable to fully comprehend why God performs any particular action, but whatever good or evil people may practice, their efforts always result in the execution of God's will and judgments." And Ben Franklin concluded, "The longer I live the more proof I see of this truth—that God rules in the affairs of men." In other words, nothing happens outside the will of God, including your belief about it, from atheism to predestination.

Theofatalism by any name is still the same. God rules in the affairs of mankind.

The creation displays uncountable species that prove this point. No one declares the brutal acts of carnivorous predators to be evil, so why pass judgment on any of God's creations, including *Homo sapiens*. The creation must display the will of God as there can be no other. There are proofs all around if you have eyes to see. There was recently discovered in China a new species of snail so small that ten of them can fit into the eye of a needle. Sea turtles lay their eggs on the same beach where they were born, and when they hatch almost simultaneously, they make a nice meal for airborne predators, except the few chosen ones among thousands that make it to the ocean. At the other extreme are blue whales that are bigger than a couple of school buses weighing sixty tons and seventy feet long. Although they are air breathing mammals, they can dive to seven thousand feet and remain submerged in the ocean for ninety minutes. Someone estimated the weight of all the cockroaches on earth would be ten times that of all the humans. Humans are continually doing things that make no sense unless you invoke the will of God in their actions. And the next time you think of it, consider that you have no control whatever over the organs in your body, including your brain. By the way, who is speaking when we say "my body or "my brain"? So what makes humans think they are the supreme creation on earth? Mmm?

Here is more. God said, "I will harden [Pharaoh's] heart, so that he will not let the (Jewish) people go" (Exodus 4:21). That decision brought a dozen plagues onto the lives of the suffering Egyptian people. Isaiah asked, "Why, O Lord, do you make us stray from your ways and harden our heart, so that we do not fear you?" (Isaiah 63:17). God said, "If a prophet is deceived and speaks a word, I, the Lord, have deceived that prophet" (Ezekiel 14:9). John writes that those who "did not believe in [Jesus] could not believe" because, quoting Isaiah 6:10, "[God] has blinded their eyes and hardened their heart" (John 12:37–40). God "hardens the heart of whomever he chooses" (Romans 9:18). "God sends [those who are perishing] a powerful delusion, leading them to believe what is false, so [they] will be condemned" (2 Thessalonians 2:11–12). "Those [Jews] who do not believe stumble because they disobey the word, as they were destined [by God] to do" (1 Peter 2:7–8). Saint/Mother Teresa said God does whatever he wants with whomever he wants and we all must take what he gives and give what he takes. So why do many preachers still claim that mankind has free will and therefore needs a savior to avoid spending eternity in hell? It keeps their treasuries full of course, and Jesus declared where your treasure is so will be your heart, and vice versa (Matthew 6:21).

It seems that our eyes are closed to the reality of creation in which we are such a small insignificant momentary but indispensable part, like a drop of water in the ocean. C. G. Jung said that life is a short pause in between two great mysteries. The ancients thought that some divine power they called God ruled their lives day by day. "A person's steps are directed by the Lord. How then can anyone understand their own way?" (Proverbs 20:24). Perhaps that pathway was laid for you as in a labyrinth before the world began. Not the manmade god in any holy books, but the prime mover in the universe—generator, operator, destroyer, GOD. It does whatever it wants with whomever it wants, and we all must take what it gives and give what it takes… ergo Theofatalism.

Choose Suffering or Contentment

C. G. Jung observed that suffering is a normal and necessary balance to happiness. The Buddha taught that suffering comes from discontent, so the way to overcome suffering is to accept what is—which really does not exist except in our own mind—which flows passed like a river, and be content with it if you want to remove suffering. The Apostle Paul claimed that he had reached that state in his personal life as he learned the secret to being content in all circumstances (Philippians 4:11–12). The Stoics of his time taught that a man of virtue would amend his will to suit the world of nature which we do not control and remain, in the words of Epictetus, "sick and yet happy, in peril and yet happy, dying and yet happy, in exile and yet happy, in disgrace and yet happy." But that is not the basic American way, which is to fix whatever we perceive as wrong, be it in politics, economics, health, religion, war, social, work, family, personal or whatever. Whenever things go wrong in our opinion, the modern mantra is "do something, do something." This is insanity. Remember the first three steps of the twelve-step programs, first applied to Alcoholics Anonymous (AA) but now being applied to many different human challenges. Step one is admitting that we are powerless over life and life has become unmanageable. Step two is believing that a power greater than ourselves can restore us to sanity. Step three is making a decision to turn our will and our lives over to God or some Higher Power. (*For more steps, visit www.12step.org.*)

When Pontius Pilate threatened Jesus with crucifixion, he declared, "You would have no power over me if it were not given to you from above" (John 19:9–11). That did not prevent him from suffering on the cross, but it explained why it had to happen—God's will. Some things are seemingly impossible to change, so they must be accepted. For example, mental illness and many disabling diseases, murder and suicide, natural disasters, and such are considered to be wrong, but the problem is there is no way yet to fix some things that are broken, and so there is suffering as well as junk yards and cemeteries and prisons. Prisons and even executions do not seem to deter criminals from breaking the law. But we keep trying. The *Big Book* of AA (1939) says, "When we admit our powerlessness and the inability to manage our own lives, we open the door to recovery."

Until they accept their total loss of control, alcoholics cannot begin the steps to recovery from their disease. (The AA movement grew out of The Oxford Group in England that had similar goals of a religious nature. It was organized in 1931 by Dr. Frank Buchman and was incorporated in 1939.)

The Buddhist solution of radical acceptance is a basic premise of Dialectical Behavior Therapy. It is derived from Zen Buddhism, which influenced Dr. Marsha Linehan who developed it while at the University of Washington. The US west coast is influenced by the beliefs of Asia while the US east coast is influenced more by the beliefs of Europe. Therefore, people on the east and west coasts of America approach the solution to suffering differently. Their culture and social mores also are different. It remains to be seen how the two cultures of east and west coast may be accommodated in the future, but they seem to be merging into a common whole on a global scale. The world, and maybe the universe, is composed of the opposite forces of stability and change—holding both and still functioning normally is a mark of human maturity. Without change, there would be no progress like calculus, concrete and smartphones and electricity and the GPS navigation system—nor nuclear bombs. No suffering—no progress, because stability and change are incompatible opposites, all in God's will of course. There are some primitive human tribes hidden in jungles on earth who prefer stability over change and some modern cultures that promote the opposite, i.e., change over stability. Some things may change rapidly during a typical human lifetime, but human nature changes much more slowly. So the more things change the more they seem to remain the same. This could be what King Solomon meant when he said there is nothing new under the sun. "What has been done will be done again; there is nothing new under the sun." Is there anything of which one can say, "Look! This is something new"? (Ecclesiastes 1:9–10). Whatever it is, God created it and only God can change it. If you don't get it, you don't get it… all in God's will of course… ergo Theofatalism. Think about it.

The Functions of Personality

People are funny. Some of them seem to act like a herd of cattle in large groups or a school of fish, running this way and that spending billions of dollars and devoting countless hours pursuing distractions from their reality, driven by some imaginary force they do not control—for what. The great King Solomon compiled great wealth and fame to conclude that it is all meaningless (Ecclesiastes 1:17–18). Some individuals cannot stand their own company and attempt to submerge it in a crowd, while others prefer their solitude—extraverts and introverts respectively. Psychiatrist C. G. Jung (1875–1961) observed that their differences could be explained by variations in their common functions of personality. We all take in information and make judgments about it—that is all—but there is more. We exhibit the function of perceiving in two separate ways, sensing/S and intuition/N and the function of judging in two separate ways, thinking/T, and feeling/F respectively. Further, we exhibit these four functions of personality in either introverted or extraverted ways. And moreover, we distribute energy among these functions in a specific ranking, which creates unique human personalities that drive their behavior throughout life. Understanding this model could help people to avoid much interpersonal conflict that otherwise can be devastating to inner peace. Jung said when two personalities meet, it is like the combination of two chemical substances. If there is any reaction, both are transformed.

This model produces 16 alternative types labeled with four letters, E or I, S or N, T or F, and J or P. My own personal type is INTJ/INTP, which filters all that is written in these essays. As St.

Paul learned, we all see things through a dark filter of our unique perception and decision making (Corinthians 13:12). Although their bodies age and change, human personalities stay relatively the same. How their lives play out are beyond their control as they are born to be who they become. Parents must all come to this conclusion as they see children grow up and take their own pathways through the labyrinth walk of life they are given. From the moment of conception, their lives are prescribed by the will of God. This is not a new idea. The ancients thought that some divine power they called God ruled their lives day by day. "A person's steps are directed by the Lord. How then can anyone understand their own way?" (Proverbs 20:24). Perhaps that pathway was laid for you as in a labyrinth before the world began. "You saw me before I was born and scheduled each day of my life before I began to breathe. Every day was recorded in your book!" (Psalm 139:16). Thus, the time and location of your birth is no accident. Perhaps we all are on the pathway just where we are supposed to be, each one walking his own labyrinth in life, aware of the past but walking into a future that is indefinitely uncertain—like riding in a train facing backward.

C. G. Jung said, "My pathway is not your pathway. Therefore, I cannot teach you. The Pathway is within us." Walking the labyrinth pathway through life cloaked in our given personalities is the process, which leads to the destination unique to everyone from which we emerged and to which we must return. Everyone must do whatever is demanded of them. But that same thought comes with the opposing notion that people are agents with free will to do and be whatever they want within the rule of law by governance voluntarily obeyed by the governed. You can find scriptures for both free will and predestination in the Bible. Necessary opposites for sure—which is one of the principles of Theofatalism. For each thought, there is an equal and opposite thought. For more on this model of human personality, Google Myers-Briggs Type Indicator or MBTI. If you do or you don't, it must all be God's will of course.

Stuff Happens

Therapist and Buddhist master David Richo says to be content, if not happy, we all must accept these necessary life essentials... (1) people disappoint us, (2) life comes with pain, (3) things do not go as planned, (4) beginnings come with endings, and (5) the future is indefinitely uncertain (*Five Things We Cannot Change*, 2006). Life definitely is unfair. As Apostle Paul learned, the main challenge is to live the life you have with contentment instead of the life you may want, because it all must be necessary or it would be different (Philippians 4:11–12). You can feel good inside no matter what happens outside/maybe. "Therefore, we do not lose heart. Though outwardly we are wasting away, yet inwardly we are being renewed day by day. For our light and momentary troubles are achieving for us an eternal glory that far outweighs them all. So, we fix our eyes not on what is seen, but on what is unseen, since what is seen is temporary, but what is unseen is eternal" (2 Corinthians 4:16–18).

Present adversity has a prior sequence of causes leading back to the first cause that makes it inevitable—which you can fight or accept, all in God's will of course. The radical acceptance of reality does not change reality, and you may still work for a better life if that is your destiny. But the Bible says God is the potter and we are the clay, some made for royal use and some for common use (Jeremiah 18:2–6, Romans 9:12). It also says that each day of our lives was written in the book of creation before we were born (Psalm 139:16). When you come to realize this is the way it is, and we really have no control of anything, including the weather, people can become outraged or depressed and suicidal, if not murderous. Depression may be the opposite side of resilience as God never made any one-sided coins. Some psychologists propose that we can change our outlook on life and develop more resilience by thinking differently—and those who don't may cause themselves and others extreme suffering. Who or what controls thinking is unknown. But here is the thing—whether you do or you don't it must be God's will or it would be different.

Indeed, this awareness can help to explain the frequent family murder-suicide tragedies that you do not get on television news. But no one has identified the command and control executive functions in the brain that would be in charge of conscious behavior. Resilience requires us to accept the things we cannot change and to move forward in spite of the indefinite uncertainty about the future, with self-efficacy and social support of friends, family, and church if possible, and alone if necessary. That is the goal of Dialectical Behavior Therapy as developed by Dr. Marsha Linehan. She wrote, "The path out of hell is through misery. By refusing to accept the misery that is part of climbing out of hell, you fall back into hell." Reality can be accepted and adversity tolerated if we realize it all must be the will of God or it would be different—but only if you are given that disposition by God, since we are the clay and it is the potter (Jeremiah 18:2–6, Romans 9:16–21). Not the manmade god in holy books but the prime mover in the universe… generator, operator, destroyer… GOD. It does whatever it wants with everything from atoms to galaxies, and we all must take what it gives and give what it takes… Ergo Theofatalism.

The Obesity Epidemic

You may have noticed that Americans are getting fatter. It is true. About one-third of us are classified as morbidly obese by the Center for Disease Control, which means at risk for premature death. Although overall life expectancy has been increasing, the additional years for the obese often are marred by chronic illnesses related to being overweight, increasing medical costs and reducing the quality of life. The body mass index was created to measure obesity, with a healthy limit set at twenty-five. Many of us post a score above thirty and climbing.

The cause, simply, is that people eat too much of the wrong things. The reasons for this cause are very complex, and there is no solution in sight. First, food is too cheap and is packaged in ways to induce people to buy processed foods that are undesirable, but more profitable for producers and sellers. Second, restaurants and fast food purveyors have conditioned people to eat too much. A brief look at the calories posted at McDonald's shows that a single meal may contain enough food energy for a half day and more. Food is the lowest cost element of operating a restaurant, so people would complain if they were served a healthy portion priced to cover all expenses and make a profit. Third, unhealthy processed foods have been flavored and packaged to appeal to the taste buds, which is not the best way to select foods for health. In spite of government-mandated content labeling, many people buy what tastes and looks most appealing without regard for nutrition. Eating unhealthy foods stimulates the desire for healthy foods, but modern suppliers respond with even more unhealthy foods laced with sugar and simple carbohydrates. So the cycle expands. Fourth, an adequate daily diet includes about 1,500–2,000 calories for the average adult person, but many people consume much more than they need. The combined result of this situation is an epidemic of obesity that begins in childhood and extends throughout life.

It is much easier to avoid gaining too much weight than it is too lose it. One pound of flesh equates to 3,500 calories, so it is logical that to lose one pound there must be a deficit of 3,500 calories. This goal can be obtained by eating fewer or burning more calories. More exercise and manual labor is not the solution because our lifestyles are becoming less physically demanding—even with the emergence of an emphasis on artificial physical activities, as in commercial gyms and such. Plus, to lose weight, one must feel a certain amount of hunger to live with the deficit. It is possible to eat healthy, tasty, attractive food if one is so conditioned, but many Americans are being conditioned to choose taste and appearance over health. The solution, obviously, would be to raise the cost of unhealthy food and its packaging, while learning to buy, prepare, and eat the more-healthy portions. But this is not happening in many affluent countries, hence the obesity epidemic. We live in a free market for food supply and demand, which says that human free will is not always a healthy way to live.

One may well ask; if we know how to select and eat healthy food and do not, why not? Aside from these foodie issues, there could be a much deeper psychological and spiritual cause of overeating—loss of relationship with God, which causes deep anxiety and worry. Food is another form of self-medication along with alcohol and drugs. If you are tempted to overeat, stop and think about this discussion from Jesus. "Therefore, I tell you, do not worry about your life, what you will eat or drink; or about your body, what you will wear. Is not life more than food, and the body more than clothes? Look at the birds of the air; they do not sow or reap or store away in barns, and yet your heavenly Father feeds them. Are you not much more valuable than they? Can any one of you by worrying add a single hour to your life? And why do you worry about clothes? See how the flowers of the field grow. They do not labor or spin. Yet I tell you that not even Solomon in all his splendor was dressed like one of these. If that is how God clothes the grass of the field, which is here today and tomorrow is thrown into the fire, will he not much more clothe you—you of little faith? So, do not worry, saying, 'What shall we eat?' or 'What shall we drink?' or 'What shall we wear?' For the pagans run after all these things, and your heavenly Father knows that you need them. But seek first his kingdom and his righteousness, and all these things will be given to you as well. Therefore, do not worry about tomorrow, for tomorrow will worry about itself. Each day has enough trouble of its own" (Matthew 6:25–34). However, all living things have a natural life cycle from birth to death, and resisting it will not change it.

Although people need food, clothing, and shelter, they need inner peace even more. C. G. Jung said he never saw a troubled patient get well who did not rediscover and reconnect with his religious roots, whatever they were. "All of my patients fell ill because they lost what living religions of every age gave to their believers, and none of them were healed who did not regain his religious outlook, which has nothing to do with creeds or church." Jung believed that the universal desire for inner peace was a natural need of everyone, which could best be provided by knowing God. Generator, operator, destroyer—GOD. So whenever you feel tempted to overeat, think on these things. Of course, whether you do or you don't must be God's will, as there can be no other. Ergo Theofatalism.

Principles of Theofatalism

Belief in Theofatalism can change your outlook on life if you can overcome a lifetime of learning faulty assumptions and accept its five principles:

1) Everything happening must be necessary or it would be different.
2) The universe is composed of necessary dialectical opposites in all things from atoms to galaxies.

3) People and all life on earth take actions based on the perceived benefits and burdens in unconscious choices they do not control.
4) The future is indefinitely uncertain.
5) God—as generator, operator, destroyer—is everywhere in everything, i.e., immaculate immanence.

It follows from these principles that to be content, if not happy, one must follow the ADTDA therapy:

1) *Accept* what is moment by moment because it must be necessary or it would be different.
2) *Detach* from what you cannot change and wish was different because it hurts too much not to.
3) *Transcend* the need for control because you don't have any as the brain has a mind of its own.
4) *Don't fight* with God because you cannot win. You must walk the labyrinth you are given.
5) *Assume* there are no mistakes, only choices and consequences, all in God's will of course.

The symbol for this belief system depicted on the title page is the ancient Chartres Labyrinth where there is only one pathway for each one to follow after emergence from birth and back again to the origin of life after the meridian is passed. Buddhist nun Pema Chodran wrote, "The spiritual journey involves going beyond hope and fear, stepping into unknown territory, continually moving forward. The most important aspect of being on the spiritual pathway may be to just keep on moving." And it all must be God's will or it would be different. The Bible says, "You saw me before I was born and scheduled each day of my life before I began to breathe. Every day was recorded in your book!" (Psalm 139:16). It is God who directs the lives of his creatures; "everyone's life is in his power" (Job 12:10). Ergo Theofatalism.

A New and Better Image of God

C. G. Jung used the word "god" to refer to the mysterious powers of the universe. "God is the name by which I designate all things which cross my path violently and recklessly, all things which upset my subjective views, plans and intentions, and changes the course of my life for better or for worse." Since we cannot see God, the only evidence of its existence is the effects of its power for good and evil. St. Clement of Rome declared, "God rules with two hands, Christ in one and Satan in the other." Do not look in the holy books for any understanding. After all, they were written by unknown authors who were merely expressing their opinions at their time in the present social circumstances in which they lived some two thousand to three thousand years ago. The Bible presents God in several different forms from the Old Testament into the New Testament. It says God is a raging fire, a spirit, and God is love in different scriptures. In the Old Testament God is jealous, vindictive, and capricious. For example, Moses in revenge on the Midianites, ordered the total plunder and slaughter of thousands of men, boys and women, and sanctioned the rape of thousands of virgin girls, at God's behest (Numbers 31). In the New Testament, God is the father and savior of sinful mankind… that he/it created in his own image with the power and freedom to disobey, knowing that they would (Genesis 1:26). He is to be loved, worshipped, and feared.

Preachers have declared that God is a disembodied person with feelings like human beings, but that really is only their assumption. They say one must accept God on faith—with faith no proof is needed and without faith no proof is sufficient. But where does such faith come from? Answer: From the same God who created all the sinners. "For it is by grace you have been saved, through faith—and this is not from yourselves, it is the gift of God" (Ephesians 2:8). Perhaps the atheists who claim there is no proof for even the existence of God are correct, and that one does not need the fear of God to live a moral life—it just is common sense, which really is not very common. Knowledge, of itself, can lead one toward or away from understanding of God, as necessary opposites. It is obvious that rampaging technology is not accompanied by increasing moral living. Witness computer hackers for example who threaten to destroy a country by disabling its vast computer-based economy.

It seems like the more knowledge, the more human suffering—because all benefits come with burdens just as King Solomon discovered and described in OT book of Ecclesiastes. "I applied myself to the understanding of wisdom, and also of madness and folly, but I learned that this, too, is a chasing after the wind. For with much wisdom comes much sorrow; the more knowledge, the more grief" (Ecclesiastes 1:17–18). God has been used throughout human history to justify all kinds of mayhem and even genocide, as presently being done by radical Islam terrorists. Perhaps it is time to retire such a god to the history books and to invoke a new image of God… actually an old one from the ancient Hindu belief in the Trimurti, gods Brahma, Shiva, and Vishnu… responsible for creation, maintenance, and destruction… generation, operation, destruction… GOD, the prime force in the universe. To imagine this God, just look around at its creation… not just the good parts, because some of it stinks pretty badly. Human nature both soars and sucks. Remember the father of the atom bomb, Robert Oppenheimer's comment at ground zero after the first test in Arizona, quoting Vishnu, "Now, I am become Death, destroyer of worlds." The God of creation does not seem to have a problem with destroying whatever it creates through wars, diseases, calamities, and such. And how about all those flesh-eating carnivores… steak, anyone? Mother/Saint Teresa declared (God) does whatever it wants with everything from atoms to galaxies and people all must "take what it gives and give what it takes." Ergo Theofatalism.

Can You Believe This?

You will not get this in church. The Bible claims that God does not just allow bad things to happen as some theologians claim, but he actually causes them. "I make peace and create evil/calamity. I, the Lord, do all these things" (Isaiah 45:7). In this context, the Hebrew word for "evil" is translated elsewhere in the Bible as, spoiled, bad, adversity, trouble, sinful, misfortune, calamity, so take your pick. "When a disaster comes to a city, has not the Lord caused it?" (Amos 3:6). "Though you build your nest as high as the eagle's, from there I will bring you down, declares the Lord" (Jeremiah 49:16, Obadiah 1:4). "Who has spoken and it came to pass, unless the Lord has commanded it? Is it not from the mouth of the Most High that good and bad come?" (Lamentations 3:37–38). The Quran says the same thing to Muslims; "No calamity comes, no affliction occurs, except by the decision and preordainment of Allah" (S:64.11). And when it comes to salvation for Christians as declared in John 3:16, Jesus said that no one can come to him unless the Father wills/enables them (John 6:44, 65). Plus, Jesus taught his disciples in coded parables so the Jews would not understand and repent and be redeemed, because that was their destiny (Matthew 13:11–13, Mark 4:10–12, 1 Peter 2:7–8). To be redeemed, once must repent of sins, which must be necessary or it would be different. In other words, sin and redemption appear to be interrelated; one cannot exist without the other.

Every individual in all forms of life on earth seems to be both insignificant and indispensable to the whole universe, in which we are just a zit in time and space. Like a drop of water in the ocean or a grain of sand on the beach, the earth would be less without each one. And the Bible says each of their lives is scheduled before they are born, "You saw me before I was born and scheduled each day of my life before I began to breathe. Every day was recorded in your book!" (Psalm 139:16). "It is God who directs the lives of his creatures; everyone's life is in his power" (Job 12:10). Moreover, Jesus said, "The spirit gives life, the flesh counts for nothing" (John 6:63). If you repeat that often, you may begin to believe it. So do not be dismayed about the life that you have been given or the labyrinth you must walk, because if it should be different it would be. Of course, if you are dismayed that also must be necessary. All in God's will of course—generator, operator, destroyer. Ergo Theofatalism.

Failing to Plan Is Planning to Fail

There is an elephant in the living room that needs attention—the aging population and their right to die on their own terms. If you don't die suddenly, the process of terminal aging can include pain, suffering, humiliation, disability, trauma, and massive expense trying to remain alive as long as possible. Dying is easy, but trying not to is hard—and very expensive. Hanging onto the body close to death only increases the fear and pain. If you cannot afford professional caregivers or lengthy assisted living, and even so, the surviving family members can be traumatized and forced to live with post trauma shock for many years if there is no advanced planning. Resources accumulated during a lifetime can be consumed by well-meaning medics, leaving the prospect of living under state controls with Medicaid sans any inheritance for family heirs. There should be a better way to exit this mortal life. Preemptive physician-assisted suicide has been legalized in California, Oregon, Montana, Colorado, Vermont, and the District of Columbia but there are so many caveats, including opposition by medical and religious zealots, it is not a popular alternative. Discussions of end of life options, including medical directives, hospice and palliative care, are fundable by physicians under Medicare, but few of them are professionally equipped for it, and many patients are too traumatized for discussions about terminal treatment during a crisis which can bring torture to patients and their families.

The late psychiatrist Elizabeth Kubler-Ross observed that dying people often need to work through various stages of shock, denial, anger, bargaining, and depression to enter the calm realm of acceptance when the inevitable ending is imminent. She could have added anxiety, fear, and even terror. Some of them get stuck in this process and need help in moving through it all. But family and medical caregivers who just do not understand often stand in the way of it or avoid it altogether until it comes. There is scant research about the anxiety of aging, which is decades behind the need for treatments of the facts and reality of it. If you are not depressed and anxious, you just don't know what is happening. Medicine is not organized to aid the dying to exit well, but only to make as much profit as possible by prolonging suffering as long as possible—except for the special doctors and nurses who work in hospice and palliative care. Many physicians withhold unfavorable information to avoid taking hope away from patients and their families, even when they know extensive treatment is futile. Some doctors act like death is a curable disease. We may say they lost the battle with the disease as though it is some kind of war to be won or lost. When all the diseases are curable, then what will people die of?

Discussing the options available to terminal patients and their families still is difficult if not impossible to many physicians. Like, would you prefer DNR or full code and life support when your heart stops beating or hospice and palliative care? Contemplating their inevitable ending is so terrifying to many people, like staring at the sun, they pursue temporary distractions and avoid end of life planning as long as possible. Even with a living will or personal medical directive, the final treatments in a hospital may be out of your control. If you have not experienced it, you have no idea what they can do to you in hospital trying to keep you alive. Read a book like *The Conversation* (2015) by Dr. Angelo Volandes to learn how bad it can get and how to make it better. He explains with all too realistic examples how terminal patients and families must choose between full code, DNR, or something in between at the last moments of life when emotions can overrule reason. Some families plan ahead, but most do not. There are no right or wrong treatment decisions in the ICU, just choices and consequences. For example, CPR in the ICU rarely works and often leaves broken ribs and collapsed lungs. But failing to plan is planning to fail, leaving many regrets and post-trauma shock behind for survivors. For more details visit www.theconversationproject.org. All in God's will of course, or it would be different. Ergo Theofatalism.

Sans Everything

There comes a natural time for everyone to exit life when their labyrinth walk is finished, so why make it more traumatic and expensive than necessary. Dying is easy but trying not to is hard. Avoiding it or denying it will not change it. Shakespeare wrote that "all the world's a stage, And all the men and women merely players; They have their exits and their entrances, And one man in his time plays many parts… Last scene of all, that ends this strange eventful history, is second childishness and mere oblivion, Sans teeth, sans eyes, sans taste, sans everything" (*As You Like It*, act 2, scene 7). The only rules for walking the labyrinth of life are to begin and continue on the pilgrimage that is your destiny, with faith that you are right where

A LABYRINTH WALK OF LIFE

you need to be up until the end. It may seem like you merely are meandering around in circles, but the pathway leads to its inevitable destination, i.e., the source from which you came. C. G. Jung proclaimed that "those who look outward dream, but those who look inward awake... In all chaos there is a secret order." We may appear to be insignificant in the scale of the universe, or indispensable like a grain of sand on the beach, but the universe would be less without each one. This discovery prompts one to make the effort to change the orientation of each life from insignificant to indispensable, from outward to inward, from sensing to intuition, from physical to spiritual after the meridian in aging is passed—say around age forty or so.

Perhaps the greatest adjustment in aging involves becoming redundant and losing control of your life. Jesus told his disciple, "When you were young you dressed yourself and went wherever you pleased, but when you are old someone else will dress you and take you where you do not want to go" (John 21:18). It is not much different today if you are fated to live through conscious aging. Some teach that we choose this walk of life for the lessons we must learn. When it ends let it go and, with assurance and confidence, say with Jesus and Apostle Paul, it is finished (John 19:30, 2 Timothy 4:6–7). Alfred Lord Tennyson wrote of his farewell thus: "Sunset and evening star, And one clear call for me! And may there be no moaning of the bar, When I put out to sea... For tho' from out our bourne of time and place the flood may bear me far, I hope to see my pilot face to face when I have crost the bar." This certainly is different from the poetic instruction of Dylan Thomas to his father, "Do not go gentle into that good night. Rage, rage against the dying of the light." Poet John Donne concluded, "Never send to know for whom the bell tolls; it tolls for thee."

C. G. Jung contended that after middle age, all human social activities merely are distractions to avoid facing the reality of inevitable death, preparation for which is the main purpose of the second half of life. Stanford professor emeritus Irvin Yalom said it is like staring at the sun. Compounding the shock is realization that no one knows what comes after and if there is any afterlife or not. Some people exit quickly and painlessly, but many suffer greatly for long periods before the final ending, leaving shock and trauma for their survivors. Anyone contemplating it must be beset with anxiety and depression at the prospect of living too long unless there is another way out. Women have the legal right to control their own bodies and to terminate an unwanted pregnancy, but suffering older adults cannot mention the suicide option without being hospitalized involuntarily under state laws by well-meaning but misguided authorities. Unless they are bridled, modern medics can keep a stone alive. At best, physicians sometimes prescribe terminal sedation, knowing that it will hasten death. So thirty thousand or more people who are given a burden too heavy to carry take the matter into their own hands each year.

Among all the advanced nations, only Switzerland permits a legal way out for anyone who wants a preemptive exit from suffering. In the United States, the issue is left up to the states, and most of them are stifled into inaction. So far, Oregon, Washington, California, Colorado, Vermont, and the District of Columbia have enacted physician-assisted exit laws. Most physicians are unprepared to serve their terminal patients this way. The Final Exit Network seeks to change this situation within the rights of free speech, but it is threatened with legal action very costly to defend. Consequently, some Americans experience the worst death in the developed world, leaving close survivors traumatized for years. We treat our aging animal pets better than that. Bottom line is the process of dying in America is inhumane and is badly in need of debate and revision. Too few doctors are able to engage this discussion about end of life care, but the few who are able may be making life much less traumatic for terminal patients and their families. You can assume it all must be God's will or it would be different or not. And when it needs to change it will. Ergo Theofatalism.

A National Disgrace

The fact is there is no recovery from life because it is a terminal condition from the instant we are conceived. After all, dying merely is the necessary opposite to procreation. Allowing death to happen naturally just is socially, politically, religiously, and psychologically unacceptable in America. Psychiatry professor emeritus Irvin Yalom concluded that contemplating your death or that of a loved one is like staring at the sun; no one can do it for long without stressing mental health so they pursue all kinds of diversions to avoid the view. That may explain the enormous amounts of money wasted and time spent on meaningless sporting events and staged entertainment and even work as momentary distractions—which seem to be part of human nature. On the other hand, C. G. Jung (1875–1961) said the entire second half of life is nothing but preparation for the end, and that is the primary goal of the psyche after the meridian is passed. If it is such an inevitable and natural ending of life, why are we made to fight it so much? Since it is socially incorrect and emotionally stressful to discuss end of life decisions in advance with families and doctors the fact is that, unless they die suddenly, the way many old Americans die in nursing homes and hospitals is a national disgrace. Unlike the old days when family doctors made house calls, medical services now are delivered by many different specialists who often do a poor job of treating the whole patient as they concentrate on very specific medical issues without coordination among family members.

This trend may improve the efficiency of treatments, which come with disabling side effects that impact the quality of life, but it diminishes the personhood of patients and families as they become case numbers in a computer database. Families often cannot let go of a beloved relative and demand "full code" treatment even though it is useless. Doctors are employed to save/extend lives and not to end them in America, and they risk legal actions to do otherwise. A few doctors are writing books about the profit driven excesses of medicine in America, but they risk their careers doing so. Even when death is unavoidable, some survivors consumed with anger accuse doctors of unethical and unprofessional behavior. Helping a terminal patient commit suicide is a felony offense in most states– except in the few states where it is legal but the prerequisites make it almost unlikely. So end-of-life suffering can be overwhelming, and useless testing can be downright fraudulent. It is not unusual for families to go bankrupt paying for terminal care. We treat our pet animals better than that. Get this: dying does not cause suffering, but resisting it does. And the more resistance the more suffering. When you confront what is happening in American medicine among the terminally ill, shock, outrage, depression, and anxiety are normal human reactions.

There is an incipient emergence of palliative and hospice care funded by Medicare for optional comfort care treatment during the last six months, but most people do not understand their benefits compared with "full code" maximum efforts to keep terminal patients alive regardless of cost or suffering. So often they demand extensive treatment that merely increases post trauma shock of survivors and does little or nothing to prolong life while inflating Medicare expenses. Hospice doctor, then professor of palliative care at Dartmouth, and author of *The Best Care Possible* (2012), Ira Byock says the passing of a loved one in the family is eased somewhat by a final conversation as follows: I forgive you, please forgive me, I love you, thanks for everything, goodbye. This of course is not how it goes in many cases. It is not easy to die peacefully in America, thanks to modern treatments that can and do prolong suffering much longer than necessary. One physician said, "I can keep a stone alive." In medical school, no one teaches doctors how to let a patient die. So doctors are so hell-bent on extending suffering at the end of life they can destroy its quality in the process, leaving lifelong trauma and bankruptcy ahead for the survivors. Most families have made no plans, such as writing a living will or medical power of attorney or discussing their wishes with the primary doctor, so the terminal stage can be very emotional as doctors try to balance treatment that is billable with what is reasonable.

Money fuels medical decisions and money motivates the whole system—the more treatment, the more profit. Doctors have a lot of monetary hope in the word "hope." They must have active imaginations. Nurses usually are left to serve the dying when doctors see their billable work is completed. Still, there are rare miracles that defy statistics, and with radical extremely expensive treatment, a few patients recover to die another day because the future is utterly unpredictable. But Dr. Byock says it is possible to feel good inside no matter what happens outside—with hospice and palliative care, i.e., treatment of the whole person, not just the illness. Choosing these alternatives is not hastening death, but choosing life without the added burdens of useless medical interventions and radical measures in the intensive care unit. Illness, death, and grief are painful, turbulent, and normal inevitable experiences of life. But they need not be as traumatic and inhumane as they have become in America. Perhaps there is a role for religion here that has been lost in our society. Jesus said, "The spirit gives life, the flesh counts for nothing" (John 6:63).

The ancient symbol of the labyrinth depicts this journey of life from the source out into the world and returning again on the pathway each one must take returning home. But it does not come easily. After he buried his wife and five of six children by his age sixty-two, Poet laureate Robert Frost (1874–1963) concluded, "It is hard to get into this world and hard to get out and what lies in between makes no sense." He petitioned the Almighty, "Lord, please forgive my many little jokes on thee and I will forgive thy great big one on me." This includes the illusion of free will because we have no control at all over life and death, medicine notwithstanding. "You saw me before I was born and scheduled each day of my life before I began to breathe. Every day was recorded in your book!" (Psalm 139:16). "It is God who directs the lives of his creatures; everyone's life is in his power" (Job 12:10). Thus it all comes down to the will of God; not the man-made god of pseudo love in holy books, but the prime mover in the universe... generator, operator, destroyer... GOD. It does whatever it wants with everyone, and Saint/Mother Teresa said, "We all must take what it gives and give what it takes." Ergo Theofatalism.

The Pathway to Inner Peace

The symbol of Theofatalism is the ancient labyrinth selected from the Cathedral of Notre Dame in Chartres, France... it shows a pathway outward from our source out into the world to midlife and then back to the source again after the meridian is passed. It is a metaphor for life and could be the spiritual pathway to inner peace. There are only two rules, begin walking and continue. The labyrinth is opposite to a maze, which is intended to confuse and frustrate. In contrast, the labyrinth presents a spiritual pathway to inner peace that begins with emergence from the source to participate in the world and then returns to the source after the meridian of life has been passed. In the end, all our journeys lead back to home. We cannot fail to end up where we are supposed to go in this lifetime, no matter where that turns out to be nor how we get there. The final goal of life is to return to the Source from which we came. Imagine that. Once done, no one can go back in time to do anything over differently, so it all must be necessary to compose the whole of human history, individually and collectively. We may feel insignificant but we really are indispensable, each and every one. Lives can only be seen looking backward, but they must be lived going forward, walking the labyrinth we are given into the great unknown future. And that comes with indefinite uncertainty, which leads to existential anxiety, called angst, if you think about it. So don't give it another thought and just go out to play. All in God's will of course.

Everyone Is a Member

Where do you turn for comfort when "do this—get that" no longer works and your life is upset and you realize that you have no control of the past, much less the future? Identical twins separated at birth who are subsequently reunited years later usually are amazed at all the similarities in their likes and dislikes, in addition to their appearance, proving this assumption. The late Beatle, John Lennon, learned that life is what happens while you are making other plans. How do you live with all the suffering and insanity in the world? Easy... well, maybe not so easy... realize it must all be God's will or it would be different, including your desire for control or wish that things were different. Not the manmade god in holy books but the prime mover in the universe... generator, operator, destroyer... GOD. Science assumes the universe is governed by the four forces of gravity, electromagnetism, and weak and strong nuclear forces, but this force appears to be a fifth force that controls everything from atoms to galaxies. It may be the assumed force of dark energy that would explain the mysterious expansion of the universe. It does whatever it wants with whomever it wants and we all must take what it gives and give what it takes. This would include the necessary but illusory belief in human free will. Leon Trotsky (1879–1940) observed, "Life is not an easy matter. You cannot live through it without falling into frustration and cynicism unless you have before you a great idea which raises you above all kinds of perfidy and baseness." Perhaps this is it. When Neil Armstrong stepped onto the moon he declared it was "a giant leap for mankind." This could be another. The community of mankind has no boundary, so you can never be outside. You might call it the Virtual Church of Theofatalism, where everyone is a member and no one can resign or be expelled. Or you might just call it life. All in God's will of course.

The World of Spirit

The existence of a duality between matter and energy has been accepted by science, but a companion duality between body and spirit still is a mystery. Jesus declared, "The spirit gives life, the flesh counts for nothing" (John 6:63). And he explained, "My kingdom is not of this world" (John 18:36). He communicated with his source, calling it Father who is in heaven (Matthew 6:9, John 17) and he thought there were heavenly beings called angels ready to defend him if he called them (Matthew 26:53). He also declared his disciples who follow him into heaven would be like the angels, neither marrying nor giving in marriage (Matthew 22:30). The Catholic Church has designated some eleven thousand deceased individuals as saints in some kind of spirit form of existence who literally are responsible for miracles, and the Vatican claims that if there is communion of the saints there must also be communications. St. Teresa of Avila (1515–1582) claimed that St. Joseph was always reliable and could be commended to others in addition to herself. Perhaps the world of spirit mimics the world of characters in drama who are separate but united with the actors who portray them. Thus, Leonard Nimoy is dead, but Dr. Spock lives. Jesus died but Christ lives. Muhammad died but Islam lives. Buddha died but Buddhism lives. Science now accepts that there could be dimensions and universes that are explainable only with mathematics, but the spirit world must be taken on faith. With faith, no proof is necessary and without faith no proof is sufficient. All in God's will of course. Ergo Theofatalism.

When Truth Is Hell

Americans are driven by the search for health, wealth, and happiness while success is measured by the price of their toys. Our form of capitalism is driven by converting luxuries into necessities—consider all the bells and whistles in modern automobiles that continually are being added, and how about the explosion of smart phones apps—just to make them more expensive and profitable. Put them together and you get a crowd of mentally unhealthy people because life really is not like the pseudo society on the little screen in your hand. Unfortunately for many people, so much of life now is consumed in fantasy that reality is shocking when it comes calling. Jack Nicholson exclaimed in the movie *A Few Good Men* (1992), "You can't handle the truth." President Harry Truman said, "People say I give them hell. I just tell the truth and they think it is hell." It is easy to acquire information but far more difficult to absorb it when reality overcomes fantasy. "With much wisdom comes much sorrow, the more knowledge the more grief" (Ecclesiastes 1:17–18). C. G. Jung saw the opposites here as in all things. "Indeed, bitterness and wisdom form a pair of alternatives: where there is bitterness wisdom is lacking, and where wisdom is there can be no bitterness." So be patient and allow the time for this enlightenment to happen in your life.

Happiness is not to be found in materialism, unless of course you happen to be a stock broker or banker or a movie celebrity or professional athlete. Even many of them are not happy. The richest person is one who needs the least. In spite of the propaganda about how exceptional we are, the fact is that the range from poor to wealthy is expanding rapidly in America, and we are no exception to the global economy. To paraphrase the late chairman of GM, what is good for business is good for America. NOT. For example, about six million jobs in the USA are dependent upon exports to Mexico, and many of the autos sold in America are assembled in Mexico. Practically all of your clothing is made in poor countries by destitute workers. Automation is expected to create 15 million new jobs in a decade while it displaces about 25 million existing jobs. One example is a machine that can make three hundred bricks per minute. Most people must seek personal resilience in the face of unexpected adversity because very few of us get the brass ring or win the lottery of life. The late oil mogul J. Paul Getty said, "Some people find oil and some people don't." Most people don't. They do not win the lottery either—in fact, for one to win many millions must lose. And yet, Americans idolize a winner, and nobody really cares who comes in second.

For many poor people, the meager benefits in life don't seem to be worth the burdens, and they slump into depression and become dependent upon government support. And yet, the poor souls keep on buying those lottery tickets because somebody always wins. Or they borrow money for worthless college educations that make them debtors for life. Or they keep on reading self-help books to learn what is wrong with them and what to do about it. Or they search the Internet trying to find the guru with all the answers. And they continue making babies. Those who think they can change just don't get it. "The Lord kills and makes alive; The Lord makes poor and makes rich; He brings some low and lifts some up" (1 Samuel 2:6–7). Nothing happens outside the will of God. Not the manmade god in any holy books, but the prime mover in the universe… generator, operator, destroyer... GOD. It does whatever it wants with whomever it wants. Ergo Theofatalism.

The Fight over Black Gold—Texas Tea

Everything God ever created comes with both benefits and burdens. Fossil fuels are prime examples. They have made modern life possible, but they also produce immense problems. All benefits come with burdens. The influence of oil driving international relations cannot be underestimated. Despite the trends toward more efficient use in transportation, it still has no real substitute. Perhaps electric vehicles will change things, but that will be far off. Ever since it was discovered under the Middle East deserts in 1938, oil has been a primary currency of international economics, separating the haves from the have-nots and making some strange bedfellows. Although the US produces a lot of oil and gas it still must import nearly half of its oil needs from countries that are Islamic theocracies that hate the modern western social style of life. The breakeven price of US and Canadian oil is about $40 per barrel, but it is much lower for Middle Eastern countries, which have abundant cheap reserves. The Organization of Petroleum Exporting Countries (OPEC) is dominated by the largest and cheapest producer, Saudi Arabia. Thus, they can afford to control international prices by controlling supplies to keep western consumers under their influence. Recent new technology has opened up vast new areas for oil production, so that US dependency on foreign sources has been reduced. Now, we export oil even though we still must import half of our needs—which makes no sense at all. Oil is a bargaining chip for international politics. Exxon/Mobil has leased land equal to the state of Wisconsin in Russia, hoping to find new profitable oil reserves. Let's face it, we are addicted to oil as President Bush said and, like any addiction, the suppliers want to keep it that way. Do not be fooled by temporary price swings due to manipulated supply and demand.

But here is the thing. Each new deposit of oil is costing more and more to discover and recover. The practice of fracking, injecting water into deep earth reserves to break up rocks and release more oil and gas, is potentially very dangerous and much more costly. Cheap oil is running out and will eventually need to be replaced with some new form of energy if not in decades, then in centuries. Whether that turns out to be solar, hydrogen, wind, or some new development as yet unimagined is uncertain. Moreover, the political controversy over global warming is impacting the demand for coal, oil, and gas in ways yet to be determined. Gas seems like an economical alternative but it also presents issues of environmental impact. Use of coal has declined because of its water pollution and global warming effects. Hope that coal could be cleaned up enough to protect its damage to human health and maintain jobs have not been successful. Until transportation is fueled by gas or electricity, the demand for oil and its derivative, gasoline, will grow and the world will be fighting over oil. In the meantime, you can expect that international relations will be driven by the struggle for oil from increasingly more expensive suppliers who are unfriendly to America. The solutions will not be easy or quick. Those who claim otherwise just don't get it. All in God's will of course… Ergo Theofatalism.

Lambs among the Wolves

The religion of Islam is in the news, so here is what you need to know. It is the second largest and fastest growing religion with about 1.6 billion members, mostly of Arabic descent. Second only to Christianity, its founder was one named Muhammad who lived in Mecca in what is now Saudi Arabia from about 570 A.D. to 632 A.D. He was a successful merchant, married to a successful woman who was fifteen years his senior, and they had two sons and four daughters. About the age of forty, he began meditations in a cave from which the angel Gabriel gave him certain instructions, which he began to teach to his closest associates. His followers grew rapidly and soon had to fight for their new beliefs because they differed so much from the established tribes in the area who felt threatened. He migrated to the adjacent city of Medina and became a winning military warrior for God, then named Allah. After his death, his followers compiled his sayings into the Holy Quran and thus began the religion of Islam, which means submission. Muhammad was declared to be the last prophet of God after Jesus, in the tradition of Moses and Abraham, possibly descending from his bastard son Ishmael, conceived with the maiden of his wife. The followers of Muhammad split into two factions over a dispute about his successor—the Sunni and the Shiite—who hate each other to this day. And they both hate the western lifestyle which they claim violates the laws of God as gifted to Moses. They developed a form of law called sharia based [on] the Mosaic laws.

There is nothing new about ubiquitous wars among *Homo sapiens*, but western cultures now face a threat based on this religion that could change the geo-political landscape. Thinking people are beginning to be concerned, and the rest should be, about the rise of militant Islam and the role of suicide bombings and other attacks by radical Muslims against nonbelievers in Allah and the prophet Muhammad. Radical Muslims have no tolerance for expressing freedom of speech when it comes to upholding their faith in Allah and his messenger, Muhammad (peace be upon him.) Attacks by Muslims on US citizens at home and abroad easily are triggered by the slightest comment or action by Americans that breach their sacred dogma—even a documentary film or a cartoon character critical of Muhammad will not be tolerated on penalty of beheading. The most radical factions among them think nothing of killing innocent women and children if it advances their cause for domination and control. The violence could easily become domestic if Imams order it. Horrific mass killings will occur so long as there are lambs among the wolves.

This is nothing less than a resurgence of the religious wars of the Middle Ages that saw Islam expand to engulf the seat of Judaism and Christianity in Jerusalem and take over much of central Europe. It bloomed through the Ottoman Empire until after WWI when the empire was disbanded and present nation-states were formed in the Middle East. However, the zeal of jihad holy war has only been dormant and was not extinguished. Now, it is rising again fueled by those conservative Muslim teachers and imams who see in the Holy Quran commandments to fight the infidel and unbelievers until they all are subdued and live under the rule of sharia as it was manifested by the prophet Muhammad. Christianity may be at risk for its survival because Jesus taught total passivism and nonviolence to enemies to the point of death and beyond (Luke 6:28–35). The Holy Quran proclaims: [4.74] "Therefore let those fight in the way of Allah, who sell this world's life for the hereafter; and whoever fights in the way of Allah, then be he slain or be he victorious, We shall grant him a mighty reward." While the Bible declares: "If your enemy is hungry, feed him; if he is thirsty, give him something to drink. In doing this, you will heap burning coals on his head" (Romans 12:20). And Jesus taught absolute passivism. So in religious conflict, guess which side wins if both are obedient to their God.

Muslims must read the Holy Quran, and it is passed time for US politicians to read it also. If they did, perhaps their claim that the first amendment of the US Constitution covers the freedom to practice of Islam could be at least debatable. The official US response is stifled because the first amendment to the US Constitution stipulates, "Congress shall make no law respecting an establishment of religion, or prohibiting the free exercise thereof…" The combination of freedom of religion and the right to bear arms in the second amendment could be the Achilles Heel of the US Constitution. Remember the Trojan horse? Those who ignore history are bound to repeat it. And it all must be the will of God or it would be different. Ergo Theofatalism.

The Evil That God Created

People just cannot believe that God does evil things. Take the pandemic of drug addictions for example. Illegal drugs—and some legal ones—ruin lives of people all the time and cost American taxpayers more than $30 billion each year trying to reverse their use by more than 27 million addicts. President Trump has declared drug addictions a national emergency. They also create havoc in Mexico where most of the traffic initiates, flooding across the southern border in all types of ingenious smuggling. The largest cash crop in Afghanistan remains the farming of poppies, the raw material of heroin distributed throughout Europe. But who created the ability of the human brain to become addicted to lethal substances, and who created the substances? Did mankind intentionally develop marijuana, or hemp, or poppies to get addicted? The growing opioid overdose epidemic was initiated by unsupported claims that painkillers were not addictive by medical scientists who should have known better. What is more, how did mankind ever learn how to farm and harvest the lethal crops and then refine them into ingestible forms of drugs and set up international markets for their distribution and sale? Mmm?

The answer applies to other such discoveries as tobacco and alcohol and the invention of concrete and steel and anesthesia and gunpowder. They all are part of the world that God created. God causes it all and only God can fix it. The Bible says, "I make peace and create evil/calamity. I the Lord do all these things" (Isaiah 45:7). In this context, the Hebrew word for "evil" is translated elsewhere in the Bible as spoiled, bad, adversity, trouble, sinful, misfortune, calamity, natural disasters, or suffering—so take your pick. "Who has spoken and it came to pass, unless the Lord has commanded it? Is it not from the mouth of the Most High that good and bad come?" (Lamentations 3:37–38). The Quran says the same thing to Muslims; "No calamity comes, no affliction occurs, except by the decision and preordainment of Allah" (S:64.11). This is not the man-made god in any holy books but the prime mover in the universe. It has three sides, which is the real trinity… generator, operator, destroyer… GOD. Ergo Theofatalism. There is no other reasonable explanation for the evil in the world. And human free will has nothing to do with it.

For All You Atheists

This essay is a bit long, so please bear with it. Christians are being duped. Here's how. Contradictions in the Bible render it unbelievable when considered rationally, including the basic dogma. If you believe the Bible is the inspired infallible Word of God, you may be shocked, so fair warning. The New Testament and church dogma claim everyone inherited sin from the first man and needs a savior who is Christ the Lord to avoid spending eternity in hell (John 3:16; Matthew 10:28; Luke 12:5; Romans 5:12, 8–19, 10:9). But Jesus claimed that only those called/enabled by God would make that choice (John 6:44, 65). Perhaps that is where John Calvin got his idea of predestination wherein some are condemned to everlasting hell fire and others get to enjoy the pleasures of heaven, at the whim of God. If God created mankind in "his" own image and likeness (Genesis 1:27) and then gave them free will, knowing they all would use it to disobey and commit sins to consign them all to hell fire unless they accept Jesus from Nazareth as Lord and Savior—this is a god to fear and not to worship. "Fear him who after killing the body has power to cast you into hell" (Luke 12:4–5). Christian dogma is based largely on the writing of Apostle Paul such as: "For just as through the disobedience of the one man (Adam) the many were made sinners, so also through the obedience of the one man (Jesus the Messiah/Christ) the many will be made righteous" (Romans 5:19, 10:9–13). But the book of Genesis does not say the disobedience of first man, Adam, was inherited by all his descendants. Instead Cain, the first son and murderer, was not punished but was protected by God and made the father of cities after killing his brother, Abel, in a fit of jealousy because God preferred the blood sacrificial gift of Abel (Genesis 4:15–17). There is no explanation for the mother of cities, so the first generations can only be explained by invoking incest.

The first six chapters of Genesis recount a mythical version of genealogy that no one can take seriously, unless God wills. God became so disappointed with his human creation that he decided to destroy them all and start over with the family of righteous man, Noah to carry on the human species, which also was a total failure because the same genes were propagated after the flood (Genesis 6:5–7). The first thing Noah did was plant a vineyard and proceed to get drunk (Genesis 9:9–21). Since his family were the only survivors, along with two of every species, the subsequent life on earth all must have emerged from incest (Genesis 11:10). As to eternal punishment, the Bible says, "He does not leave the guilty unpunished; he punishes the children and their children for the sin of the parents to the third and fourth generation" (Exodus 34:7). No mention of sending them to hell or passing the punishment to all generations to come.

Elsewhere, the Old Testament says that each person will be judged for himself alone and not his ancestors (Ezekiel 18:19–20, Deuteronomy 2:16). However, the whole genealogy of Israel is based upon the stolen blessing of his father, Isaac, by Jacob who cheated his older brother Esau out of his rightful inheritance, which was not labeled a sin. Jacob was renamed Israel and had twelve sons with his two wives, Rachel and Leah plus each of their servants (Genesis 35:23–26). From among their descendants rose David, the forebear of Jesus. Moreover, King David was not punished for his adultery with Bathsheba and the murder of her husband Uriah in battle but was ordained as the slayer of "tens of thousands," and became the original ancestor of Jesus the Messiah/Christ (1 Samuel 18:7, Matthew 1:6–16). Actually, the first son of his adulterous conception died at birth as punishment, but his second son became the next king of Israel, Solomon. The Catholic Church says that unbaptized infants who die go directly to heaven, even though the Bible states, "In sin did my mother conceive me" (Psalm 51:4–6, KJV). However, Jesus said the Kingdom of Heaven belongs to such as little children, so they cannot be born sinners to make this work (Luke 18:26). He also said neither the man born blind nor his parents had sinned so the "power/works of God" could be shown in his healing (John 9:3). Apparently, some people do not need a savior because Jesus said, "Learn what this means. I have not come to call the righteous, but sinners" (Matthew 9:12–14).

Moreover, Jesus declared the second commandment to love your neighbor as yourself is equal to the first one to love God with all your being (Matthew 22:38–40, Mark 12:30–32). But he also said, "Greater love has no man than this: to lay down his life for his friends" (John 15:13). And then he admonished his disciples to hate their families and even their own lives to be his disciples and take up their cross and follow him… presumably into martyrdom (Luke 14:26). The Gospel of Mark, the oldest one and closest to the recorded events, does not even mention any divine virgin birth of Jesus, which was added later in Matthew and Luke gospels with differing details. Neither does the Gospel of John declare Jesus was born of a virgin. Some scholars think the word "virgin" should be translated as "young woman." When Jesus went off to pray alone in the

Garden the night before he was betrayed, there were no witnesses, so how could the writer quote what he said? (John 17). And lastly, Jesus said human genealogy is worthless because "The spirit gives life, the flesh counts for nothing" (John 6:44, 63). So it appears that the Bible scribes were more than a little confused. Apostle Paul said that God is not the author of this confusion (1 Corinthians 14:33)… so why is the Bible full of it?

Here is some basic history you may not get in church. The New Testament was compiled from many circulating hand copied manuscripts almost four hundred years after the ministry of Jesus from Nazareth. The earliest papyrus manuscripts from Egypt date to the fourth century. Only fragments exist of earlier parchment copies. In 331 CE, the Roman Emperor Constantine sent a letter, the text of which has survived, to Bishop Eusebius in Caesarea—who was a recognized historian—asking him to arrange for the manual production of fifty Bibles using the approved canon in koine Greek. Eusebius was an advisor to and confidant of the emperor. The first official adoption of Christian doctrine occurred at the Council of Nicaea (Iznik, Turkey) convened by Constantine I from May 20 to June 19 in 325 CE and turned on the argument between two debating bishops from Alexandria, Arius, and Athanasius—Athanasius won the debate, and we got the Roman Catholic Church. If Arius had won, things would be different because some theologians prefer Arianism to this day—which rejects the doctrine of a trinity combining father, son, and holy ghost into one. The Latin translation emerged at the end of that century as the Vulgate, but it was not adopted by the Roman Catholic Church as the official inspired version until the Council of Trent in 1545. Before then, countless secular scribes and monks made copies of individual books by hand, inserting editing and translation variations along the way, which practice was continued until invention of the printing press in 1440 by Johannes Gutenberg in Germany. The Bible was divided into chapters in the thirteenth century, and verses were itemized in the sixteenth century. A primitive incomplete version was first printed in 1516 of dubious quality and origin. Prior versions include translations attributed to Wycliffe, Coverdale, and Rheims. The first edition to be published in English was a translation by Tyndale about 1534–1536 that was never actually completed.

Martin Luther kicked off the Reformation in 1511 with his ninety-five criticisms of the Roman Catholic Church, of which he was a priest who was excommunicated and isolated with a price on his head. He translated the Bible into German in 1522–1532 after which it was translated into the King James Version in English in 160–1611 when James I and the pope disagreed over his primary obedience to God/pope and him alone. Apostle Paul claimed that all authorities are appointed by God and should be obeyed. "Let everyone be subject to the governing authorities for there is no authority except that which God has established" (Romans 13:1–7). So King James organized the Church of England under the doctrine of the divine right of kings to purge the popular Geneva Bible of its marginal notes. The Geneva Bible went out of print in 1640 after it was translated into English, possibly because it contained footnotes disavowed by King James, which were appended by John Calvin, John Knox, and other leaders of the Reformation.

Since then, many different translations have been published and endless commentaries and interpretations as well. The New International Version claims to be the most authentic. So the versions of the Bible we have today may not even be close to the intentions of the original writers of the first century. After all, the first manuscripts were probably written in Hebrew and koine Greek and none of them exist in totality today, except for a few scraps. The earliest complete manuscript of the Old Testament is the Septuagint in Greek that dates to the fourth century. Those who claim the Bible is the divine Word of God are driven by personal faith. With faith, no proof is necessary and without faith, no proof is sufficient. But where does faith come from if not the will of God? (Romans 10:14-15, Ephesians 2:8).

If God knows everything, including the future, then he orchestrated the fall of mankind (and everything else) before setting his plan into motion. In the beginning, God created everything—including belief in free will—thus mankind is not responsible for anything (Genesis 1:1) The mystery is why are not Christians smart enough to question this obviously flawed theology? They appear to be driven to churches and many traditions that transcend and overcome rational logic by some force beyond reason. They seem to be possessed by so much God-given guilt and fear they cannot help themselves in hopes of a blissful hereafter in heaven with the Lord if they just acknowledge and obey him and him only. "You shall have no other gods besides me" (Exodus 20:30). "Fear him who after killing the body has power to cast you into hell" (Luke 12:4–5). However, Christians amount to only about one-third of all humans on earth, so what about all the other forms of religion? The belief in God seems to be a continuing part of human evolution that has not moved very far from the tribal ancestors who made up some higher power to explain acts of nature they could not understand. Some of them, i.e., astrologers in the Middle East and the Maya in Central America, tried to connect the earth with the stars, which could be the origin of belief in heaven above the earth and hell beneath it. However, science claims the tides on earth are controlled by the moon, so perhaps the stars influence life on earth more than we know.

Here is the thing… it all must be God's will or it would be different. "A person's steps are directed by the Lord. How then can anyone understand their own way?" (Proverbs 20:24). "Does not the potter have the right to make out of the same lump of clay some pottery for special purposes and some for common use?" (Jeremiah 18:2–6, Romans 9:16–21). Perhaps it is time for a new theology—

one that accommodates the reality of all creation from atoms to galaxies, including all the various religions in the world. But that must be a different God and one superior to the God of Christianity plus all other religions, which *are* cleaved with controversy to this day. How about the prime force in the universe, generator, operator, destroyer… GOD. It does whatever it wants with whomever it wants, including duping of Christians. Hence… wait for it… THEOFATALISM.

Pretending Nothing Happened

All beginnings come with endings, it is true. Losses come in various ways and intensities, but they all require a transition from the past to the present and walking the labyrinth of life into the future. Deaths and other losses are part of life, and some are more difficult to process than others. The Holmes-Rahe scale of stress puts death of a spouse highest on the scale of one hundred. This is surprising because death is a consequence of living and thus should not be so traumatic for survivors, but it is. People all need to learn to grieve their losses as it is not a naturally endowed skill. Physicians are programmed to preserve life and so are disabled when all their efforts come to failure so they are not much help. They are happy to turn the consequences over to professional morticians, leaving the survivors to look after themselves. Churches are not much help either as services usually go on as usual after the funeral. Mourning, and all its emotions, seems to be contagious and to be avoided because mirror neurons in the brain absorb the pain of suffering when observed in others—called empathy. It is not unusual for acute stress to cause a fatal heart attack from the reactions that some people experience after unexpected shocks, both positive and negative, called stress induced cardiomyopathy.

A LABYRINTH WALK OF LIFE

Anthropologist Margaret Mead (1901–1978) said, "We celebrate at weddings and we rejoice at births but when someone dies we pretend nothing happened." People in western cultures would rather think about anything but death, especially their own or a loved one. The late Steve Jobs, founder of Apple Inc., observed that "even people who think they are going to heaven don't want to die to get there." Death is a giant elephant in the living room that people just pretend is not there until it happens. Even losses of close loved ones are pushed into the past, possibly leaving damage to the psyche left unhealed while they jump into substitutes and distracting activities as soon as possible to avoid the feelings and painful memories. Pretending it did not happen is not healthy, and as one gets older, ungrieved losses can pile up until the psyche almost breaks from unexpressed distress. Shakespeare wrote this instruction in *The Tragedy of Macbeth*, "Give sorrow words, the grief that does not speak knits up the over-wrought heart and bids it break." Perhaps that was the beginning of the modern form of therapy because sharing your painful thoughts and feelings does appear to be helpful in absorbing human tragedies. If families and friends cannot be helpful, then professionals may be needed for grief counseling. In fact, it is normal for close friends and relations to avoid the impact of a family loss if it threatens their personal stability and intrudes into their lives. So it may be useful to keep a private daily journal to track your progress. For one such example, read *A Grief Observed* by C. S. Lewis (1963).

It may be traumatic to witness death of a loved one—even horrific—but learning to grieve our losses is necessary for mental health. If they are not grieved, the impact of accumulated post traumatic shock may be disabling. Some survivors liken loss of a loved one to an amputation, which can be substituted with a prosthesis, but never replaced. When someone enters your heart they never really leave. The process of grieving can be learned, but only in very small chunks over a period of time that varies for each survivor because it is like staring at the sun. There are five tasks in recovery from loss: (1) acknowledge the loss, (2) accept the feelings, (3) detach from investment in the past, (4) find and arrange for substitutes, and (5) reconstruct a life with new relationships side by side with the memories that may fade, but never totally leave. This is much easier said than done. Mourners all navigate this process according to their unique personality traits, employing sensing, thinking, feeling, and intuition in their own ways, i.e., physical, intellectual, emotional, and spiritual resources as coping mechanisms. You may recognize this process as being one application of the theory of personality proposed by C. G. Jung and implemented through the Myers-Briggs Type Indicator© by CPP Inc. Google "MBTI" for details. There are no established social institutions that help mourners conduct this process, so each survivor is left alone to continue living sometimes in a broken condition that cannot be fixed, like Humpty Dumpty. To visit this model of grieving, read *Recovery from Loss* co-authored by this writer.

Even those who think they are prepared can be blindsided with the impact of a major loss. It is possible in our culture to live into midlife without ever facing death of a loved one, so it can be a great shock. For the Christian, grief presents a conundrum, a difficult and confusing problem that has never been resolved. If God is all loving and omnipotent, how come suffering is so ubiquitous among his creation? After untimely death of his wife, British writer and Christian apologist C. S. Lewis (1898–1963) lamented when he needed the help of God to survive, the door of grace seemed to be closed, locked, and barred on the other side, the lights were out and no one seemed to be present. He died of a broken heart soon after he wrote *A Grief Observed* (1963) in which he declared, "No one told me that grief feels so much like fear." Lewis summarized the problem of pain and grief thus: "If God were good, He would make His creatures perfectly happy, and if He were almighty He would be able to do what he wished. But the creatures are not happy. Therefore, God lacks either goodness, or power, or both… There is not much chance I will stop believing in God. What I fear is coming to believe such terrible things about him. So this is what God really is like; deceive yourself no longer… Tortures occur… if there is a loving God then tortures must be necessary." The ancients thought God was all powerful, i.e., omniscient and therefore caused all forms of suffering. "The Lord kills and makes alive; The Lord makes poor and makes rich; He brings some low and lifts some up" (1 Samuel 2:6–7). "I make peace and create evil/calamity. I the Lord do all these things" (Isaiah 45:7). The Quran says the same thing to Muslims: "No calamity comes, no affliction occurs, except by the decision and preordainment of Allah" (S:64.11). Job declared, "The Lord gives and the Lord takes away" (Job 1:21). This dark view of God is very difficult for surviving mourners to accept when your life has been shattered, like Humpty Dumpty.

Grief is considered to be a natural part of being human, which kindles a new compassion that did not exist before for others mourning a loss. And it must be necessary or it would be different. All in God's will of course—generator, operator, destroyer. Ergo Theofatalism.

Oh, Wow

Science says what separates humans from animals is the size of our brains. No one can count all the neuron cells it contains, and exploring its operations is like looking at the moon with a telescope. fMRI scans are showing where the hot spots are during mental processes but the inner workings of the human brain are unknowable. When you add the concept of nonmaterial mind, the whole thing gets even more complex. Consciousness also is unexplainable, although we seem to know when it is not working. When the brain goes awry, strange behaviors often result. The function of the brain in controlling human behaviors is confusing. When an organ is transplanted, all the nerve connections are cut, so how can the brain control the functions of the transplanted organ? Since modern medicine can keep a defective heart and lungs pumping blood and processing air, the brain is left to determine life or death. But death is a mystery because organs can be transplanted several hours after removal, and some rare humans have been rejuvenated after being unconscious for lengthy periods. Thus, life and death are enigmas with no easy explanations. The one thing certain is that medical doctors will try to keep one going so long as someone will pay for the treatments that are possible, because they swore to "do no harm." But keeping someone alive in agony and humiliation may be doing more harm than good. Even though most doctors would choose to not be on life support, ventilators, feeding tubes, etc., they still are uneasy discussing palliative and hospice care alternatives to patients, for professional, personal, and cultural reasons.

Hospice with palliative care is a fundable alternative under Medicare, but often it is hopelessly confused with euthanasia and so to be rejected in favor of interminable suffering before the merciful release of death. Since contemplating our own death is like staring at the sun, final arrangements often are decided in a state of panic and acute distress. Churches leave the subject mostly untouched, so everyone is left to their own end-of-life planning. One option is to create a living will or medical directive that tells your medical providers what you want them to do and not do when the end is near—but many people leave that undone causing more trauma for survivors. And if you go to an emergency room, there is no guarantee they will honor your wishes for fear of a lawsuit. According to his sister, the last words of the late Steve Jobs, co-founder of Apple Inc. were "Oh wow, wow, wow." No one can know what he might have been experiencing as his brain shut down. It is common for patients who survived approaching death to describe a similar experience of euphoria and peace with images of loved ones gone before. Brain death can actually take several hours after there is no possible return, but what happens then is the ultimate mystery. The late physician-aided suicide advocate Dr. Jack Kevorkian said, "After all, how painful can oblivion be?" Jesus said, "The spirit gives life, the flesh counts for nothing" (John 6:63). So perhaps brain death is nothing to fear. But we have not yet come to terms with death individually or culturally. Living the mystery is part of being human. And here is the thing: if it could be different it would be. Ergo Theofatalism.

Mutually Exclusive Dichotomies

The world of humanity seems to be approaching an existential crisis. On the one side are conservative Christians who seem to dominate the dogma of the religious right, claiming the Bible as their authority to regulate life as they interpret the scriptures, which leaves little room for revisionist progressives to agree with. On the other side are the radical conservative Sunni Muslims who are dominating the silent Shiite majority in Islam with their dogma of conversion by conquest no matter how brutal or inhumane it must be. These seem to be mutually exclusive dichotomies with no room for compromise or negotiation, hence ubiquitous wars and terrorism are on the horizon. Anthropologist Margaret Mead said, "Never doubt that a few dedicated people can change the world. Indeed, that is the only thing that has." And yet, Jesus declared, "Blessed are the peacemakers for they shall be called sons of God" (Matthew 5:9). However, he also declared the world will always see wars and preparations for wars (Mark 13:7). God created it and only God can fix it. The challenge facing humanity is how to reconcile divergent religious dogma with some common conscience that will enable a form of morality and ethics we can all live with. It seems like that will have to be an act of God. Ergo Theofatalism. Get it?

A Drop of Water in the Ocean

The universe is a very big place with lots of stuff going on. Stars are being formed by gravity from gas and dust while others are dying out as their hydrogen fuel is consumed in the process of fusion. Billions of billions of stars are grouped into billions of billions of galaxies as far as science can see. In the center of them all appears to be a "black hole" sucking up all the matter around it—so dense that even light cannot escape. The space of the universe is measured by how far light can travel in a year at the speed of 186,000 miles per second. One light-year is about 5,865,696,000,000 miles. It was assumed that light travels in a straight line until Albert Einstein set up an experiment that proved that light actually is bent by the gravity field around stars, like the sun. So what is seen in one place among the stars may actually be someplace else or not even existing anymore, since the light we see could have been extinguished long, long, ago. The age of the universe is uncertain but is estimated at nearly 14 billion earth years, but nobody knows because its origin is clouded in vague theories of matter being created from nothing, which taxes human imagination. Time, itself, is an arbitrary division of the rotation of the earth and its orbit about the sun. The standard basis for time is based on vibrations of the cesium atom located at the US Naval Observatory in Washington, DC. If motion did not exist, time would not either. Moreover, the universe seems to be expanding at an increasing rate of speed, which cannot be explained by existing rules of physics, and nobody knows where it is going. Scientists now estimate they can explain less than 5 percent of matter in the universe as computed from gravity, and the rest may be dark matter and dark energy, which so far are undetectable. Could this unseen universe be the realm of spirit where the physical body of matter has no further purpose?

There may even be an unknown number of such universes, limited only by the extension of mathematical models. If so, they also must be controlled by God, the prime force of all. So what makes *Homo sapiens* on this lonely planet in this lonely solar system think they are anything special? From stellar dust, we are and to stellar dust we shall return (Genesis 3:19). Why we are here and where we are going nobody knows. Each sentient being on earth seems to be both insignificant and indispensable, like a drop of water in the ocean. We may be the pinnacle of creation, and maybe not. Jesus said the spirit gives life, the flesh counts for nothing (John 6:63). F. Scott Fitzgerald stated in *The Crack Up* (1936) that a mark of maturity is holding the opposites—as in creation and destruction—and still functioning normally. The more we learn the more questions are raised. As the great King Solomon concluded, with much wisdom comes much sorrow, and with more knowledge comes more grief. What you don't know cannot hurt you, and ignorance is bliss. If you can, just enjoy life and die with a smile on your face because nothing happens outside the will of God—generator, operator, destroyer, the prime force in the universe and controller of everything from atoms to galaxies. Ergo Theofatalism. Can you handle that?

One Prime Source of All

There are more forms of life on planet earth than anyone knows, and new ones are being discovered all the time. Science claims that life came from some biological and chemical processes that converted elements from inanimate into animate over billions of years in some unknown process of evolution, but the Bible claims all life forms were created at one time by the supreme creator by merely commanding it to happen. "In the beginning God created the heavens and the earth" (Genesis 1:1). Take your pick. Species have come and gone, with possibly the remaining ones now on the planet being merely the remnants of many more now long extinct. Most curious are the blind deep-sea creatures living in total darkness at pressures that no manmade device can withstand. Somebody estimated the weight of all the cock roaches is ten times that of human beings. And bacteria may be one of the earliest forms of life that both supports and threatens human beings. *Homo sapiens* are the most recent arrivals, dating back only fifty thousand years from a valley in Africa in their present forms. Hunter-gatherer tribes gave way to farming about seven thousand years ago. Metallurgy and ceramics date back to 4,000 BC. Archeology has discovered ancient construction projects—like the great pyramids of Egypt and Stonehenge in England—so complex that only some unknown knowledge was used to construct them—some claiming they could have been advanced beings from outer space.

Humans occupy the planet in wide-ranging climates and geologies with extremely different forms of culture, language, and government and religion. There are so many variations one could not explore all of them in a lifetime, even if you had the time and the money. Some of them pose infinite mysteries—like how the original natives arrived on the islands of Hawaii in the middle of the Pacific Ocean?? Or how did the Sahara Desert come to occupy the northern third of the African continent? Or how did people learn to harvest the minerals of the earth for all their uses? Or how did one discovery linked to another lead up to space travel and smart phones? Shakespeare said life's a stage and people merely are players. But who is the playwright? Each individual of all the species must be indispensable, even though insignificant, like a drop of water in the ocean. So why would anyone think their particular spot and time on earth is somehow the world's best to be defended and extended to all the others, by wars if necessary? Could there be many gods or only one? If there is only one prime source of all then it must control this universal zoo of life forms for some purpose and destiny that only it can understand. In Theofatalism, it is called GOD, the generator, operator, and destroyer of everything from atoms to galaxies. And if you don't get it, you don't get it. All in God's will of course.

The Four Quadrants of Life

Four is some kind of special number—four seasons, four points on the compass, four gospels, four horses of the apocalypse, four quadrants on the labyrinth used for the symbol of this work. Four also can help describe the life-long development of *Homo sapiens*. From beginning at birth, life progresses with (1) physical and sensing skills for basic survival, to (2) intellectual learning for lifetime careers, to (3) making healthy relationships for healthy families, to (4) reaching for spiritual enlightenment at the end of life. The pathway seems quite standard, once you are aware of it. We leave the source and grow through four stages of infant, child, youth, and adult until midlife. Then at the meridian we return to the source through four stages of maturity, seniority, retirement, and contemplation. The symbol for the walk of life could be the ancient labyrinth—the symbol for Theofatalism—that passes from birth through four quadrants into the world and then returns to the source after the meridian is passed. Some churches and spiritual traditions use the four-quadrant Chartres Labyrinth to symbolize the walk of life each of us is given. Also, Swiss psychiatrist, C. G. Jung developed a theory of human personality that included four functions: perception in the forms of sensing and intuition, and judging in the forms of thinking and feeling. These four functions can be either introverted or extraverted—creating sixteen different personality types. Each person has a definite preference for a combination of these four functions that is uniquely their own. This model was developed into the Myers-Briggs Type Indicator (MBTI), which is used extensively in family and career counseling, conflict resolution, stress management, and leadership training. If you need help in those areas, maybe it is time for you to try it too. It could help to prevent many divorces and even wars to know who you really are. Google "MBTI" for all the details. All in God's will, of course.

Four Particular Memes

Contagious ideas, called memes, seem to have a life of their own. How they are born, grow, and propagate throughout a culture is one of the mysteries of the universe. In the USA, four particular memes are changing the society and for good or ill nobody knows for sure, because the freedom of speech opens the possibility of burdens exceeding the benefits. One is the change from single mothers being a social disgrace to some badge of honor in just one generation. The urge to reproduce is stimulated with government monetary rewards as in aid to dependent children. Now, nearly half of all children are being raised in single parent families usually without any father role models, except for the rapper types, actors, and professional athletes who display a total lack of parenting skills. In some inner cities, fully 70 percent of black children are born to single mothers. So long as government pays for child support, guess what? There is a vast difference between mating and parenting, but many seem to have lost that distinction. People do not need to demonstrate any minimum level of intelligence to reproduce. While genetics has a role in human physical development, their family and social environment influences their behavior, so we can expect more of the same. One may argue about the causes, but only time will tell what kind of society will be created by all these fatherless children. The growth of street gangs may be a model of things to come.

Another meme is the rapid trend toward legalizing same-sex marriages with all that means for changing families. It only took a few decades for the LGBT community to go from social outcasts to being respected and accepted members of society, at least officially. Our grandparents never would have thought that to be possible. There must be some power greater than social rejection to make such things happen. In addition, there is the incipient meme of legalizing marijuana as with alcohol and tobacco, while deaths from drug overdoses soar. States that have legalized sales of weed take in revenue from taxes that derive from the profits of growers and sellers. The jury is still out on whether the buyers benefit from weed or not. They seem to think that that they do. Evidence indicates that some medical benefits may justify its use, so it appears that the benefits outweigh any burdens attached with legal marijuana.

The fourth meme is driven by the need for human beings to worship some power greater than themselves. The solution has been the creation of various religions throughout history. Now, it seems that certain celebrities in sports and entertainment are replacing religious figures as the Internet makes it possible to follow the lives of rich and famous people, even to the point of virtually stalking them on social media. A new mental disorder called celebrity worship syndrome is being used to describe people who revere them as some kinds of faux deities, or at least some larger than real life human beings, which they seem to be. Advertisers have used this syndrome to employ celebrities to help sell products and services of all types with television, social and print media. Why some people are selected for this quasi-religious role must be God's will or it would be different. The best current example could be the mindless worship of

Kim Jong-un, the "great leader" of North Korea, by his 22 million subjects.

With the unregulated and ubiquitous Internet and smartphones, revolutionary ideas can propagate globally at the speed of light, good or bad, so round and round it goes and where it stops is anybody's guess. What incubates a meme and how they become contagious ideas, only God knows for sure… unless of course you do not believe in God. Which is another meme, come to think of it. God makes agnostics and atheists too. Ergo Theofatalism.

An Amazing Creation

Did you ever wonder how you got to be the human being that you are? How does a sperm and an egg develop into a *you* inside the womb during nine months of gestation? How come that specific egg and sperm united at that instant of time and space? Was that a random event or the inevitable outcome of all previous events? The same can be asked of all living species on earth. If fertilized, alligator eggs hatch into alligators, and snakes into snakes, birds into birds, etc. Plant seeds remain dormant until they are given the right combination of soil, water, and sunlight to burst into life again. Consider the human body. It is an amazing creation. At the instant a female egg is pierced by a male sperm your physical destiny apparently is set. Science claims it must all come from a protein combination in each cell called DNA, which makes everyone unique among each species on earth. And how come all their respective organs go about their work sans any conscious efforts by the sentient being? And how to explain feelings, the experience of which is real but not material? Science has not and possibly cannot explain the mind-brain problem or the brain-body problem. Organs can be transplanted from one body to another, and even though the nerves are cut they seem to transfer functions normally from the host body to the recipient. British biologist Rupert Sheldrake concluded there must be some, as yet undetected, form of information transfer which transcends the physical cells in living things like the waves of information broadcast in radio and television through the medium of electromagnetism. He calls it morphic energy fields. If the brain is an electro-chemical transmitter, it could be possible. Perhaps this explains the instant attraction and repulsion some people feel upon first meeting. Science has not yet accepted this theory, and atheists claim it all must be just random developments in the universe through evolution by natural selection. But Albert Einstein said he did not believe that God plays dice. Randomness or God's will? Are these necessary opposites or what?

If you were raised in India you probably are Hindu, if you were raised in Italy or South America you probably are Catholic, if you were raised in Utah you probably are Mormon. If you were raised in North Korea you definitely worship the Dear Leader. Are these just random events, or is something more deterministic behind them? "You saw me before I was born and scheduled each day of my life before I began to breathe. Every day was recorded in your book!" (Psalm 139:16). "It is God who directs the lives of his creatures; everyone's life is in his power" (Job 12:10). Perhaps that includes Democrats and Republicans, in addition to atheists.

Although science still cannot explain how it happens, your body will develop in the womb just as intended, abnormalities and all. The human body is thought to be composed of some ten billion individual cells. But it is host to possibly ten times that many in various forms of parasites, bacteria, and viral life forms. They go about co-existing so long as the immune system keeps it all in balance. The human body functions through several interactive systems. There is the endocrine system, the skeletal system consisting of 206 bones, the digestive system, the reproductive system, and so on. They all are fueled by the circulatory system that transports nutrients through blood and the pulmonary system that filters oxygen from the air we breathe. Nothing is more amazing than the sensing system, the way we take in information and make uses of it, converting electrochemical blips in the neuron cells of the brain into conscious awareness of colors, sounds, objects, ideas, concepts, etc.

All this complex flesh seems to know how to carry out its many functions that provide life for its host—the human spirit. Jesus said, "The spirit gives life, the flesh counts for nothing" (John 6:63). It all works perfectly until it malfunctions and stops working. Each human body has a beginning and ending, but perhaps the spirit is like a mobius with a continuous existence in a spiritual universe not yet discovered. "But who are you, a human being, to talk back to God? Shall what is formed say to the one who formed it, 'Why did you make me like this?' Does not the potter have the right to make out of the same lump of clay some pottery for special purposes and some for common use?" (Jeremiah 18:2–6, Romans 9:16–21). If people do not control who they are then they are not responsible for what they do. So what appear to be subconsciousness decisions may be driven by some force yet to be discovered, like the top of an iceberg that must go wherever the bottom takes it. Perhaps some things really are unknowable… yet. Just saying. All in God's will of course. Ergo Theofatalism.

The Divine Rule of Kings

American founder Ben Franklin (1706–1790) concluded, "The longer I live the more proof I see of this truth—that God rules in the affairs of men." And when asked what kind of government they gave us he replied, "A republic, if you can keep it." Perhaps that government is being tested now, as never before. In *Citizens United v.*

Federal Election Commission, the US Supreme Court ruled (5–4) on January 21, 2010, that laws preventing corporations and unions from using their general treasury funds for supporting electioneering communications violate the First Amendment's guarantee of freedom of speech. Since the ruling, the US government is being bought by the very wealthy, including the Koch Brothers, who pour millions of dollars into political campaigns of ultra-conservative candidates to preserve their corporate kingdoms. So those who call it a democracy—rule by the majority—are mistaken. The founders did not want rule by the majority, which they saw as potential tyranny. Getting elected and sustaining public office in America has become insanely expensive. It costs billions of dollars and nearly two years to elect a president. Political elections are very big business in America. Once elected, politicians must reward their main contributors. The late comedian Will Rogers (1879–1935) said, "Whenever Congress makes a joke it is a law and whenever they make a law it is a joke." Two things you should avoid watching being made are sausage and laws. Congress is graded on how many laws they pass in each session, which seems to be odd for a country that prizes personal freedom and liberty. The founders never intended for political office to be a lifetime career. If it is the greatest form of government, how come no other nation has adopted it? Neither did we set up this form of government in Japan or Germany after WWII.

The survival of a republic depends on an informed electorate but in spite of news overload, more and more people are less and less informed. Reported surveys indicate that one out of four natural born Americans could not pass the test required of immigrants to become citizens. The late social commentator George Carlin (1937–2008) said the average American is pretty dumb, and half of the rest are even dumber. Put them together and you get a situation that bodes ill for the future. British Prime Minister Winston Churchill once said, "You can count on Americans to do the right thing, but only after they try everything else first." So if you think elected officials are running the government by will of the voters, think again. It all must be God's will or it would be different. Apostle Paul claimed that all authorities are appointed by God and should be obeyed. "Let everyone be subject to the governing authorities for there is no authority except that which God has established" (Romans 13:1–7). From this opinion, we got the divine rule of kings and dictators. Think Adolf Hitler and Nazism. But when he was accosted and threatened by the Jewish leaders for teaching about Jesus, Apostle Peter replied, "We must obey God rather than human beings" (Acts 5:29). So it seems that obedience to God must trump the rule of man… or does it? If God is the supreme source of all, then opposing dialectical views such as these must be necessary or they would be different. So we are left with Theofatalism—nothing happens from atoms to galaxies outside the will of God, the generator, operator, and destroyer. Get it?

If the Lord Wills

Some people seem to think they can bend the will of God to fulfill their own desire. Prosperity preachers claim you can have all you pray for, if you claim God's favor and have the faith of a mustard seed, like Jesus said (Matthew 17:20). And if two of you agree on a request in prayer it will be more powerful with God (Matthew 18:19). But Jesus said God knows your needs and will provide just as he does for the birds and the wild flowers in the fields, so there is no sense in worrying about tomorrow—apparent opposites. And he said there would be false prophets, false teachers, and false prophecies to deceive even the elect—perhaps they wrote some of the Bible (Matthew 24:23–25, 2 Peter 2:1–22). Apostle Peter claimed if your prayers are not answered it is because you ask with the wrong selfish motives. And he said your plans should always be prefaced with submission to God's will. Apostle James proclaimed, "Go to now, you that say, today or tomorrow we will go into such a city, and continue there a year, and buy and sell, and make money: Whereas you know not what shall be on the morrow. For what is your life? It is even a vapor, which appears for a little time, and then vanishes away. Therefore, you ought to say, if the Lord wills, we shall live and do this or that" (James 4:13–15). Perhaps that is why Muslims preface their plans with "Lord willing."

In contrast, Jesus told his disciples that if you believe it, anything you pray for is yours—including throwing mountains into the sea (Matthew 17:20–23). But sometimes it appears that God is absent when we suffer innocently and wish that things were different. Jesus was crucified as atonement for sinners by the will of God, and he felt abandoned on the cross by his Father, "My God, why have your forsaken me" (Matthew 27:46). If God is omnipotent and omniscient, then he is everywhere in everything as immaculate immanence, i.e., panentheism. So what are you gonna believe? Answer: whatever you are given. When Peter declared he thought that Jesus was Messiah, it was an act of God in heaven and not of man (Matthew 16–17). As Jesus said, "Not my will by thine" (Luke 22:42). Ergo Theofatalism. If you don't get it, you don't get it.

The Wages of Sin

Sin is an interesting subject. There are various interpretations, depending upon one's religious orientation, or lack thereof. The Bible claims sin originated soon after creation as the first humans disobeyed God by eating the prohibited fruit of knowledge of good and evil, for which all mankind inherited the penalty of death. They were expelled from the Garden called Eden so they would not eat the tree of life and live forever (Genesis 3:22–24, Romans 5:12). When once asked, "What is the definition of sin?" the celebrated Christian evangelist, Billy Graham gave the following answer:

A sin is any thought or action that falls short of God's will. God is perfect, and anything we do that falls short of His perfection is sin. The Bible actually uses a number of examples or word pictures to illustrate what this means. For example, it tells us that sin is like an archer who misses the target. He draws back his bow and sends the arrow on its way—but instead of hitting the bull's-eye, it veers off course and misses the mark. The arrow may only miss it a little bit or it may miss it a great deal—but the result is the same: The arrow doesn't land where it is supposed to. The same is true of sin. God's will is like the center of that target—and when we sin, we fall short of His will or miss the mark. And this is something we do every day; as the Bible says, "For all have sinned and fall short of the glory of God" (Romans 3:23). Even when we aren't aware of it, we commit sin by the things we do (or fail to do), or by the way we think." That seems to be a very tall order which no normal person can live up to. Hence, everyone is a sinner to some extent by this definition.

Perhaps, you were taught that disobedience of the "Ten Commandments" given by Moses is sinning. Or possibly that disobeying any of his 613 rules for living imposed on the nation of Israel is sin. Punishment for disobedience was very harsh. A woman guilty of adultery or a homosexual was stoned to death. A disrespectful and disobedient teenager might also lose his life. A slave who disobeyed his master may get many lashes. A thief might have his offending had cut off (Exodus 22, Leviticus 20). Indeed, Jesus spoke of such punishment: "If your hand or your foot causes you to stumble, cut it off and throw it away. It is better for you to enter life maimed or crippled than to have two hands or two feet and be thrown into eternal fire. And if your eye causes you to stumble, gouge it out and throw it away. It is better for you to enter life with one eye than to have two eyes and be thrown into the fire of hell" (Matthew 18:8–9). When Jesus spoke of his second coming and judgment, he warned that among those deserving punishment some would "be beaten with many blows" and others "with few blows" (Luke 12:47–48). He also reserved his most fierce denunciations for the pride and unbelief of the religious leaders, calling them hypocrites and vipers (Matthew 12:34, 23:13–36). This enraged them and set him up for the crucifixion.

But consider that if sin is breaking the law of God, without the law there could be no sin—as it was before the laws of Moses. "Sin is not charged to anyone's account where there is no law" (Romans 5:13). No one can break a law that does not exist. The humanist or atheist may have a different view of sin. They may see sin as the opposite of morality and assume that any normal, logical person would know the difference. The famous author Ernest Hemingway (1899–1961) said, "What is moral is what you feel good after doing." Of course, the opposite of that is what you feel bad about after doing is immoral. However, that gets into a discussion of conscience, and whether there is an inherent aspect of humans that can tell the difference between good and evil or not. It does appear that some people are more disposed to doing good, and others are disposed to doing evil. In the extreme, the sociopath and the psychopath seem to have no conscience, while some sacrifice their lives for others. Jesus declared, "Greater love has no man than this: to lay down his life for his friends" (John 15:13). If the wages of sin is death, or life in prison, or even execution, why would anyone in their right minds do something to get there?

Perhaps, Apostle Paul faced just such a dilemma in his own life as he lamented, "I do not understand what I do. For what I want to do I do not do, but what I hate I do. And if I do what I do not want to do, I agree that the law is good. As it is, it is no longer I myself who do it, but it is sin living in me. For I know that good itself does not dwell in me, that is, in my sinful nature. For I have the desire to do what is good, but I cannot carry it out. For I do not do the good

I want to do, but the evil I do not want to do, this I keep on doing. Now if I do what I do not want to do, it is no longer I who do it, but it is sin living in me that does it. So I find this law at work: Although I want to do good, evil is right there with me. For in my inner being I delight in God's law; but I see another law at work in me, waging war against the law of my mind and making me a prisoner of the law of sin at work within me. What a wretched man I am!" (Romans 7:7–21).

Since we all are born sinners to some extent, the only solution offered by the Rev. Graham was to place our faith in the forgiveness of God obtained through acceptance of Jesus Christ as Lord and Savior (Romans 10:9). But what if sinning or not sinning is beyond the power of individuals to choose? There could be another side to this story. St. Clement of Rome said, "God rules with two hands, Christ in one and Satan in the other." C. G. Jung said the tragedy of Job was not because of his sin as his friends thought, but rather that "God required of Job to look at His dark side. One must be able to suffer God." The Bible says that God causes all of it. "I make peace and create evil/calamity. I, the Lord, do all these things" (Isaiah 45:7). Viewed from this perspective, it appears that sin must be necessary for God to have something to forgive. Not the manmade god of holy books, but the prime force in the universe—generator, operator, destroyer… GOD. Ergo Theofatalism. Now, go outside and play.

The First Trinity

Nothing is more uncertain than what causes life and what happens after death. C. G. Jung said that life is a short pause between these two great mysteries. There are many ideas and dogmas, but nobody really knows the answers for sure. This is just one of the many indefinite uncertainties that we must live with as human beings—which creates much angst if you think about it. Philosopher and theologian, the late Paul Tillich said the cause of such anxiety is the awareness of fate and death, self-criticism and guilt, and a feeling of emptiness and lack of purpose. His antidote was belief in the "God above Gods" as the source of all being. Religions merely add more confusion because there are so many that collectively they make no sense. There are many contradictions and confusions in the Bible, even though Apostle Paul claimed that, "God is not the author of confusion" (1 Corinthians 14:33). So it may follow that God did not write the Bible, or he needed a better editor. Atheists go to the extreme and conclude there is no God and we must do the best we can without him. But what if there is a prime force in the universe that controls everything from atoms to galaxies… holy books included. The ancient Hindus worshipped three gods called the Trimurti, those responsible for creation, maintenance, and destruction as possibly the first trinity—Shiva, Vishnu, and Brahma. In modern terms, this could be the unified force of generation, operation, and destruction that controls everything from atoms to galaxies… GOD. This is like gravity, there from the beginning waiting to be discovered. Now may be its time. Ergo Theofatalism.

Cherry Picking and Proof Texting

There are many teachings of Jesus in the gospels that would drive people out of church if they were taught in Sunday school and preached from the pulpits. And yet he said, "If you love me keep my commandments" (John 14:15). Read Luke 6 to learn what he taught. The truth is that church leaders have cherry picked and proof texted what they want people to get to preserve their careers and treasuries. If they preached the full gospel, the churches would be empty. Thus, all Christians are hypocrites, more or less. How this could be must be the will of God or it would be different. Ergo Theofatalism. If you don't get it, you don't get it.

Necessary Complementary Opposites

Arguments about predestination and human free will have occupied philosophers for centuries. You can find both in scriptures. The Jews were made to reject Jesus as Messiah because "this is what they were destined for" (1 Peter 2:7–8). Even Jesus could not change the willful destiny of the Jews. "Oh Jerusalem, how often I have wanted to gather your children together as a hen gathers her chicks beneath her wings, but you wouldn't let me" (Matthew 23:27). But Jesus taught his disciples in mysterious parables just so the Jews would not understand, repent, and be redeemed (Matthew 13:10–11, Mark 4:10–12). Apostle Paul instructed them to obey their rulers as appointed by God (Romans 13:1–7). Nevertheless, they revolted against Roman occupation and were vanquished in 135 AD and banned from residence in Jerusalem until Israel was again recognized in 1948 by the United Nations. Compare John 3:16 with John 6:65. One implies free will while the other text removes it. God gave his only son so that whoever believes in him will be saved, but no one can come to him unless they are called/enabled/granted by the Father. Go figure. It seems that God created belief in free will to offset his creation of the opposite belief in predestination. We have no free will, so we must believe in free will.

The ancient Chinese used the symbol of yin and yang to illustrate the universe is composed of necessary complementary opposites… like sweet and sour, hot and cold, good and bad, legal and illegal, in and out, up and down, war and peace, saints and sinners, suffering and compassion, Christ and Antichrist, etc. St. Clement said God rules the world with two hands, Satan in one and Christ in the other. Necessary opposites. F. Scott Fitzgerald concluded that a mark of maturity is the ability to hold the opposites in mind and still function normally. This is one of the five principles in Theofatalism. Read the book by this writer, *Voices of Sedona*, for all the details. Spiritual maturity requires holding both/and rather than either/or because that is the truth. The bottom line is that no matter which you believe, it must all be God's will or it would be different. God makes atheists and agnostics too. Not the one in holy books, but the prime mover in the universe—generator, operator, destroyer. Ergo Theofatalism.

The Dark Side of the Moon

The labyrinth walk of life includes traversing some ups and downs, joys and sorrows, success and failure, pain and pleasure, war and peace, etc. God never made any one-sided coins. In fact, the Bible claims that God created the tree of knowledge of good and evil which started it all (Genesis 2:9, 2:17). Just as the earth goes through phases of light and dark, so does the lives of its creatures. While this observation seems to be self-evident, there is an aspect of human life that poses a difficult question. We know nature requires that each species must consume food to live and that the carnivores must consume the flesh of other species to exist, but how to explain the willful acts of harm that one human often visits upon another. We call it a crime when some action occurs outside of the lawful boundaries of social behavior, from a traffic violation to robbery, assault, rape, and even murder. We try to reduce such actions by courts of law that impose penalties intended to deter such antisocial behaviors. However, the same actions that incur penalties in one situation may obtain praise in another. Thus, harming your neighbor without provocation is bad but harming your enemy in time of war is laudable.

In the extreme, killing another human being or several may get you either executed or decorated with the Congressional Medal of Honor, depending upon the situation. Whether your neighbor is friend or foe depends upon the citation of government. And governments are institutions of God which deserve obedience (Romans 13:1–7). It is clearly possible to convert normal citizens into killing machines through a period of training for battle as with the current recruitment by radical Islam of loyal subjects to commit horrific acts of terrorism, even including their own suicide. If they survive combat, it is often difficult for battle veterans to return to normal social life without serious adjustment problems, called post trauma shock disorder. But sociopaths actually seem to enjoy a role of outlaw behavior, which has been evident since recorded history. How to explain the difference between lawful mayhem and the unlawful kind, that is the question. The Bible commands "thou shalt not kill/murder," which seems to imply some freedom of choice, but what if that is an illusion and humans under some conditions lose control and just must harm each other regardless of the consequences?

Theodicies were developed by writers to reconcile the existence of a perfectly sinless, benevolent god with the existence of evil and suffering—which is impossible to imagine. Nothing happens outside the will of God. For example, printing this book requires paper, which destroys trees, which depletes the earth, which requires the sun, which requires the universe, which was created by God. The purpose of guns is to kill something alive. They fire bullets propelled by black powder composed of sulfur, charcoal, and saltpeter—all products of earth. They are made of metal, which is a product of the earth which was created by God. Generating electricity burns coal to make steam, which creates deadly waste products that are the elements of earth, which was created by God. Consider that the global marketplace for products made overseas that have destroyed American jobs would not be possible without ocean transportation based on those amazing container ships. The largest ones weigh 224,000 tons and carry 12,000 containers. They began with a McLean trucking company executive who wanted to streamline the transfer of goods from one tractor trailer to another using portable reusable containers, which requires the production of steel, which is an alloy of iron and other metals, which are natural elements of the earth, which was created by God. And consider what the Wright brothers, who were bicycle mechanics, unleashed with their demonstration of heavier than air flight that has led to space travel in just one century which would not be possible without the laws of gravity and aerodynamics, which mankind did not create, but God did. Mankind had imagined flying for centuries before they made it happen. People suffer and die from many causes not of their own making. In order to survive and reproduce, all life forms on earth must kill something, be it plant or animal. One may conclude that suffering in the world is evidence for the dark, but necessary, side of God.

Swiss psychiatrist C. G. Jung pondered this dilemma during his active duty service in prisoner of war camps during WWI and observed "the secret order" in all chaos. He concluded there was an opposite force at work in people from the "Golden Rule." It negates the commandment to "love your neighbor as yourself" and empowers them to project fear and loathing upon their neighbors, often for no reason at all. Adolf Hitler learned from his service in WWI the winning army in a battle was not necessarily the troops who were the best armed or trained, but the most disciplined. He used this tactic to mobilize the entire nation of Germany in WWII, causing the deaths of more than 50 million people throughout Europe. The worst example was the Holocaust attempt at extermination of the Jews. Jung would say that he recognized and used the "shadow" of human personality both individually and collectively to project his own desire for revenge onto the Nazi party and by extension onto the battle field. When they were defeated, he condemned them for their unwilling ability and desire to execute his orders, and they got what they deserved.

Jung concluded that everyone has a dark side to human nature that under certain conditions will take over and turn an otherwise law-abiding citizen into a psychopath unconsciously. Such a person is "standing in his own light," as with the dark side of the moon which we cannot see, but is there nevertheless. Even Apostle Paul lamented that he neglected things he should do and did what he should not, driven by the law of sin within him. "What a wretched man I am" (Romans 7:22–25). Jung wrote, "A certain amount of suffering and unhappiness is our lot, and no one can escape all the dark phases of life. It is understandable that people should get panicky, or that they eventually become demoralized under a chronic strain, or despair of their hopes and expectations. It is also understandable that their will-power weakens and their self-control becomes slack and begins to lose its grip upon circumstances, moods and thoughts. It is quite consistent with such a state of mind if some particularly unruly parts of the patient's psyche then acquire a certain degree of autonomy." In other words, desperate people can do desperate things.

Thus, Jung seemed to assume a perpetrator of violence and crime is being controlled by the evil part of human nature created by God. Indeed, if God created man in his own "image and likeness," to see man is to see God (Genesis 1:26–28). It has been shown in controlled experiments that normal people are capable of breaching the norms among and within social groups. One college experiment, in which some students portrayed prison guards and some others portrayed prisoners, had to be stopped because the "guards" became too brutal. Human violence seems to be the inevitable consequence of nature as it is. If one believes in a higher power, it may be as St. Clement of Rome said, "God rules with two hands, Christ in one and Satan in the other." Only by recognizing this evil side of human nature and bringing it into consciousness can it be bridled and controlled by reason instead of emotion. This process seems to be impossible for some people, so incarceration and even execution have not erased violence from human nature. Jesus said there would always be wars and rumors/preparation for wars until the end (Mattthew 24:6). It is an act of God, and only God can change it. Not the manmade god in holy books, but the prime mover in the universe, generator, operator, destroyer—GOD. Ergo Theofatalism.

Muslims Win and Christians Lose

The world seems to be facing a new war between Muslims and Christians. If you read the Holy Quran and the Holy Bible, you will see that peaceful Muslims and warlike Christians both are hypocrites to their faith. Muslims are commanded to fight and kill for Allah until everyone submits and declares there is no God but Allah and Muhammad is his messenger. The Holy Quran proclaims: [4.74] "Therefore let those fight in the way of Allah, who sell this world's life for the hereafter; and whoever fights in the way of Allah, then be he slain or be he victorious, We shall grant him a mighty reward." On the other hand (there always is another hand), Christians are commanded to love their enemies and turn the other cheek, give their cloaks as well as their coats to a robber, and forgive those who do not repay a loan or harm them (Luke 6:27–31). "Do not take revenge, my dear friends, but leave room for God's wrath, for it is written: 'It is mine to avenge; I will repay,' says the Lord" (Romans: 12:19). "Give thanks in all things for this is the will of God for you" (1 Thessalonians 5:18). So it follows that if Muslims are faithful and Christians are faithful, Muslims win and Christians lose. If there is only one God and source of all, then it must be driving both sides in this war as it has in all the others. Ergo Theofatalism.

The World That God Has Made

Have you ever watched a hungry python squeeze an alligator to death and then consume it head first? It can take several hours. Or how about watching a pride of lions taking down a rhinoceros for dinner? One of the most efficient predators is the night owl. Its favorite meal is the small ground shrew and its newly born litter. Watching a cheetah chase down its prey, grab it by the neck, and choke it to death is not much fun. It would not be much fun to visit a slaughterhouse where they process pork, beef, and chickens either. Nature has decreed that male animals must compete for procreation, and species must fight for territory and hunting rights. If human males had to compete for breeding rights, perhaps we would be a better species. So we get murders and rapes and hurricanes and tornadoes and earthquakes, wars, diseases, accidents, computer scams, and financial frauds. This is the world that God has made. "In the beginning, God created the heavens and the earth" (Genesis 1:1). Never mind there are two different accounts of the creation in chapters 1 and 2. Poor editing, or God's will? Apostle Paul instructed to give thanks in all things/circumstances for that is the will of God for you (1 Thessalonians 5:18). If anything should be different it would be. Life is dangerous to your health, and birth sentences you to death. But Jesus said, "The spirit gives life, the flesh counts for nothing" (John 6:63). The late poet, Robert Frost (1874–1963) wrote, "It is hard to get into this world and hard to get out and what lies in between makes no sense." He also wrote, "Lord, please forgive my many little jokes on thee, and I will forgive thy great big one on me." But here is the thing. You can feel good inside no matter what happens outside, if you believe in GOD as generator, operator, destroyer, i.e., the prime force in the universe, or maybe all possible universes. It controls everything from atoms to galaxies. However, that belief may not be your choice to decide because nothing happens outside the will of God. Not even belief in free will or atheism. Ergo Theofatalism. Unless, of course, you know of a better idea.

The Secret

C. G. Jung said, "Because a personal secret may cause suffering, it is best to keep it to one's self." But I cannot resist, so please forgive me. Suffering seems to be included in the lot of mankind, but there is a secret to suffering, if you can accept it. Jung said it was a necessary counter pole to happiness, i.e., the universal law of necessary opposites. If you live long enough, you might learn life comes with pain, people often disappoint us, plans sometimes fail, beginnings come with endings, and life is unfair... among other things... and it all must be God's will or it would be different. That is life. If you are not prepared in advance, the shock of reality can be very depressing. Willis Carrier, inventor of air-conditioning, said the way to happiness is to imagine the worst and prepare to accept it. Indeed, nothing can change unless you first accept it. And that includes accepting the cause of it. Jung said, "Job did not suffer for his sins as his friends thought; it was rather God who required of Job to look at His dark side. One must be able to suffer God." The Bible says that God causes all of it. "The Lord kills and makes alive; The Lord makes poor and makes rich; He brings some low and lifts some up" (1 Samuel 2:6–7). "I make peace and create evil/calamity. I, the Lord, do all these things" (Isaiah 45:7). The Quran says the same thing to Muslims; "No calamity comes, no affliction occurs, except by the decision and preordainment of Allah" (S:64.11). It also says, "Allah, wielder of the kingly power; thou givest that power to whomever thy will and thou taketh the power from whomever thy will, Thou dost exalt whom thy will and thou doth abase whom thy will... Thou over all things are most powerful… and if Allah shall help you then none can defeat you, but if He abandon you who will help you?" (S.3:25, 3:154).

The Buddha discovered the secret to living with trouble is to close the gap between desire for things to be different with the radical acceptance of what is, both the good and the bad. John Stuart Mill (1806–1873) stated, "I have learned to seek happiness by limiting my desires rather than attempting to satisfy them." The Apostle Paul declared, "I have learned to be content in whatever situation I am in. I know how to be humble, and I know how to prosper. In each and every situation, I have learned the secret of being full and of going hungry, of having too much and of having too little" (Philippians 4:11–12). Pity that he never told us what his secret was to such accommodation of dialectical opposites, except to accept the divinity of Jesus. To paraphrase the serenity prayer by the late Rev. Reinhold Niebuhr, "Lord, please grant me serenity and inner peace, grace to accept what I cannot change, the courage and ability to change what I should, and the wisdom to know the difference." F. Scott Fitzgerald concluded in *The Crack Up* (1936), "The mark of maturity is to hold the opposites in life and still function normally."

Thus, contentment must be matched with discontent, joy with sadness, happiness with grief, wealth with poverty, freedom with enslavement, and rage with acceptance, etc. All benefits come with burdens and vice versa. God did not make any one-sided coins. Jung said, "Suffering is not an illness, it is the normal and necessary counter pole to happiness. One must not avoid unhappiness. Every real solution is only reached through intense suffering. One must accept suffering; it is a great teacher. Whoever can suffer within himself the highest united with the lowest is healed, holy, whole." The question we cannot answer is why we must suffer at all. Perhaps, if there were no suffering we could not hope for anything better in heaven, which God wants us to seek. This may be why every human society seems to need some form of religion, even if it is atheism. When you realize that nothing in the universe from atoms to galaxies happens by random accidents, you may feel insignificant… everything has its cause and every cause has its cause, etc. You and every other sentient creature on earth must be indispensable to the whole or you would not exist, regardless of the situation you are in. But Jung said suffering must be overcome, and the only way to overcome it is to endure it. All in God's will of course. Ergo Theofatalism. Think about it.

Kisses Aren't Contracts

We live in an ever-changing culture, and one of the ubiquitous changes is in human intimate relationships. In the movie *Oklahoma* (1955) a song lyric stated, "Love and marriage go together like a horse and carriage," but not now. Quite often, people are hooking up for ad-hoc relations with no intention of life-long commitments. At the onset of puberty, children become conscious of their sexuality, and many of them become capable of reproducing by middle school. Since it takes them several more years to become self-sufficient, the pressure for hooking up precedes their economic ability to support themselves, and that creates tensions in families and society. The birth control pill liberated females from the threat of unwanted pregnancy, which in turn removed the social and religious stigma that previously had restrained young people from otherwise irresponsible sexual behavior. In addition, the stagnation of middle incomes and growth of poverty have pushed couples into cohabitation, which was previously taboo. Thus, possibly half of young adults live in some form of ad-hoc cohabitation well into their maturity, sans marriage. Even those who do get married have been given an easy out with no-fault divorce laws, which has resulted in about half of all children being raised in single-parent households. Besides, who wants to declare loyalty "for better or worse, in sickness and in health, for richer or poorer, forsaking all others, till death do us part?" Moreover, the education system has all but ignored the need for preparing young people for family life to fill the void created by the loss of traditional family values. So here is a summary of what they need to know.

People bring three resources based on their experience into intimate relationships. One is the native personality they were born with, another is the values and cultural life imparted by their family conditions, and third is the social environment, including education, in which they grew up. It is highly unlikely that any two people will be matched up on all three aspects. So without some conscious awareness of where they stand and the ability to communicate their needs and negotiate for what they want, they will discover that kisses aren't contracts. They need to revise the "Golden Rule" and do unto others as others would be done unto, if matchups are to have any chance of lasting. When two people honestly try to meet the needs of psychiatry, magic happens—and if not, it doesn't. Even though there are some useful commercial matchmaking services available on the Internet, things change with time, and meeting those changes successfully requires the ability to adapt and to recommit as needed to adjust. When some disagreements are not negotiable, it is necessary to practice the serenity prayer of the late Rev. Reinhold Niebuhr, "Lord, please grant me serenity and inner peace, grace to accept what I cannot change, the courage and ability to change what I should, and the wisdom to know the difference."

Relationships come in four flavors and all of them can be successful if both partners want them to. One is the independent-independent pairing, which has two people sharing the world from differing perspectives—from housing to careers to religion, finances, and politics. They agree to disagree and in the extreme to accept open marriage. C. G. Jung said the glue that holds such a marriage together is the freedom to be unfaithful. He had five children with his wife, Emma, and two mistresses. Another style is the independent-dependent partnership where one needs the other moreso. This one helps to explain—if not condone—the battered partner style where one needs to be controlled and the other needs to be the controller. A third style is the dependent-dependent partnership where each one relies on the other so much that neither one could be whole without the other. This is called the co-dependent relationship. And then there is enmeshment, where each one fills up all the holes in the other so completely that they feel like soul mates. There is little for them to disagree about so they can last a long time. Any style of relationship can provide either a growth experience or a stifling form of imprisonment. When the burdens exceed the benefits, it may be appropriate to break up, grieve, and go on.

The government requires everyone to study the traffic laws and pass an exam before driving a car. It is beyond tragic that no such preparation is needed to hookup and create children—which has many consequences for society. As former Secretary of State, John Kerry said, "Americans are free to be stupid and crazy." So half of all first marriages end in divorce and even more of second marriages. One may wonder why this is so, and the only reasonable answer is it must be necessary or it would be different. Some force more powerful than our lawmakers must be in control of the evolution of society, as in everything else from atoms to galaxies. That force may be the prime mover in the universe: generator, operator, destroyer—GOD. Ergo Theofatalism.

What's Happening—Que Pasa

Somewhere some people are getting married, some people are getting divorced, some people are dying, some are smoking pot, some are gambling, some are eating, some are sleeping, some are waking, some are sowing, some are reaping, some are buying, some are selling, some are cold, some are hot, some are drinking, some are eating, some are starving, some are obese, some are bulimic, some are blind, some are peaceful, some are resting, some are working, some are robbing, some are raping, some are fighting, some are praying, some are singing, some are waking up, some are on the land, some are on the sea, some are under the sea, some are in the air, some are on the mountains, some are on the plains, some are on the deserts, some are making things, some are destroying things, some are attending funerals, some are alcoholics, some are rich, some are poor, some are smart, some are dumb, some are hateful, some are kind, some are crazy, some are religious, some are atheists, some people are eating, some are defecating, some are urinating, some are building, some are demolishing, some are disabled, some are beautiful, some are ugly, some are changing diapers, some are wetting diapers, some are reading the paper, some are watching TV, some are inventing things, some are writing essays, some are doing schoolwork, some are cooking at McDonald's, some are eating at McDonald's, some are cooking at the White House, some are making laws, some are breaking laws, some are swiping their cell phones, some are walking, some are swimming, some are rock climbing, some are dreaming, some are teaching, some are harvesting, some are butchering, some are mating, some are rich, some are poor, some are tall, some are short, some are running, some are walking, some are sitting, some are driving, some are riding, some are boating, some are camping, some are hiking, some are thinking, some are feeling, some are bathing, some are selling drugs, some are buying drugs, some are shooting drugs, some are shooting people, some are happy, some are sad, some are healthy, some are sick, some are laughing, some are crying, some are making money, some are spending money, some are gambling money, some are loving, some are hating, some are making jigsaw puzzles, some are doing crossword puzzles, some are reading, some are playing games, some are watching games, some are cooking at home, some are driving cars, some are taking cabs, some are riding buses, some are riding tractors, some are riding horses, some are riding camels, some are sleeping on streets, some are truthful, some are lying, some are suffering, some are alone, some are in crowds, some are in hospitals, some are despondent, some are elated, some are content, some are discontent, some are here and now, some are there and then, some are making sense of this and some are not. And it all must be God's will or it would be different. Not the manmade god in holy books but the prime mover in the universe: generator, operator, destroyer… GOD. It does whatever it wants with whomever it wants. Ergo Theofatalism.

A Necessary Illusion

Americans are free to be stupid and crazy. The late comedian George Carlin observed that the average American is pretty dumb and half of the rest are even dumber. Scientist, Albert Einstein said the difference between stupidity and genius is there is a limit to genius. He also said the world is a dangerous place, not because some people are evil but because most people do nothing about it. Of human society, Arthur Schopenhauer (1788–1860) wrote, "No one shows himself as he is, but wears a mask and plays his part. Indeed, the whole arrangement of society may be likened to a perpetual comedy; and this is why a man who is worth anything finds society so insipid, while a blockhead is quite at home in it." When people do crazy, dumb things that make no sense and are not in their own best interest there is only one reasonable explanation… it must be God's will or it would be different. People are driven unconsciously to actions by assuming the benefits will be worth more than the burdens, even if it sends them to prison or to a mental hospital. The conscious mind must go where ever the subconscious takes it… like an iceberg with most of it below the surface. The top must go wherever the bottom takes it. Thus, beliefs in free will and freedom of choice are questionable. Einstein said man can do what he wills, but he cannot will what he wills. Whatever they choose to do, people all can be assured that the perceived benefits are more powerful than the perceived burdens… even if they are not aware of this subconscious process at work. But we have no free will, so we must believe in free will. Free will is a necessary illusion to maintain law and order in society, but it does not exist in nature. So why should it be different among *Homo sapiens*? It must all be God's will or it would be different. Ergo Theofatalism.

The Cause of It All

Although Jesus taught that those are blessed who mourn, the meek and the peacemakers, the poor and the persecuted and otherwise who suffer in this life have a great reward in heaven, the Bible claims that God is not your friend, comforter, or protector. It is your master. Not the manmade god in holy books, but the prime mover in the universe—generator, operator, destroyer… GOD. The earth is a very dangerous place to live with hurricanes, tornadoes, earthquakes, volcanoes, tsunamis, diseases, accidents, wars, murders and such. If you think about it you would naturally become very depressed to realize you do not control any of it.

The Bible says that God causes all of it. "The Lord kills and makes alive; The Lord makes poor and makes rich; He brings some low and lifts some up" (1 Samuel 2:6–7). "I make peace and create evil/calamity. I the Lord do all these things" (Isaiah 45:7). In this context, the Hebrew word for "evil" is translated elsewhere in the Bible as, spoiled, bad, adversity, trouble, sinful, misfortune, calamity, natural disasters, or suffering—so take your pick. "Who has spoken and it came to pass, unless the Lord has commanded it? Is it not from the mouth of the Most High that good and bad come?" (Lamentations 3:37–38). The Quran says the same thing to Muslims: "No calamity comes, no affliction occurs, except by the decision and preordainment of Allah" (S:64.11). It also says, "Allah, wielder of the kingly power; thou givest that power to whomever thy will and thou taketh the power from whomever thy will, Thou dost exalt whom thy will and thou doth abase whom thy will… Thou over all things are most powerful… and if Allah shall help you then none can defeat you, but if He abandon you who will help you?" (S.3:25, 3:154). "His is the kingdom of the heavens and the earth; He gives life and causes death; and He has power over all things" (S57:52).

Jesus used the metaphor of winemaking to show that God prunes the creation to ensure a better crop of fruit, just like they do in orchards and vineyards. It hurts to get pruned but it must be necessary or it would be different (John 15:1–2). One must conclude that the suffering of mankind, and all the sentient beings, must be the will of God. As for loving God who is perfect love, Jesus declared, "Fear him who after killing the body has power to cast you into hell" (Luke 12:4–5). Although Jesus is claimed to be Messiah/Christ, he declared that no one can come to him unless the Father wills/calls/enables them (John 3:16, 6:65). Apparently, what God wants is a broken spirit, remorse and penitence, a broken and contrite heart (Psalm 51:16–18). Sorry about that, but that is what it says. Ergo Theofatalism.

Necessary Reality

The primary commandment is to love God with all your being because "God is love" (Matthew 22:36–38, 1 John 4:8). But he/it did not make any one-sided coins—we inhale at birth and we exhale at death. There is another side of God described in the Bible that you won't get in church because most people cannot stand this alternative scripture, and it might send them running to the exits. "The sacrifices/desires of God are a broken spirit, and a broken and contrite heart" (Psalm 51:17). "Be afflicted and mourn and weep, let your laughter be turned to mourning and your joy to heaviness. Humble yourselves in the sight of the Lord and he shall lift you up" (James 4:9–10). "Do not be afraid of those who kill the body but cannot kill the soul. Rather, be afraid of the One who can destroy both soul and body in hell" (Matthew 10:28). "Fear him who after killing the body has power to cast you into hell" (Luke 12:4–5). "The spirit gives life; the flesh counts for nothing" (John 6:44, 63). "The Lord makes poor and makes rich; He brings some low and lifts some up" (1 Samuel 2:6–7). God is the potter and we are the clay… some to be made for royal use and some for common use. "But who are you, a human being, to talk back to God? Shall what is formed say to the one who formed it, 'Why did you make me like this?' Does not the potter have the right to make out of the same lump of clay some pottery for special purposes and some for common use?" (Jeremiah 18:2–6, Romans 9:16–21). "You saw me before I was born and scheduled each day of my life before I began to breathe. Every day was recorded in your book!" (Psalm 139:16). "It is God who directs the lives of his creatures; everyone's life is in his power" (Job 12:10). So neither praise nor blame are appropriate in judging the behaviors of mankind because free will is an illusion, necessary at this stage of social evolution, but still an illusion. Every event has a preceding causal event and so on back to the original event, thus everything is inevitable. Think about it. The way to contentment—if not happiness—is to accept what is as being necessary reality—including belief in free will—because it must be God's will or it would be different. Ergo Theofatalism.

What Is Truth

When actor Jack Nicholson screamed, "You can't handle the truth" in the movie *A Few Good Men* (1992) few really appreciated the complete impact of his statement. The fact is that not only can we not handle the truth, but we cannot know it either. What we assume to be the truth is nothing more than the compiled body of information that we have gathered up to here and now, and a lot of it merely is opinions and interpretations. Eye witness testimony in court is known to be grossly unreliable. That fact is not new as Roman Emperor Aurelius wrote in his *Meditations* during the second century CE, "Everything we hear is an opinion, not a fact. Everything we see is a perspective, not the truth." The full complete truth cannot be known because it is evolving constantly in time, and it changes with circumstances and new discoveries. Greek philosopher and father of stoicism, Heraclitus wrote in 500 BC that no man ever steps into the same river twice—for it is not the same river or the same man—thus knowledge never is static. In modern quantum mechanics, merely observing something changes it. When Jesus was asked by Pilate during his inquisition, "What is truth?" he remained silent and gave no reply. Some things really are unknowable, and even God cannot know the unknowable. The ancient Greeks developed the system of logical reasoning to help determine the truth of an assumption, but very few students study classical logic anymore, so people often draw false conclusions. Problems occur when they act upon them.

In epistemology, the Münchhausen trilemma is a thought experiment used to demonstrate the impossibility of proving any truth, even in the fields of logic and mathematics. If it is asked how any knowledge is known to be true, proof must be provided. Yet that same question can be asked of the proof, and any subsequent proof, ad infinitum. We must live with the truth that truth is relative and not of our own making, especially about what the future will bring into our lives and that makes for existential anxiety—called angst—the curse and affliction of being alive and the bane of human existence. Some prosperity preachers and a few psychologists claim if you think positive thoughts your future will be positive and if you think negative thoughts your future will be negative. But nobody knows where thoughts come from or who or what can control them. Many people exhibit grandiosity, believing they are more than they really are. But some people seem to have all their dreams come true with uncanny ability. However, if you look into it, you find that many decisions and actions by others were needed to make their dreams come true. No one is an island in human affairs. That's the truth.

Thus, decisions often are made from subconscious forces we cannot control that are compiled from assumptions, perceptions, and experiences, like the tip of an iceberg that must go where the submerged base takes it. The base is composed of all those perceptions, experiences, and interpretations of events compiled since childhood and before birth from our ancestors that makes each one see and react to the world in their unique way, called schema. Since there are no courses required for parenting, most kids grow up with some of their needs unmet, leaving them with faulty adult coping skills. However, two kids growing up in the same household can take away much different experiences. These unconscious forces drive behavior in response to current events beyond the conscious control of the individual. Each event adds more material to the compilation of schema, which evolves as we go through life. Becoming a healthy adult requires identifying faulty schema, forgiving the past, and developing effective coping skills. In this process, everyone does the best they can under the circumstances. So it follows that all of our choices and decisions are made under conditions of indefinite uncertainty about the future results or outcomes. There may be no mistakes, just choices and consequences. Like playing blackjack at a gambling casino, we must play the cards we are dealt and walk the labyrinth of life we are given without knowing how it will all turn out. And it must all be God's will—generator, operator, destroyer—or it would be different. Ergo Theofatalism. Think you can handle that?

Nothing Happens Outside the Will of God

You don't have to search for the purpose of your life because you cannot avoid it. Everyone must do whatever is demanded of them. Each person seems to have a calling that is unique to them, which must be necessary or it would be different. The Rev. Rick Warren wrote in *The Purpose-Driven Life* (2002), "God made you for a reason, he also decided when you would be born and how long you would live. He planned the days of your life in advance, choosing the exact time and place of your birth and death." The Bible says, "You saw me before I was born and scheduled each day of my life before I began to breathe. Every day was recorded in your book!" (Psalm 139:16). It is God who directs the lives of his creatures; everyone's life is in his power" (Job 12:10). The Rev. Warren did not realize it, but he found the basis for belief that nothing happens outside the will of God, including the suicide of his youngest son who suffered from incurable depression. Not the manmade god in holy books but the prime mover in the universe: generator, operator, destroyer—GOD… it controls everything from atoms to galaxies and we all must take what it gives and give what it takes. This is not a god to be worshipped, but rather one to be feared because what appears to be free will merely is a God-given illusion. Of course, you can believe just the opposite and probably find some scriptures to prove that opinion also. God never made any one-sided coins. But it takes a lot of maturity to hold the opposites and still function normally. All in God's will of course. Believe it or not. Ergo Theofatalism.

Immaculate Immanence

God is everywhere in everything as immaculate immanence, i.e., the prime force in the universe. If God—the generator, operator, destroyer—wanted anything to be different it would be. "For since the creation of the world God's invisible qualities—his eternal power and divine nature—have been clearly seen, being understood from what has been made, so that people are without excuse" (Romans 1:20). To paraphrase Deepak Chopra and C. G. Jung, "It is very difficult to find God, but it is impossible to avoid him." To see God, look around at its creation… all of it. Some of it stinks, pretty badly. If the god of the Bible is the creator of this mess and world of tears, he/it has a lot to answer for. Just saying. So there must be a prime mover in the universe more powerful than this. One that is everywhere in everything *as immaculate immanence*. Nothing happens outside the will of God from atoms to galaxies… generator, operator, destroyer… GOD, and we all must take what it gives and give what it takes. Ergo Theofatalism.

Your Inalienable Rights

The founders of America wrote into the US Constitution that all mankind are endowed by their creator with certain inalienable rights; among these are life, liberty, and the pursuit of happiness. They also wrote that all men are created equal, but we know how that has not worked so far because that is not for man to decide. In fact, people are not created equal in any way, shape, or form. In addition, the first ten amendments to the Constitution were necessary to add and specify more clearly the actual rights that were intended for citizens. You can read them if you Google the Bill of Rights. The founders declared that the purpose of the Constitution was to "create a more perfect union" between the various states. This obviously still is a work in process. They created a bicameral congress to make the necessary federal laws and a court system to enforce them and to assure they would be interpreted within the intent of the Constitution. The Supreme Court was established to settle disagreements among the lower courts about the applications of the various laws. Federal judges are appointed for life by the incumbent president as elected by the voters through a process that is called the electoral college which assures some balance of power between the larger and smaller states. Thus, it is possible for the President to be elected with fewer than a majority of the votes cast. In recent times, this happened with the election of G. W. Bush and Donald J. Trump. He is trying to govern with a 48 percent majority and a questionable mental condition. The challenge for understanding is how did he ever get elected unless it was the will of God.

Each state employs a police force to apprehend law breakers and the federal government employs the Department of Justice and the Federal Bureau of Investigation for enforcement of federal laws. In addition, people in America are subject to many laws passed by the various states and their local jurisdictions, which makes for a wide range of legal services. The total number of laws imposed upon each individual probably is in the hundreds, if not the thousands. Some of them are so archaic they no longer are enforced and should be repealed, but they seldom are. They claim we are a nation under the rule of law and that no one is above the law, which means that personal liberty that was claimed by the Founders is not the prime objective of the US government. If Congress does not pass new laws every session they are criticized for not doing their job. The more laws, the less liberty. But I digress.

That the US form of government is not the most preferred among the nations is shown by the fact that none of them have copied it. The most popular option is the parliamentary form which has roots in the British Empire and its many colonies during its period of expansion. The others are mostly dictatorships in one form or another. But no matter what government you live under, it must all be the will of God or it would be different. Apostle Paul wrote, "Let everyone be subject to the governing authorities, for there is no authority except that which God has established. The authorities that exist have been established by God. Consequently, whoever rebels against the authority is rebelling against what God has instituted, and those who do so will bring judgment on themselves. For rulers hold no terror for those who do right, but for those who do wrong. Do you want to be free from fear of the one in authority? Then do what is right and you will be commended. For the one in authority is God's servant for your good. But if you do wrong, be afraid, for rulers do not bear the sword for no reason. They are God's servants, agents of wrath to bring punishment on the wrongdoer. Therefore, it is necessary to submit to the authorities, not only because of possible punishment but also as a matter of conscience" (Romans 13:1–5).

Recall he wrote this to the Christians in Rome who were living under the rule of Caesars. When the disciples of Jesus asked him who they should obey he replied, "Give to Caesar what is Caesars and to God what is Gods" (Mark 12:17). But when the apostles ran into opposition from the local governing temple rulers in Jerusalem, Peter declared, "We must obey God rather than human beings" (Acts 5:29). Ever since then, theologians have been trying to decide how to apply these scriptures to current times. The solution varies from place to place and from time to time subject to various interpretations, and yours is as good as any others. American founder Benjamin Franklin (1705–1790) thought the American Revolution was an act of God. He wrote in his autobiography, "The longer I live, the more convincing proofs I see of this truth—that God governs in the affairs of men."

So here is the thing. It all must be necessary or it would be different as nothing can happen outside the will of God. Not the man-made god in holy books, but the prime mover in the universe—generator, operator, destroyer… GOD. It does whatever it wants with whomever it wants and we all must take what it gives and give what it takes—as said by Mother/Saint Teresa. Ergo Theofatalism.

A Different Pathway

Very few people can handle the truth because the world of illusion feels much safer, so please feel especially gifted if you are reading this. If you don't get it, it doesn't matter. The truth is all relative to time and place and is likely to change depending on the pathway you are given. Poet Robert Frost (1874–1963) wrote, "I took the road less traveled, and it made all the difference." If after reading all these instructive essays, you do not agree with Theofatalism, never fear. People lived under the law of gravity without knowing it before Isaac Newton proposed it in 1687, and it was not confirmed until 1798, seventy-one years after his death. Perhaps this belief will be confirmed at some future time or maybe not. St. Thomas a Kempis wrote in *The Imitation of Christ* (1427), "It is better to leave everyone to their own way of thinking rather than give way to contentious discourse." Mystical writer Abd-ru-shin, a.k.a. Oskar Bernhardt (1875–1941), who was big on free will, intuition, and personal volition declared in *The Grail Message* (1941), "All teachings/thoughts/ideas were at one time willed by God, precisely adapted to the individual peoples and countries, and formed in complete accord with their actual spiritual maturity and receptivity." Thus, some people are Atheists, some are Mormons, some are Muslims, some are Buddhists, and some are Christians—Democrats and Republicans, saints and criminals, and some believe in free will and some don't.

So there is no benefit in judging anyone who follows a different pathway because each one must take the labyrinth walk of life they are given, and no one can take the walk for another. C. G. Jung said, "Your pathway is not my pathway. Therefore, I cannot teach you. The pathway is within." This would include parents who cannot control the lives of their children who must walk the pathway of life they are given. If it is all God's will, then you can feel good inside no matter what happens outside, because Jesus said, "The spirit gives life, the flesh counts for nothing. The words I have given you are full of spirit and of life" (John 6:63). He also said before you criticize the speck of sawdust in the eye of another to remove the plank in your own vision (Matthew 7:3). The road to enlightenment can be a lonely struggle. The ocean of knowledge never is full because there always is more to learn. Like Jung, we might say, "I confess I am afraid of a long-drawn-out suffering. It seems to me as if I am ready to die, although as it looks to me some powerful thoughts are still flickering like lightnings in a summer night. Yet they are not mine, they belong to God, as everything else which bears mentioning… One must be able to suffer God. That is the supreme task for the carrier of ideas. We must be the advocate of the earth. God will take care of himself."

Life is not fair, the good suffer with the bad and everyone leaves the body to return it to the stellar dust from which it came, but God's justice is unimpeachable. The creation has no power to criticize the Creator. We are the clay and it is the potter, making some for common use and some for royal use (Jeremiah 18:2–6, Romans 9:12). Get it? Saint/Mother Teresa (1910–1997) concluded, "God does whatever he wants with whomever he wants, and we all must take what he gives and give what he takes… with a smile." And the late Helen Schucman (1909–1981), scribe of *A Course in Miracles* (1975) concluded, "Disobeying the will of God is meaningful only to the insane. In truth, it is impossible." So if you don't get it, that must be the will of God, which may be the most important piece of wisdom that you can possibly learn.

Great King Solomon learned that with much wisdom comes much sorrow and the more knowledge the more grief (Ecclesiastes 1:18). Enlightenment has its price. After his own discoveries about the human psyche, Jung was borderline despondent. "I suffer from the fact that I can so seldom have a conversation with an adequate partner. I have suffered enough from incomprehension and from the isolation one falls into when one says things that people do not understand." I also have felt such isolation in trying to get even a few people to understand the message of theofatalism. I am a man on the riverside yelling at people floating by having a party on a houseboat while heading for a waterfall. But even if they heard me it would not change anything. As with the law of gravity, it is what it is.

A great sage said, "Before enlightenment, I carried water and chopped wood, and after enlightenment, I carried water and chopped wood." So perhaps it is best just to observe destiny because we cannot change it anyway. For Jung, the labyrinth walk of life is not about the pursuit of happiness but rather the pursuit of consciousness. "The development of consciousness (awareness of God as generator, operator, destroyer) is the burden, the suffering, and the blessing of mankind." In other words, all benefits come with burdens and vice versa. So be careful what you ask for. All in God's will of course. Ergo theofatalism.

The Bottom Line

God never made any one-sided coins. Jesus said there would always be poor people as well as rich people, warmakers and peacemakers—necessary opposites for sure. For every action, there is an equal and opposite reaction. Such is the law of physics. The late comedian

George Carlin observed the average American is pretty dumb and half of the rest are even dumber. Such is the law of statistics. Every bell curve has a bottom half, and it seems that everyone does what is necessary to occupy the position they are assigned in the labyrinth of life—like a small piece in a gigantic jigsaw puzzle fits into only one place. The Bible says, "You saw me before I was born and scheduled each day of my life before I began to breathe. Every day was recorded in your book!" (Psalm 139:16). "A person's steps are directed by the Lord. How then can anyone understand their own way?" (Proverbs 20:24). Do you get the picture? The richest man in India lives next to squalid slums. Saint/Mother Teresa, patron saint of Calcutta, said, "Heaven will be full of slum people." The richest person is not the one with the most, but the one who needs the least. Jesus said in the Kingdom of God the last shall be first and the first shall be last (Matthew 19:30, 20:16). Can you believe that? Bottom line is it must all be God's will or it would be different. Generator, operator, destroyer… GOD. Ergo Theofatalism. Believe it or not, because that also must be the will of God as there can be no other. Amen.

Epilogue
The Book of Ecclesiastes
Chapter 1

¹The words of the Teacher, son of David, king in Jerusalem:
²"Meaningless! Meaningless!" says the Teacher.
  "Utterly meaningless!
  Everything is meaningless."
³ What do people gain from all their labors
  at which they toil under the sun?
⁴ Generations come and generations go,
  but the earth remains forever.
⁵ The sun rises and the sun sets,
  and hurries back to where it rises.
⁶ The wind blows to the south
  and turns to the north;
  round and round it goes,
  ever returning on its course.
⁷ All streams flow into the sea,
  yet the sea is never full.
  To the place the streams come from,
  there they return again.
⁸ All things are wearisome,
  more than one can say.
  The eye never has enough of seeing,
  nor the ear its fill of hearing.
⁹ What has been will be again,
  what has been done will be done again;
  there is nothing new under the sun.
¹⁰ Is there anything of which one can say,
  "Look! This is something new"?
  It was here already, long ago;

it was here before our time.
¹¹ No one remembers the former generations,
and even those yet to come
will not be remembered
by those who follow them.
¹² I, the Teacher, was king over Israel in Jerusalem. ¹³ I applied my mind to study and to explore by wisdom all that is done under the heavens. What a heavy burden God has laid on mankind! ¹⁴ I have seen all the things that are done under the sun; all of them are meaningless, a chasing after the wind.
¹⁵ What is crooked cannot be straightened;
what is lacking cannot be counted.
¹⁶ I said to myself, "Look, I have increased in wisdom more than anyone who has ruled over Jerusalem before me; I have experienced much of wisdom and knowledge." ¹⁷ Then I applied myself to the understanding of wisdom, and also of madness and folly, but I learned that this, too, is a chasing after the wind.
¹⁸ For with much wisdom comes much sorrow;
the more knowledge, the more grief.

PART II

Contemplation in Aging

Introduction

Aging progresses slowly on the walk of life until one day it becomes a startling reality. The challenges come in various ways, and many people are poorly prepared for them. Clearly, there is a need for such preparation. As one possible intervention, this essay explores the use of Jungian personality functions in a discussion of the aging process during the latter years. This is a field that is void of research and publication, possibly because it is too stressful to contemplate, and many people would prefer to avoid it as long as possible. This reaction may be understandable as a defense mechanism, but to be forewarned is to be forearmed. So perhaps this discussion will stimulate more work on this subject, which is a new and unique application of Jungian psychology.

(*Note: Coping with aging challenges may involve issues that are outside the scope of this work, which is not a substitute for professional care. It is important to recognize that aging is a chronic condition, and you need all the help you can get to manage it well.*)

Swiss psychiatrist Carl Gustave Jung (1875–1961) suggested that aging begins after the meridian is passed as one may shift from counting the time since birth to contemplating the time left until death. The first half of life may be viewed as four stages of growth through infancy, childhood, youth, to adulthood. The second half of life may be marked off in four stages of maturity, seniority, retirement, and contemplation—possibly overlapping and not necessarily correlated with chronological age. The cycle of life is symbolized by labyrinth—leaving the source at birth out into the world and returning again back to the source. The work in this essay leaves active aging to editors of the AARP national magazine and focuses on challenges in aging transitions during the latter stage life, which ends in mortality. Thanks to a better standard of living and modern medicine, life expectancy has increased by a decade or more during the past century, but with a cost. The World Health Organization estimates up to 75 percent of the life extension will be spent in "chronic illness, disability and suffering."

The situation is becoming acute as the aging 76 million "baby boomers" born from 1946 to 1965 present a "silver tsunami," which is changing the demographics of many western nations and is creating a growth industry for aging services plus stress on government programs for their support. Some estimates say 40 percent of those over age sixty-five are living on Social Security payments alone. And the combined unfunded liability of SS and state pensions is estimated by Motley Fool at $20 trillion—while the attempts to legislate the best medical care system money can buy for everyone flounders in never land. Both Medicare and Medicaid seem to be threatened by the current political winds. One side wants a single payer system for everyone and the other wants a free market. If we get free market health care, it will be like the personal transportation business. Some will be able to buy a Rolls Royce, some will buy a luxury car, some will have to settle for an economy car, some will only get a used car, some will have to take Uber or the bus, and some will die in the streets. It is a mystery why the US Congress cannot convene organizations of the health care industry to create a plan that is best for all the factions involved, with care of suffering people paramount. Oh, I forget, the primary goal is maximum profits.

There are about 2.6 million funerals annually in America, 7,123 per day and 296 per hour, but you would not know it unless your family is one of the statistics. However, we are programmed to live and not to die. The late founder of Apple Inc., Steve Jobs (1955–2011), observed that "even those who think they are going to heaven don't want to die to get there." Humans seem to push their mortality off into some distant future. Moviemaker Woody Allen said, "I don't want to live forever in my work, I want to live forever in my apartment. I don't mind the idea of dying, I just don't want to be there when it happens." Although it is the inevitable end to life, preparation for aging and death is a taboo in many western countries, so it has not been integrated into normal family living as it is in some other cultures. Stanford professor emeritus Irvin Yalom said facing death is like "staring at the sun." It can only be viewed through a dark lens or in very short glimpses. But eventually, it cannot be avoided as the process of aging takes its toll on individuals and families.

Half of the people in America die by age eighty and most of the rest by age ninety, and the final years may not be very pleasant. The Bible says, "Our days may come to seventy years, or eighty if our strength endures; yet the duration of them are but trouble and sorrow, for they quickly pass, and we fly away" (Psalm 90:10). If dying is a natural transition in the life cycle, why do we fear it and fight it so much? Like the lyrics in Old Man River from the musical *Show Boat* (1927, 1951), "I'm tired of livin,' but scared of dyin'… I must keep livin' until I'm dyin." Or the Paul Simon lyric, "Don't know where I'm going, but I'm on my way." Perhaps the shock of aging cannot be totally avoided, but maybe it is time to seek a better way to get prepared. The challenges of aging may be understood and managed better if they can be related to the Jungian theory of human personality. So perhaps this can be the genesis of a new meme, a contagious idea whose time has come.

Jung said there is the thing and the symbol of the thing. The ancient symbol of a labyrinth displayed here as the Chartres Labyrinth from the thirteenth century may serve as a mandala for each of us in the walk of life. Unlike a maze with its many random dead ends, everyone is given a labyrinth without options to walk through life, so let us count the ways of walking through it. Four seems to be a very significant number, four seasons, four points to the compass, four gospels, four horsemen of the apocalypse… as with the four quadrants of the labyrinth through which one must traverse from the source out into the world and then back to the source, there are possibly four aspects or challenges in aging. Jung identified them as four functions of personality. For this purpose, they are discussed as the physical/sensing, spiritual/intuition, cognitive/thinking, and emotional/feeling functions of personality. They can either be introverted, keeping them inside and private or extraverted, preferring to share them with anyone possible. People approach aging with the same unique personal resources they used throughout their lives, so these four functions are arranged in a top to bottom ranking of ability and preference by each individual. They are discussed here in the familiar "Z" pattern. Your own preference in ranking them may be different from the order presented here. My own type preference is INTJ/p so that is reflected in this work. This discussion follows the Jungian personality model called the Myers-Briggs Type Indicator (MBTI). ©CPP Inc. Google MBTI for the details. Sources are cited in the text, except those from Internet sites that are posted with the references. (*All quotations and sources are included under the fair use doctrine of US copyright law.*)

A LABYRINTH WALK OF LIFE

Challenges in Aging

Note to caregivers: The following information relates to the experience of aging from within. As a caregiver of a loved one or family member or a client or patient, your perspective may be one of observer and facilitator. Like gravity or other laws of nature, which mankind has observed without changing them, having this information may improve your role as a witness and helper. It is not meant to change anyone as that would be impossible. Change must come from within as nature intended for each person. Everyone must take the labyrinth walk of life alone for themselves. The key seems to be accepting changes and seeking ways to enjoy the life you are given, each to his own. Jung wrote in The Red Book (2009, 2012), "My path is not your path; therefore, I cannot teach you. The pathway is within us."

First and most observable are the *physical changes* that are visible and measurable with the senses (S). They include the obvious changes and slowing down that even exercise and diet cannot deter forever. The hidden challenges may be invisible and gradual, but eventually they cause physical symptoms to appear. As F. Scott Fitzgerald at age thirty-nine described in *The Crack Up (1936)*, "There is a sort of blow that comes from within—that you don't feel until it's too late to do anything about it, until you realize with finality that in some regard you will never be as good again." Self-management becomes a necessary skill to keep the body functioning as long as possible. It is important to plan a right-carb diet and exercise to maintain muscle tone and balance to avoid dangerous falls. Getting the right amount of sleep and taking naps will help sustain your physical condition. Having regular medical check-ups and treating illness also is important. You may need to consider moving to a safer place where your physical needs are part of the service package. The main problem with mortality is something has to kill you. The most likely offenders are heart disease, cancer, stroke, and diabetes with Alzheimer's disease close at hand. One can debate which is worse, losing your mind in a healthy body, or losing your body with a healthy mind. The social stigma attached to some disorders may pose a limitation on the open display of disability in some situations. This physical challenge will be marked with increasing doctor appointments and eventually the need for such aids as canes, walkers, and wheelchairs. The final blow may be losing your driving privilege, so it may be necessary to make arrangements for needed transportation and home care. Slowly losing the self-image or persona in life may be difficult to accept, but necessary. As Shakespeare described it: "One man in his time plays many parts… Last scene of all, that ends this strange eventful history, is second childishness and mere oblivion, sans teeth, sans eyes, sans taste, sans everything" (*As You Like It*, act 2, scene 7).

This physical aging process seems to be regulated by the length of something called telomeres appended to the chromosomes we are born with. In 1975–1977, Elizabeth Blackburn, working as a postdoctoral fellow at Yale University with Joseph Gall, discovered the nature of telomeres. Telomere shortening is associated with aging, mortality, and aging-related diseases. In 2003, Richard Cawthon discovered that those with longer telomeres lead longer lives than those with short telomeres. As cells die and are replicated, the telomeres dry up, which controls our individual longevity and senility. What regulates telomeres, nobody knows. You can get an evaluation of your own condition by space-age DNA technology from Telomere Diagnostics Inc. Visit www.teloyears.com. You can accept it or fight it and maybe defer it, but you cannot change it. To quote the late Muhammad Ali, "You can run but you can't hide." It will be necessary to adapt to the physical changes that will challenge the coping resources of us all, controlling what you can and accepting what you cannot.

The *second* challenge in aging comes from the *spiritual/intuition* or human imagination (N) which drives all creativity. Active imagination is one of the practical tools that Jung offered to help us tap into our creativity in the second half of life. It can see around corners, and it can anticipate the future, which comes with benefits and burdens. Nothing is done by humans that is not first imagined, both the good and the bad. The mind may focus on the worst-case scenario or anticipated catastrophe. Knowledge that mind and body are changing may induce a loss of control and a feeling of futility. The motivation to change may be driven by what Jung called intuition. Albert Einstein (1879–1955) thought that intuition is more important than knowledge. "The intellect has little to do on the road to discovery. There comes a leap of consciousness, call it intuition or what you will, and the solution comes to you and you don't know how or why. The intuitive mind is a sacred gift and the rational mind is a faithful servant. We have created a society that honors the servant and has forgotten the gift." Napoleon Bonaparte (1769–1821) concluded, "Imagination rules the world." It was a delight when the future held promise and accomplishment, but a future leading only to suffering, humiliation, and oblivion eventually may erode the mind and produce anxiety and depression accompanied with fear and anger. Intuition/imagination can produce both positive and negative results.

Those with a spiritual belief in some blissful life after life may find comfort in their imagined spiritual transition. For them, the best is yet to come. Jung wrote in *Commentary on The Secret of the Golden Flower* (1929), "All of my patients in the second half of life fell ill because they lost what living religions of every age gave to their believers, and none of them were healed who did not regain his religious outlook, which has nothing to do with creeds or church… As a doctor, I make every effort to strengthen the belief in immortality, especially with older patients when such questions come threateningly close. For, seen in correct psychological perspective, death is not an end but a goal, and life's inclination toward death begins as soon as the meridian is past. If you sum up what people tell you about overcoming distressing experiences, you can formulate it this way: They came to themselves, they could accept themselves, they were able to become reconciled to themselves, and thus they were reconciled to adverse circumstances and events. This is almost what used to be expressed by saying, he has made his peace with God, he has sacrificed his own will, he has submitted himself to the will of God." French philosopher Pierre T. de Chardin (1881–1955) said, "We are not humans having a spiritual experience, we are spirits having a human experience." Jesus said, "The spirit gives life, the flesh counts for nothing" (John 6:65).

The *third* challenge in aging emerges from thinking (T) and is *cognitive or mental.* Learning new stuff eventually becomes more difficult and tedious and less rewarding—keeping up with all the new technology becomes less and less exciting as the burdens exceed the benefits. Managing all the cognitive details of living can become burdensome and sometimes neglected as the world becomes increasing complex. Once done, nothing in the past can be redone differently so thoughts of remorse and regrets may become a part of aging. The most common regret may be not saving enough money for retirement—about 40 percent of seniors live on Social Security payments alone. If such things could be different, they would be. My father said, "Talking about the past will not change anything, and I think I did the best I could under the circumstances." Dreams can invade your restless sleeping cycles leaving you more tired when you awake and troubled by their mysteries. Thoughts of pending disability and worries about the impending future can invade normal life so that mental activities once pleasurable lose their zest. There may be a slow but persistent mental decline—and loss of interest in current events, or even loss of grip on reality and an overall withdrawal from mental activities. Forgetfulness may be helped with written post-it reminders and placing personal things in designated places.

It may be helpful to downsize living space and remove cherished personal possessions to reduce housekeeping to manageable routines, keeping only precious family heirlooms to pass on. Clubs, social activities, and maintaining hobbies and volunteer projects may help in keeping the mind active. Chronic mental diseases are frightening and gruesome to contemplate, and their social stigma still needs to be overcome. The diagnostic manual (DSM-V) for psychiatry describes dozens of ways the brain can go awry. Unfortunately, mental illness carries a social stigma and so may not be diagnosed or treated effectively. Joan Erikson (1903–1997) wrote at her age ninety-three, "Being incompetent because of aging is belittling and makes elders like unhappy small children of great age." Realizing the future is indefinitely uncertain leads to worry and angst if you think about it. Normal mental resilience that met and resolved problems of living in the past now can induce irritability, anxiety, and outrage as the options for personal care, medical treatment, housing, and estate management become more confusing, as control may be passed to others. Some seniors may need help in creating a will or trust and designating a power of attorney for medical and financial decisions.

Fourth, the *feelings and emotions* (F) that were the source of many pleasures and excitement that make life worth living may become dull and retreat into a shrunken atrophy, or possibly expand and take control of the mind. Feelings often are confused with thoughts as when people say, "I feel that…" We can feel hot or cold, happy or sad, etc., but we cannot "feel that" tomorrow is Thursday. Feelings are related to emotions as in love, sadness, shame, guilt, fear, anger, happiness, jealousy, anxiety, envy, anger, depression, and such. They can upset your comfortable life and render impotent your logical reasoning. As the reality of aging sinks in, enjoyment of entertainment and pleasures of the past are replaced with recurring fears and panic attacks as the realization emerges that each day is one day less to live, and what comes after nobody knows. Social support fades away as lovers, friends and relatives move away and succumb to the grim reaper, one after the other, leaving no doubt about your own impending demise. All beginnings come with endings, and we must grieve our losses. The death of a spouse is usually a particularly powerful loss. A spouse often becomes part of the other in a unique way: many widows and widowers describe losing half of themselves. The days, months, and years after the loss of a spouse will never be the same and learning to live without them may be a harsh challenge in the new normal walk on the labyrinth of life. Sharing and building a life with another human being, then learning to live singularly, can be an adjustment that is exceedingly complex. On the highly-validated Holmes-Rahe scale of forty-three life events that cause illness, death of spouse was rated the highest (100) with divorce a distant second (73). No matter how many years together, they are never enough if the partnership was one of mutual respect and love. Because woman was made from the rib of a man, the Bible declares, "For this reason a man will leave his father and mother and be united to his wife, and the two will become one flesh. So they are no longer two, but one flesh. Therefore, what God has joined together, let no one separate" (Genesis 2:24, Matthew 19:4–6). With Dr. Gary Harbaugh, I wrote *Recovery from Loss*, also based on Jungian Type resources (CAPT).

Family relationships may strengthen or get distorted as social and generational gaps replace solidarity and mutual support with estrangement and loss. Some relatives may shy away from aging caregiving because they assume the symptoms are contagious—which they are. Regrettably, some people cannot handle their own emotions around a loved one who is showing their age. Personal losses may include loss of confidence, loss of self-esteem, loss of independence, loss of lifestyle, loss of self-image, loss of appearance, etc. Giving them up, grieving and eventually letting go of your own body may be the last great adventure. It may be necessary to direct your love to others… if you cannot be near the ones you love, then love the ones you are near, i.e., love your neighbor as yourself (Matthew 22:29). Sometimes, a pet may become a loving companion in old age, but that too must be grieved when it is gone. When someone, including a pet, enters your heart, they never really leave. All beginnings come with endings.

But beware of the difference between love and cathexis. Cathexis is driven by the instinct for reproduction and striving to get conditionally, but love is striving to give unconditionally. The late poet Maya Angelou said love does not hold, love liberates. "Love is patient, love is kind, it does not envy, it does not boast, it is not proud, it does not dishonor others, it is not self-seeking, it is not easily angered, it keeps no records of wrongs, it always protects, always trusts, always hopes, always perseveres" (1 Corinthians 13:4–8). The four natural passions—joy, hope, fear, and grief—all must be integrated during the second half of life. You may also experience a cascade of such emotions as frustration, loneliness, anxiety, sadness, plus some positive ones including a sense of peace, the joy and thankfulness for being alive and unfortunately being invisible to the social environment, requiring a rediscovery of your sense of humor and tolerance for the ignorance of others. Their time will come. It may be helpful to practice mindfulness meditation living in the here and now moment by moment, living neither in the past or the future.

Anthropologist Margaret Mead (1901–1978) said, "We celebrate at weddings and we rejoice at births, but when someone dies we pretend nothing happened." Jung thought this denial was not healthy for the psyche. Shakespeare advised Macbeth to "give sorrow words because the grief that does not speak knits up the oe'rwrought heart and bids it break." It may be helpful to process the emotional challenges of loss with aid of a qualified counselor if relatives and trusted friends are unable or unwilling to help you hold these strong feelings and life changes, which they see coming in their own futures. As aging progresses, the male hormone testosterone and the female hormone estrogen decline so that each gender may display some behavioral traits of the opposite, what Jung called the anima in males and the animus in females. Thus, older men may become a little more collaborative, and older women may become a little more competitive. (This transition is seen among the population of transgender folks.) Joan Erickson (1903–1997) observed at age ninety-three, "The years of intimacy and love often are replaced by isolation and deprivation. Relationships become overshadowed by new incapacities and dependencies." However, she did not condone assisted living and nursing homes because "aging is the process of becoming free and should not be treated as the opposite." Thus, becoming freer to be who we really are sans any social constraints may be one of the positive benefits of aging.

Personal Responses

Everyone perceives the world and reacts to it through the filter of their individual personality. Jung observed that what appears to be random human behavior can be the result of individual perceiving and judging functions of personality, which have their genesis in previous generations. There are four functions described by Jung which are operative in everyone, divided into two activities of perceiving and two activities of judging. The job of the perceiving functions—sensing (S) and intuition (N) is to continually collect information. The job of the decision/judging functions—thinking (T) and feeling (F)—is to close that process and come to some conclusions about it. Either the preferred perception or the preferred judging function can be dominant. Thus, they occur in eight preferred combinations of perceiving and judging, i.e., sensing/thinking (ST), sensing/feeling (SF), intuition/thinking (NT), and intuition/feeling (NF). They also can be reversed, i.e., thinking/sensing (TS), thinking/intuition

(TN), feeling/sensing (FS), and feeling/intuition (FN). Jungian theory would say that people respond to the challenges in aging by employing their preferred personality type, favoring their most developed function. Thus, people preferring sensing may likely do better on the physical issues, those preferring intuition on the spiritual/imaginative issues, those preferring thinking on the intellectual/mental issues, and those preferring feeling on the emotional issues. More work is needed on the way various personalities cope with the challenges in aging, possibly expanding to cover the sixteen types in the Myers-Briggs Type Indicator.

Although they are not strictly age related, here are some possible type-related responses to the respective challenges using "I" statements as developed in the *Coping Resources Inventory* by Allen L. Hammer and M. Susan Marting (1988, 2004) (www.mindgarden.com).

Sensing/Physical: (S) I have plenty of energy. I do not eat junk food. I exercise vigorously three times per week. My weight is within five pounds of where it should be. I like the way my body looks. I am rarely tired. I do stretching exercises daily. I eat well-balanced meals. I do not snack between meals. I get enough sleep and rest. I keep in fairly good physical shape. I have regular medical checkups and manage medications and their side effects. I use physical aids as necessary. I enjoy social events with significant others who share my activities. I can enjoy the beauties of nature alone at times.

Intuition/Imagination: (N) I accept the mysteries of life and death. I can make sufficient sense of the world. I believe in a power greater than myself. I accept problems that I cannot change. I know what is important to me in life. Family and social/cultural traditions play an important role in my life. I attend church or believe in some form of religion. I seek to grow spiritually though not religious. I pray or meditate regularly. My values and beliefs help me to meet daily challenges. I take time to reflect on my life experience. I can live in the moment and be comfortable with future uncertainty. I am both insignificant and indispensable to the universe, like a grain of sand on the beach and a drop of water in the ocean.

Thinking/Cognitive: (T) I like the person I am. I am as worthwhile as anyone else. I see myself as fairly normal and lovable. I actively look for the positive aspects of people and every situation. I accept compliments easily. I am aware of the good qualities in myself and others. I actively pursue things, ideas, and activities that make me happy. I rarely put myself down. I am optimistic about my future. I can usually solve my problems and find ways to accommodate things I cannot change. I can find logical ways to explain sufficiently why things are as they are. I challenge negative thoughts to check their validity. I seek professional help as in cognitive behavior therapy to challenge automatic negative thoughts with more realistic appraisals. I am energized by learning new things about the world and current events. I can set goals and plan how to achieve them.

Feeling/Emotional: (F) I can identify my emotions. I say what I need to without making excuses or dropping hints. I am mostly happy. I have friends who are willing to listen when I talk about my feelings. I can show it whenever I am upset. I openly express my feelings to my friends. I can tell other people when they hurt me. I can cry when I am sad and grieving my losses. I can say what I need to without putting other people down. I admit and accept it when I am scared or angry. I express my feelings directly and clearly. I express my feelings of joy. I can laugh wholeheartedly. I show others when I care about them. I find ways of being of service to others. I work on finding things that I can be thankful for.

In addition to these personal responses, Hammer and Marting recommend an active social life by initiating contact with people who care about you, with whom you feel comfortable, with whom you can confide, who you enjoy being with, who share in your preferred activities, and who genuinely like you. Also, it is useful to practice the PEAA rule with the people in your life: praise, empathy, approval, and attention. This is powerful medicine, and a little of it goes a long way. The human ego loves it. If you do the opposite, it will drive people away and turn them into enemies. In his practical book *How to Win Friends and Influence People* (1930), Dale Carnegie (1888–1955) emphasized that most people are more interested in their own lives than in yours, so it pays to treat others the way they want to be treated. So ask open-ended questions and be responsive with attention, praise, and approval. The late poet Maya Angelou (1928–2014) said people may not remember what you say, but they will remember how you made them feel. Practice the modified golden rule: "Treat others as they want to be treated." And if you don't know, ask.

Everyone uses all four Jungian functions (sensing, iNtuition, thinking, feeling) but not with equal skill. Moreover, Naomi Quenk described in *Was That Really Me?* (2002) how those who are stressed beyond limits with physical, imagination, cognitive, and emotional challenges may be observed to shift into the least preferred functions if the primary functions are disabled, flipping as it were into the inferior/opposite personality. Of this shift Jung wrote, "It is understandable that people should get panicky, or that they eventually become demoralized under a chronic strain, or despair of their hopes and expectations. It is also understandable that their will-power weakens and their self-control becomes slack and begins to lose its grip upon circumstances, moods and thoughts. It is quite consistent with such a state of mind if some particularly unruly parts of the patient's psyche then acquire a certain degree of autonomy." He may have been describing a takeover by the "shadow" or least preferred parts of ourselves, although unconsciously—what he said was "standing in our own light." This change can enhance the distress more so if one feels alone and inadequate to the challenges without adequate social or family support. Some may retreat into harmful activities and distractions trying to avoid the distress of aging, but if functional stressors are identified and managed, life can proceed more normally until the stress is resolved. Professional therapy may be needed to help work through the "dark night of the soul." Marsha Linehan wrote in *Dialectical Behavior Therapy—Handouts and Worksheets* (2015), "Seek activities that are fun and meaningful. Contribute by adding value to the life of someone else. Compare yourself to the less fortunate as there always will be someone worse off and better off. Shift your attention to laughter, enjoyment, pride in your accomplishments. Push the hurt to the background and focus on something useful and self-affirming. Stimulate your senses, taste, smell, sounds, visions of things you enjoy. Practice these skills."

When the primary functions of personality are disabled, it may be useful if one can develop the less preferred ones, as a football coach may send in the backup quarterback when the star is sidelined. Thus, the ST will need to work on the NF, the SF will need to work on the NT, the NT will need to work on the SF, the NF will need to work on the ST, and the TS will need to work on the FN, the TN will need work on the FS, the FS will need to work on the TN, and the FN will need work on the TS. Such self-development may be aided with the help of a qualified counselor. Unfortunately, even when pending mortality is acknowledged, some families are unable to deal with it. Actually, denial of a mortal threat seems to be a beneficial coping defense for some people who cannot tolerate stressful events very well. Surgical patients seem to recover more quickly with less pain if they deny how sick they really are. The goal seems to be radical acceptance of reality, with contentment and thankfulness for a life well lived, no matter how it is lived. This could be an application for the serenity prayer of the late Reinhold Niebuhr, "Lord, please grant me serenity and inner peace, grace to accept what I cannot change, the courage and ability to change what I should, and the wisdom to know the difference." My father said, "In life we don't always get what we like, so we have to be satisfied with what we get."

An anonymous patient wrote to Jung, "By keeping quiet, repressing nothing, remaining attentive, and by accepting reality, taking things as they are and not as I wanted them to be, by doing all this unusual knowledge has come to me and unusual powers as well. I always thought if we accepted things they overpowered us in some way or another, but this turns out to be untrue. So now I intend to play the game of life, being receptive to whatever comes to me, also accepting my own nature with its positive and negative sides. Thus, everything becomes more alive to me." Everyone does the best they can under the circumstances, weighing the benefits against the burdens of each decision, albeit unconsciously. Like an iceberg, the top must go where the bottom takes it. Whether decisions in aging as in life are predetermined or driven by free will has been debated for millennia with no resolution. You can find evidence for both in the Bible. We have no free will so we must believe in free will. Perhaps, there may be no mistakes on the labyrinth walk of life. If this is true, then you don't have to search for your purpose in life, because you cannot avoid it.

Eventually something breaks that cannot be fixed, time runs out, and we must enter the event horizon that sucks everyone into the infinite black hole of the unknown. This is like the white water that presages the water fall ahead from which there is no escape. The late author and atheist Christopher Hitchens said the hardest part about dying was realizing the party is going on without you. The longer you live, the faster time seems to pass; as the years pile up, each one becomes a shorter interval of your life. During the second half of life, time is measured toward death instead of away from birth as in the first half. Geriatric medical and psychology resources slowly are acknowledging the special needs of aging as the 76 million baby boomers—born from 1945 to 1965—enter retirement poorly equipped to navigate these troubling waters. By some reports, half of them have no money, half of them are divorced, and one-fifth of them have no teeth. Although hospice and palliative care are available to reduce suffering, most people are unaware of these alternatives and actually spend far less than the Medicare allotted six months in terminal comfort care. So many people fear death that hospice often is not considered until the end is nigh. But those survivors who experience the compassion of hospice staffs and the comfortable passing of their loved ones all seem to recommend it.

Unfortunately, technology, medicine, and commerce have created some of the most painful, expensive, and prolonged ways of dying known to human history. The medical industry will not give up so long as someone will pay for extended treatment, unless patients and families choose otherwise. Some doctors seem to think aging is a curable disease and focus on treating symptoms without much attention to the quality of life. Recall that medicine in America is a profit-making business and the more treatment costs the more profit. Drugs often are prescribed off-label to treat symptoms which the side effects address, even though unapproved for the purpose. Thus, a drug approved for allergy relief is prescribed to enhance sleep because it causes drowsiness. A drug approved for treating BPH is prescribed for growing hair, and a drug approved for ED is prescribed for BPH. Chronic conditions may require several pills for treatment and more pills to counter their side effects. Patients need to become competent self-managers, in the physical, spiritual, cognitive, and emotional personality functions.

Premature ending of life carries a stigma that doctors cannot condone. Jung expressed conflicting opinions about preemptive suicide. "It is really a question whether a person affected by a terrible illness should end her life. It is my attitude in such cases not to interfere. I would let things happen as they were so, because I'm convinced that if anybody has it in himself to commit suicide, then practically the whole of his being is going that way. I have seen cases where it would have been something short of criminal to hinder the people because according to all rules it was in accordance with the tendency of their unconscious and thus the basic thing. So I think nothing is really gained by interfering with such an issue. It is presumably to be left to the free choice of the individual." On the other hand, he also wrote, "The idea of suicide, understandable as it is, does not seem commendable to me. We live to gain the greatest possible amount of spiritual development and self-awareness. As long as life is possible, even if only in a minimal degree, you should hang onto it in order to scoop it up for the purpose of conscious development. To interrupt life before its time is to bring to a standstill an experiment which we have not set up. We have found ourselves in the midst of it and must carry it through to the end. Without it, we cheat the psyche from attaining its eventual goal."

Although Jung was conflicted about suicide, one may argue that there is a death instinct within us, hence a death archetype, i.e., the grim reaper. Crucial to this archetype of a death instinct is that regression is as much a part of life as is growth and progress—like a bell curve has an up phase and a down phase. Jung wrote, "By bearing the opposites we can open ourselves to life in our humanity. We have to realize both the good and evil in us. (St. Clement of Rome) said God rules with two hands, Satan in one and Christ in the other. We have to risk life to get into life, then it takes on color. Otherwise, we might as well read a book." The universe is composed of such necessary opposites. However, doctors are hired to extend life and not to end it, and aiding suicide still is illegal in most states, but that is changing. People who commit suicide want to escape something perceived as worse than death. Recall the intentional passing of actor, Robin Williams after he was diagnosed with Lewy Body Dementia, possibly to avoid the pending catastrophe for himself and his family. There should be a better way. Physician assisted suicide now is legal in the District of Columbia, Oregon, Washington, Montana, California, Colorado, and Vermont but the procedures are expensive, cumbersome and highly restrictive. Also, many physicians are opposed. Failing this, a humane way to exit may be just stopping eating and drinking to let nature take its course after a fatal diagnosis when suffering is unbearable.

Doctors can be paid for end-of-life discussions under Medicare, but very few are professionally prepared for that role. They confuse the oath to "do no harm" with their ability to sustain the trauma of dying, while religious dogma claims that assisted suicide is a mortal sin which induces old people to refuse treatment to save their money for their heirs. Opponents of assisted suicide invoke the word euthanasia to add emotions to their case. But Jesus declared, "There is no greater love than this; to lay down one's life for his friends (family)" (John 15:13). Sometimes, love is best expressed by letting a family member pass on when the time has come without extensive treatment that only bankrupts families and ensures more trauma for survivors. The Final Exit Network was organized to help promote this goal. For more details, visit www.finalexitnetwork.org.

Some resilient souls will discover resources they could not imagine during their aging and learn to radically accept the inevitable losses and possible social isolation, while they pass through phases of shock, denial, anger, bargaining, and depression before reaching acceptance of their mortal reality. (*On Death and Dying* (1969) Elizabeth Kubler-Ross (1926–2004). Professor emeritus, Stan Goldberg described in *Lessons for the Living* (*2009*) his experience and personal growth working as a hospice volunteer, which often includes high drama at the end of life as families deal with their shocking emotions. He advocates making plans in advance with medical doctors and family so there will be less confusion in the end. In his recent book *Dealing with Doctors* (2017) retired oncology doctor, Aroop Mangalik (in addition to others) discusses the many medical and ethical issues involved in end of life planning. He says aggressive treatment beyond hope merely is "sanctioned torture." Families must feel tragically guilty to put a loved one through such an ordeal unless, of course, the patient actually wants to prolong life as long as possible. Dying actually is easy, but trying not to is hard and very expensive. Without careful planning and discussions ahead of time, the terminal phase of life can leave post trauma shock for survivors that can become a permanent part of life. Since it is impossible to predict the future, patients and doctors and families must work together to seek the best quality of life in a bad situation. Most people hope to die in their homes among family, but 70 percent die in hospitals, often alone, connected to life support hardware that is not very comfortable because they did not plan ahead. Dr. Mangalik quoted Pope Paul VI who said, "The physician's duty consists of endeavoring to soothe the suffering rather than prolonging as long as possible a life that is obviously approaching its natural conclusion." Hospice physician Dr. Ira Byock has said the final conversation should hover around these four topics: Please forgive me, I forgive you, thank you, I love you, goodbye.

The Existential Pathway

An existential crisis occurs when a person questions the very foundations of their beliefs: whether this life has any meaning, purpose, or value—sometimes referred to as the "dark night of the soul." Religion has its place, but sometimes it is more depressing than comforting if faith is shaken by the reality of life, even causing some theologians to become agnostics or atheists. "You aren't interested in offerings burned before you on the altar. It is a broken spirit you want, remorse and penitence. A broken heart OH God you will not ignore" (Psalm 51:16–18). Poet laureate Robert Frost (1874–1963) prayed, "Lord, forgive my many little jokes on thee, and I will forgive thy great big one on me." He lost his wife and four of six children by his age sixty-four and lived until age eighty-six to think about it. After the untimely death of his beloved wife, C. S. Lewis wrote in *A Grief Observed* (1963), "Go to Him when your need is desperate, when all other help is vain, and what do you find? A door slammed in your face, and a sound of bolting and double bolting on the other side. After that, silence. You might as well walk away. There is not much chance I will stop believing in God, but I fear what I may come to believe about him. So this is what God is really like. Deceive yourself no longer." C. G. Jung commented about the role of religion in suffering thus: "There are millions who have lost faith in any kind of religion. Such people do not understand their religion any longer. While life runs smoothly without religion, when suffering comes, it is another matter. That is when people seek a way out and to reflect about the meaning of life and its bewildering and painful experiences."

Although Job declared, "Though he slays me I will still trust in him" (Job 13:15), at his age of thirty-nine, F. Scott Fitzgerald wrote in *The Crack Up* (1936), "In the real dark night of the soul it is always three o'clock in the morning." The late pathologist and preemptive suicide advocate, Dr. Jack Kevorkian (1928–2011) resolved his own demise by concluding, "After all, how painful can oblivion be?" And psychiatrist, Dr. Viktor Frankl (1905–1997) who survived the Nazi concentration camps, said if you have a "why" to live you can tolerate almost any "how" (*Man's Search for Meaning*, 1946). This idea, unfortunately, failed millions of souls who were lost against their own will during WWII. Willis Carrier, inventor of air-conditioning, said "the secret to happiness is imagining the worst that can happen and planning to accept it." Apostle Paul accommodated his own aging intuitively thus: "We glory in our sufferings, because we know that suffering produces perseverance; perseverance, character; and character, hope... Though outwardly we are wasting away, yet inwardly we are being renewed day by day. For our light and momentary troubles are achieving for us an eternal glory that far outweighs them all" (Romans 5:3–4, 2 Corinthians 4:16).

Jungian analyst, Dr. James Hollis has explained that turbulent emotional shifts can take place anywhere between the age of thirty-five and eighty when we question the choices we've made, realize our limitations and feel stuck—commonly known as the "midlife crisis" (*Finding Meaning in the Second Half of Life*, 2005). He shocks some readers by saying, "Sooner or later life brings each of us not only disappointment, but something worse, a deep disillusionment regarding the 'contract' that we tacitly presumed and served to the best of our ability, the friendship we counted on, the protection we assumed would be there perpetually, the comfort that someone would pick us up and make it all right when we fell. You really only grow up once you accept the world as a chaotic and random disaster that is full of good and bad at the same time as necessary opposites." God never made any one-sided coins. You will have to confront your "magical thinking" that if you do right, think right, eat right that you'll be spared the worst of it. Perhaps, you are searching for some relief from the intense feeling of apprehension, anxiety, or inner turmoil, called angst, which C. G. Jung said, "sets in during the middle of life and is actually a preparation for death. If viewed correctly in the psychological sense, death is not an end but a goal, and therefore life toward death begins as soon as the meridian is passed. Death is psychologically as important as birth. Shrinking away from it is something unhealthy and abnormal which robs the second half of life of its purpose."

Jung expressed a disdain for clinging to youth in old age and saw human development as continuing throughout life. Both a zest for living in youth and a contemplation of death in old age are normal, but we may worship the former and repress the latter. One of the great privileges in later life is to reconnect to the unencumbered child within and to discover your natural personality and to find others who accept you as you are. Jung saw in the second half of life a transition that includes: facing the realities of aging with acceptance and possibly even relief from the incessant competition and striving in life, reviewing one's life and reconciling both the sweet and the sour, the sun and the shadow, finding harmony and peace within ourselves and with others, getting beyond the self-ego need for keeping score and turning instead to compassion and service, a shifting of world view from the external and physical to more inward focus on the eternal and spiritual, a shift in finding meaning from things and physical activities to one of internal contemplation, and facing the last transition with less fear and even anticipation.

Fr. Richard Rohr has observed that many people in this culture attempt to remain in the first half of life all their lives. The AARP national magazine promotes this view. Jung's view was that the second half of life must not be governed by the principles of the first half of life; that the afternoon of life is just as full of meaning as the morning, only its meaning and purpose are different. "A human being would certainly not live to be 70 or 80 years old if this longevity had no meaning for the species to which he belongs. The afternoon of human life must also have a significance of its own and cannot be merely a pitiful appendage to life's morning… An ever-deepening self-awareness seems to me as probably essential for the continuation of a truly meaningful life in any age, no matter how uncomfortable this self-knowledge may be… The greatest potential for growth and self-realization exists in the second half of life…the privilege of this time is to become who you really are." (The MBTI model of personality is intended to help you find that person.) Unfortunately, our culture is obsessed with youth, activity, and productivity for as long as a person lives. In Western cultures, there is the implication that the best way to age is to do everything we can to continue doing what we've always done for as long as possible—and to look young while doing it. That's why it is important to realize that aging *socially* is not always the same as aging consciously or well. The air brushed models on the AARP magazine covers eventually all will become the true image of aging—like *The Picture of Dorian Gray* by Oscar Wilde. Perhaps, the need to display a persona to be successful in society can be merged into a more authentic experience during the latter stages of life.

For some people, this mortal phase of life can offer increased appreciation of past generations, review of personal experience, less interest in material things and social events and new enjoyment of solitary contemplation of nature. With a more cosmic and transcendent vision, the individual no longer considers him/herself particularly significant but has a growing feeling of being an indispensable part of a larger world like a grain of sand on the beach. There also may be an awareness of spiritual communion with the universe in relation to time and space—what is being called "gerotranscendence" as developed by Lars Tornstam, professor of sociology at the University of Uppsala in Sweden (*A Development Theory of Positive Aging*, 1978, 1995, 2005). The awareness that everyone is united in suffering and impermanence begins to gain acceptance. This concept is perhaps more accepted in Eastern cultures than in the West. We regard elderly people who want peace and quiet and limited social contact as disengaged. Old people who withdraw into solitary contemplation are considered to be in need of help to increase their social activity—possibly confusing introversion with extraversion. They say if you don't know what an extravert is thinking you have not listened, and if you don't know what an introvert is thinking you have not asked. Our western culture ignores that and continues to spread the idea that aging is best either denied or concealed, making it obvious that the biggest denial of all is the inevitability of death. The Jungian model offers alternatives to the traditional understanding of the elderly and may contribute to a redefinition of aging, one that accommodates variations in personality.

Along with the emerging global economy, some therapists have attempted to integrate concepts of mental health from east and west. Jung investigated Eastern philosophy and thought the common key to mature aging is to turn inward during the second half of life. It is a journey that few in the West ever make of self-exploration and unique inner discovery that Jung called "individuation," i.e., the realization of the wholeness of human self, integrating the conscious with the unconscious, the good with the bad, the saint with the sinner, the visible with the shadow, which is the central concept of his analytical psychology. (One can only wonder what Jung would say about the modern megacity lifestyles of both east and west.) During most of life, we encounter dis-individuation to integrate with various organizations that require loyalty, subordination, and conformity. In other words, social success requires that we subvert our own authentic self to become lost in the maddening crowd. Just observe the rush hour commute in any major city. While wearing so many different social persona, we lose touch with who we really are or were born to be as human beings because we are too busy being human doings. Observe the spontaneous behavior of an infant, whether happy or distressed—smiling or crying, to see an authentic human being. Unfortunately, adults immediately force the infant into conformity and the authentic self quickly becomes submerged into the subconscious. We have the opportunity to rediscover it during the contemplation stage of aging. Jung said "the person who looks outward dreams, but the person who looks inward awakes."

One of the great privileges in later life is to reconnect to the unencumbered child within and to discover your natural personality and to find others who accept you as you are. In some sense, it is like a rebirth from one persona into another one or the recovery of ingredients from past generations that make us who we are—what

Jung called the personal unconscious. Perhaps, the feelings from bitter-sweet memories of the past with loved ones gone help to develop the humanity in each of us that was submerged in the façade of civilization, which is very thin. Jung spent his own life in this endeavor and wrote an illustrated diary of his inner journey in *The Red Book* (2009, 2012*)*. We can discover and build on our inner life at any age, welcoming new ideas and experiences, continuing to grow and learn as we age, leading to a new sense of meaning and purpose in our lives. This process of looking inward can present new ways of thinking about ourselves, our identities and the past and lead to the formation of new values and goals that can bring a different vitality and spiritual maturity to our lives as we age. We can be open to conscious grieving and let go of goals that we did not achieve earlier in life and remorse for things we might have done differently. We can refocus our energy on those things that we can still enjoy during the second half of life and let go of the persona in the past, physically, spiritually, mentally, and emotionally.

Maybe you will be given the necessary resilience and determination to survive whatever challenges come with aging—what is called in psychology, self-efficacy—and find a life worth living up until the inevitable ending. Prof. George Bonanno of Columbia University has found that resilience is a natural adaptive mechanism in humans, suggesting that it cannot be taught through specialized programs. There is virtually no existing research with which to design resilience training, nor is there existing research to support major investment in such things as military resilience training programs (*The Other Side of Sadness*, 2009). Some people have more than others. The challenges in aging can provoke positive or negative responses depending upon the personal resilience and personality type development of the individual. As noted above, each of the eight Jungian dominant types—Sei, Nei, Tei, Fei—likely will approach each of the challenges in their own most preferred way. This model says the S type will focus on the physical, the N type will focus on the spiritual, the T type will focus on the cognitive and the F type will focus on the emotional. Problems can occur when there is a mismatch between the needs of the situation and the preference of the individual. The best decisions require that all four of the functions be used to determine the best choice. This can be a complex process, and few are even aware that it is happening, so most decisions under stress are faulty.

A general four-step model for coping may be useful for everyone facing a terminal illness: Understand what is happening, express your fears, set some goals, and make some plans, including a conversation with family and doctor about your wishes—physical, spiritual, mental, and emotional. You need a medical advocate who can speak for you when you can speak no longer. A survey by *The Conversation Project* reported 90 percent of respondents agreed that discussing their aging desires with family and doctors is important but only 28 percent did the former and less than 10 percent did the latter. This process may benefit with help from a counselor qualified in Jungian personality psychology, and it may be a fertile new opportunity for clinicians, as well as educators. In her book, *Extreme Measures* (2017) Dr. Jessica Zitter, an intensive care doctor, advocates for death education in middle schools, along with sex education. She advocates for more palliative care of terminal patients instead of concentration on fighting the disease at all costs, but don't hold your breath. So long as the profit motive drives medicine, people still will suffer needlessly with treatments that merely extend the dying.

The greatest adjustment in aging may involve becoming redundant and losing control of your life. We live in a culture that prizes control, but Jesus told his disciple, "When you were young you dressed yourself and went wherever you pleased, but when you are old someone else will dress you and take you where you do not want to go" (John 21:18). It is not much different today, if you are fated to live through conscious aging. Families who are unprepared often put

A LABYRINTH WALK OF LIFE

their dying loved ones through hell to protect their own fragile egos. When life ends, let it go and, with assurance and confidence, say with Jesus and Apostle Paul, "It is finished" (John 19:30, 2 Timothy 4:6–7). Perhaps, death may be seen as a transition and not a termination. The late actor Charlton Heston explained during his last days, "I must reconcile equal measures of courage and surrender." From a traditional hymn, "O Lord, you know I have no friend like you. If heaven's not my home then Lord what will I do? The angels beckon me from heaven's open door, and I can't feel at home in this world anymore." Alfred Lord Tennyson wrote of his farewell thus, "Sunset and evening star, And one clear call for me! And may there be no moaning at the bar, When I put out to sea… For tho' from outh our bourne of time and place the flood may bear me far, I hope to see my pilot face to face when I have crost the bar." This certainly is different from the poetic instruction of Dylan Thomas to his father, "Do not go gentle into that good night. Rage, rage against the dying of the light." Poet John Donne concluded, "Never send to know for whom the bell tolls; it tolls for thee."

Jung saw in the chaos of living a secret order. He served in WWI as a military officer in POW camps and saw the chaos firsthand. The symbolic walk through the thirteenth century Chartres Labyrinth, a mandala or metaphor that symbolizes the walk of life on the book covers by this writer, may provide some order amidst the chaos. Unlike the dead ends and random pathway of a maze, the labyrinth has no barriers, and it definitely is not a random walk. The Rev. Lauren Artress (*Walking a Labyrinth*, 2011) has said, "Walking the Labyrinth has reemerged today as a metaphor for the spiritual journey and a powerful tool for transformation. This walking meditation is an archetype, a mystical ritual found in many religious traditions. It quiets the mind and opens the soul. Each step unites faith and action as travelers take one step at a time, living each moment in trust and willingness to follow the course set before them."

There are many forms of labyrinths as well as interpretations dating back to ancient times. In its adoption for this use, the traditional interpretation of walking into the center and then back out is reversed. We leave the source at birth (depicted as a lotus blossom in the center) and traverse the four segments of the labyrinth through life as they are given to each of us: infant, child, youth, and adult out into the world—each one building upon the others. Then after midlife, we retrace the pathway in return to the source through integrating stages of maturity, seniority, retirement and contemplation to approach death, wondering what it is all about. Everyone must take the walk of life they are given alone for themselves. Jung wrote in *The Red Book* (2009, 2012), "My path is not your path; therefore, I cannot teach you. The pathway is within us." It seems that the pathway cannot be learned, only experienced. The only rules are: begin and continue until the final transition emerges while becoming redundant and losing control of your life—or merely giving it up. Some churches are practicing the labyrinth walk as a spiritual medium. Many say they feel comfort and inner peace along the pathway. You can make a copy of the graphic on this cover and trace it with a pencil. With a small finger labyrinth, you can begin at the center depicting the source to "walk" out into the world and then reverse at midlife back to the source. (*You can buy a finger-walking labyrinth for personal use at www.bwatsonstudios.com.*)

Perhaps this venture through aging is described by the late prime minister of Israel, Golda Meir (1898–1978), "Life is like taking a plane trip, once they close the door there is nothing you can do about it." To quote the movie character Forrest Gump, "Life is like a box of choclats, you never know what you're gonna get." Celebrated humanist Helen Keller (1880–1968) although deaf and blind, wrote in *The Open Door* (1957), "Security is mostly a superstition. It does not exist in nature, nor do the children of men as a whole experience it. Avoidance of danger is no safer in the long run than outright exposure. Life is either a daring adventure, or nothing." And it all must be necessary or it would be different—Ergo Theofatalism. Perhaps the bottom line is focusing your energy on thankfulness and contentment as the time of life approaches its end. St. Paul said he had found the secret to feeling content regardless what his circumstances were (Philippians 4:11–12). He also advocated to "give thanks in all things, for this is the will of God for you" (1 Thessalonians 5:18). All burdens come with benefits, so if you are suffering, consider that each day is one day less to go. Life is too short to let circumstance determine your joy. All in God's will of course—if you believe in God. (Otherwise, it is what it is.) The labyrinth walk of life contains no mistakes. "You saw me before I was born and scheduled each day of my life before I began to breathe. Every day was recorded in your book!" (Psalm 139:16). "A person's steps are directed by the Lord. How then can anyone understand their own way?" (Proverbs 20:24). Bon voyage.

The Functions of Personality

Personality drives human behavior, so the benefits of its discovery are potentially immense. Nations are composed of individuals, so the healthier the people are, the healthier the nation will be. The functions of personality were originally discussed by psychiatrist Carl G. Jung (1875–1961) in *Personality Types* (1921, 1960). He said people take in information and make judgments about it—that's it. These functions are two ways of perceiving, i.e., sensing (S) and intuition (N), and two ways of decision making, i.e., thinking (T) and feeling (F), each being either extraverted or introverted thus composing eight different types of personality. Everyone uses all the eight functions, but they prefer to use one for perceiving (S or N) and one for decisions (T or F) in combination more than the others. Either perception or decision functions will be dominant with the other providing support and backup, while each function may be introverted (i) or extraverted (e). This situation leaves the other four functions less preferred and less developed, and mostly unconscious. Examples of possible function combinations: Sei with Tei or Sei with Fei or Nei with Tei, or Nei with Fei, or Tei with Sei, or Tei with Nei, or Fei with Sei, or Fei with Nei. When you invoke introversion or extraversion to each function, there results 16 possible combinations thus: SiTe, SeTi, TiSe, TeSi, etc. This is the approach developed by the Myers-Briggs Type Indicator.

Type dynamics is the process of recognizing your own preferred type functions and working to develop the others, thus creating a more balanced and more effective life. If this model of personality is not understood by family members and social or work groups, they can be very argumentative and disagreeable. Opposite personality types may attract each other, but the tension that creates may not be worth the benefits. Similar types may feel comfortable with each other, but find little stimulation for growth. Following are some brief descriptions of each function as originally envisioned by Jung and updated by Berens and Hartzler to compile the basic eight personality types. They are derived from the Myers-Briggs Type Indicator. For a more thorough application to individuals, Google MBTI.

Four ways to collect information, i.e., perception.

Sensing—Extraverted, Se: Perceiving the world using the five senses, seeing things as they really are in the here and now. Seeing a pencil, observing its structure, size, color, sharpness, etc. While eating, one may observe the taste, texture, and presentation of food. Listening to music in concert or walking in nature would include sounds and observations. Experiencing the immediate context, taking action in the physical world, noticing changes and opportunities for action, accumulating experiences, scanning for visible reactions and relevant data, recognizing "what is." The key here is conscious awareness of the sensory world.

Sensing—Introverted, Si: Recalling previous sensing experiences including memories of personal reactions stimulated by current observations. The pencil may stimulate recalling similar pencils in general as new in their packaging, unsharpened or fully sharpened and ready for use. The key here is internal awareness of the here and now as it is impacted by previous observations. Reviewing past experiences; "what is" evoking "what was"; seeking detailed information and links to what is known; recalling stored impressions; accumulating data; recognizing the way things have always been. Being more energized by things than people and ideas.

Intuition—Extraverted, Ne: Realizing patterns, relationships, and possibilities in the moment. Imagining new uses for observations, as in seeing around corners to use objects and situations for different purposes. Seeing some vacant land with buildings potentially erected on it. Or coming up with ways of improving utensils, tools, and necessities, like converting crank windows in cars into electrical ones. Napoleon (1769–1821) said, "Imagination/intuition rules the world." Interpreting situations and relationships; picking up meanings and interconnections; being drawn to change for what could possibly be, noticing what is said and threads of meaning emerging across multiple contexts.

Intuition—Introverted, Ni: Being oriented to the future, perceiving abstract meanings and symbols of things, ideas, and information, both positive and negative. Scientist Albert Einstein (1879–1955) described it: "The intellect has little to do on the road to discovery. There comes a leap of consciousness, call it intuition or what you will, and the solution comes to you and you don't know how or why." The key here is internal awareness of future possibilities. Foreseeing implications and likely effects without external data; realizing what will be, conceptualizing new ways of seeing things;

envisioning transformations; getting an image of profound meaning or far-reaching symbols.

Four ways of organizing information, i.e., judging.

Thinking—Extraverted, Te: Acting within rules and guidelines to achieve logical and reasonable goals. Observing mathematical precision or scientific principles to assure that "do this, get that" behavior produces desired outcomes. Moves and shakes people and things as needed to accomplish their goals. Likes to extend trend lines into the future with little to no variations. Organizing for efficiency; systematizing; applying logic; structuring; checking for consequences; monitoring for standards or specifications being met; setting boundaries, guidelines, and parameters; deciding if something is working or not, balancing the benefits against the burdens, and evaluating the consequences.

Thinking—Introverted, Ti: Designing or determining a model of how things should be done to achieve goals logically. Introverted thinking often involves finding just the right word to clearly express an idea concisely, crisply, and to the point. Having an internal sense of the essential qualities of something, noticing the fine distinctions that make it what it is. Likes to take ideas apart to figure out how they work or how they can be improved. Enjoys looking at different sides of an issue and seeing where there is inconsistency. Analyzing; categorizing; evaluating according to principles and whether something fits the framework or model; figuring out the principles on which something works; checking for inconsistencies; clarifying definitions to get more precision.

Feeling—Extraverted, Fe: Acting to preserve relationships in the group, family, social circle, community, and intimate others. Often driven by a desire to connect with or disconnect from others by expressions of warmth or displeasure and self-disclosure. Being polite and considerate, and being appropriate with concern for being dependable and helpful are important whether expressed or shown by actions. Avoids confrontations and feels uncomfortable in situations of conflict. Considering others and the group; organizing to meet their needs and honor their values and feelings; maintaining societal, organizational, or group values; adjusting to and accommodating others; deciding if something is appropriate or acceptable to others. Considering what would be appropriate for the situation.

Feeling—Introverted, Fi: Determining what feels right and avoiding hurting anyone or anything. Feels hurt when a value is threatened or breached but not likely to express it. May seek peace and acceptance by others before self- acceptance. Processes what feels right as moral integrity. Is more likely to flee when threatened rather than stay and fight. Valuing; considering importance and worth; reviewing for incongruity; evaluating something based on the truths on which it is based; clarifying values to achieve accord; deciding if something is of significance and worth standing up for.

"Everything good is costly, and the development of personality is one of the most costly. It is a matter of saying yes to oneself, of taking oneself as the most serious of tasks, of being conscious of everything one does, and keeping it constantly before one's eyes in all its dubious aspects—truly a task that taxes us to the utmost" (*The Collected Works of C. G. Jung*, vol. 13, para. 24). If you see the benefits in learning more about personality functions, there are numerous resources available on the Internet. Google "MBTI."

References:
  Abd-Ru-Shin, *The Grail Message* (1941)
  Artress, *Walking a Labyrinth* (2011)

Berens, *Understanding Yourself and Others* (2004)
Bonanno, *The Other Side of Sadness* (2009)
Carnegie, *How to Win Friends and Influence* People (1930)
Chodran, *When Things Fall Apart* (1996)
Goldberg, *Lessons for the Living* (2009)
Frankl, *Man's Search For Meaning* (1946)
Hammer-Marting, *Coping Resources Inventory* (1988, 2004)
Hartzler, *The Functions of Type* (2005)
Hogan, *Way of the Winding Path* (2003)
Hollis, *Finding Meaning in the Second Half of Life* (2005)
Kubler-Ross, *On Death and Dying* (1969)
Linehan, *Dialectical Behavior Therapy* (2015)
Lorig, et al. *Living a Healthy Life With Chronic Conditions* (2012)
Mangalik, *Dealing with Doctors*—2017
Quenk, *Was That Really Me?* (2002)
Zitter, *Extreme Meaures* (2017)
www.16personalities.com
www.bwatsonstudios.com
www.cognitiveprocesses.com
http://lifetransitionslifecompletion.blogspot.com
www.mindgarden.com
www.personalitypage.com
www.veriditas.org
www.theconversationproject.org
www.personalityrelationships.net
www.finalexitnetwork.org

Lewis Tagliaferre co-authored *Recovery from Loss* with Dr. Gary Harbaugh and *Kisses Aren't Contracts*, plus *Voices of Sedona, Baby Boomer Lamentations, Theofatalism*, and several blogs on the philosophy of theological fatalism. For details, visit www.theofatalism.org and www. facebook.com/theofatalism.

Epilogue

In the Christian tradition, some people have composed hymns to help them and others to walk the labyrinth pathway of life they are given. In the process of singing these hymns, many have felt a calm inner peace that says no matter what happens, they are in good hands. The lyrics to three of my favorites follow. I hope they will help to grant you serenity and inner peace. (*Note: These lyrics were obtained on the Internet and are included under the fair use doctrine of US copyright law.*)

This is My Father's World
Malthie D. Babcock

This is my Father's world, and to my listening ears
All nature sings, and round me rings the music of the spheres.

This is my Father's world, the birds their carols raise,
The morning light, the lily white, declare their Maker's praise.

This is my Father's world: I rest me in the thought
Of rocks and trees, of skies and seas;
His hand the wonders wrought.

This is my Father's world. O let me ne'er forget
That though the wrong seems oft so strong, God is the ruler yet.

This is my Father's world: why should my heart be sad?
The Lord is King; let the heavens ring!
God reigns; let the earth be glad!

This is my Father's world: He shines in all that's fair;
In the rustling grass I hear Him pass;
He speaks to me everywhere.
In the rustling grass I hear Him pass;
He speaks to me everywhere.

This Ole House
Christy F. Smith, et al

I ain't a gonna need this house no longer ain't a gonna need this house no more
Ain't got time to fix the shingles, ain't got time to fix the door
Ain't got time to oil the hinges nor to mend the window panes
I ain't gonna need this house no longer, I'm gettin' ready to meet the saints

This ole house once I knew my children this house once knew my wife
This ole house was joy and comfort as we fought the storms of life
This ole house once rang with laughter, this ole house heard many shouts
Now she trembles in the darkness when the lightnin' walks about
I ain't a gonna need this house no longer...

Now my old hound dog lies a sleepin' he don't know I'm gonna leave
Else he'd wake up by the fireplace and he'd sit there, growl and grieve
But my huntin' days are over, ain't gonna hunt the coon no more
Gabriel done brought in my chariot when the wind blew down the door
I ain't a gonna need this house no longer...ain't gonna need this house no more.

A LABYRINTH WALK OF LIFE

I'll Fly Away
Alfred E. Brumley

I'll fly away, oh glory, I'll fly away
When I die, hallelujah by and by, I'll fly away

Some bright morning when this life is over, I'll fly away
To a land on God's celestial shore, I'll fly away

When the shadows of this life have gone, I'll fly away
Like a bird from these prison walls I'll fly, I'll fly away
I'll fly away, oh glory, I'll fly away
When I die, hallelujah by and by, I'll fly away

Oh, how glad and happy when we meet, I'll fly away
No more cold iron shackles on my feet, I'll fly away

Just a few more weary days and then, I'll fly away
To a land where joy will never end, I'll fly away

I'll fly away, oh glory, I'll fly away
When I die, hallelujah by and by, I'll fly away

And so it is.

About the Author

The author's autobiography is included as one of the essays in Part I. He provides this book as the completion of a series of books which, at his age of 84 years, document his personal search for inner peace after many challenges, losses, and some success resulting in his discovery of Theofatalism. His career included researching and publishing many magazine articles and technical journals in the fields of energy and electrical construction. However, it is not about the author, it is about the message. The author merely was the scribe who was given the message to sow as seeds thrown among the grains of sand on the desert of human suffering. Some of them will be blown away, some will rot and decay, and a few seeds will take root and grow to produce new seeds, and so it will be. All in God's will of course. Amen.